Changing african
family project series
Monograph No

7

Women, education
and modernization
of the family
in West Africa

edited by

Helen Ware

The Department of Demography
The Australian National University

Canberra 1981

First published in Australia 1981

Printed in Australia by
The Australian National University Printing Unit
for the Department of Demography

National Library of Australia
Cataloguing-in-Publication entry

Women, education and modernization of the family in West Africa.

Bibliography
ISBN 0 909409 12 9

1. Family - Africa, West - Addresses, essays, lectures.
2. Women - Africa, West - Addresses, essays, lectures.
I. Ware, Helen.   II. Australian National University.
Department of Demography.   (Series: Changing African
family project series: monograph; no.7).

306.8'0966

Library of Congress No. 81-68948

Distributed by The Australian National University Press
CANBERRA, AUSTRALIA.   MIAMI, FLORIDA.
and by The Department of Demography,
P.O.Box 4, Australian National University,
Canberra, Australia 2600.

iii

CONTENTS

CONTRIBUTORS

Dr. Helen Ware

Department of Demography, Research School of Social Sciences, Australian National University, P.O.Box 4, Canberra, Australia 2600.

Dr. O.O.Arowolo

Department of Sociology, University of Ibadan, Ibadan, Nigeria.

Dr. Susan H. Cochrane

Population and Human Resources Division, World Bank, 1818H Street,N.W., Washington D.C., 20433, U.S.A.

Dr. Wambui Wa Koranja

Department of Sociology, University of Lagos, Lagos, Nigeria.

Dr. Dolores B. Koenig

Department of Anthropology, American University, Washington D.C. 20016, U.S.A.

Dr. Susan Soyinka

Department of French, University College, Ilorin, PMB 1515, Ilorin, Kwara State, Nigeria. (Linby, Hucknall, Notts.U.K.NG15 8DE)

Dr. Virginia De Lancey

American Embassy (USICA), B.P.817, Yaounde, Cameroun. (20, Hillstar Court, Columbia, S.Carolina 29206, U.S.A.)

Dr. I.O.Orubuloye

Nigerian Institute of Social and Economic Research, Private Mail Bag No.5., U.I.Post Office, Ibadan, Nigeria.

LIST OF TABLES AND FIGURES

Contd...

TABLES AND FIGURES Contd

Contd...

LIST OF TABLES AND FIGURES Contd

PREFATORY NOTE

The Changing African Family Project began in 1972 as a collaborative project of the Department of Sociology, University of Ibadan, Nigeria (then headed by the late Professor Francis Olu Okediji) and the Department of Demography, The Australian National University. Subsequently collaborators in eleven other African Countries undertook projects. All twelve national projects, Cameroun, Congo, Ghana, Kenya, Nigeria, Senegal, Sudan, Togo, Tunisia, Uganda, Upper Volta and Zaire, were funded by the Population Council.

These research projects were based on the belief that demographic behaviour reflects the nature of society, and particularly the nature of its families. Hence they focused, from the stance of various disciplines, on the family in conditions of stable high fertility, immediately before the onset of fertility decline, and also during the early stages of fertility decline. This strategy has proved rewarding.

The whole project was described in "The Changing African Family Project: A Report with Special Reference to the Nigerian Segment", published in Studies in Family Planning, 7:5:1976, and written by Francis Okediji, John Caldwell, Pat Caldwell and Helen Ware. The Nigerian segment has been described and analysed in many published papers, in the first three volumes of The Changing African Family Project Monograph Series and in the first two publications of Family and Fertility Change: Changing African Family Companion Series.

However, the findings of the other Segments have to date not been nearly as readily available, although five (Ghana, Nigeria, Cameroun, Kenya and Sudan) were represented by chapters in a publication in the latter series, The Persistence of High Fertility.

The first non-Nigerian national report, however, was A Case of the Akamba of Eastern Kenya, which was the fifth monograph in The Changing African Family Project Monograph Series; followed by the sixth monograph by Israel Sembajwe in which he examines the relationship between fertility and child mortality amongst the Yoruba of Western Nigeria.

We now have this seventh volume, edited by Helen Ware, which is a collection of works focused on women and the family in West Africa. The authors are drawn from a wide range of disciplines from sociology and anthropology to demography and comparative literature and cover areas from Cameroun and Nigeria to Mali and Guinea. Its publication has been funded by the Department of Demography, The Australian National University, as will be the succeeding national volumes (a further Nigerian study on rural Yoruba women and also a volume on fertility change in the Sudan are in preparation. Work towards the Final Report has been funded by the Rockefeller Foundation, and will be completed during 1981.

The typing and preparation for press of this volume has been carried out by members of the Department of Demography of The Australian National University.

J.C.Caldwell
Series Editor

INTRODUCTION

THE ORIGINS OF THIS BOOK

Woman's Place is Everywhere

Helen Ware

INTRODUCTION

THE ORIGINS OF THIS BOOK

Helen Ware

WOMAN'S PLACE IS EVERYWHERE

Every academic discipline has both a central focal area and a certain number of peripheral areas which tend to be neglected. In the social sciences the areas in which women are prominent are very often amongst those which are left to one side. Frequently it would almost appear that the involvement of women was in itself sufficient to ensure the classification of the topic as unimportant. Equally, in studies with global titles referring to subjects such as development, migration or the workforce it is only too common to find that women are either altogether ignored or cast aside in a few passing references.* In traditional cultures, despite the central place of kinship in anthropological studies, women's lives and opinions have often been entirely ignored by researchers. Indeed there is now a considerable literature devoted to redressing the male-centred bias of much anthropology (see the reviews of Quinn 1977; Rogers 1978 and Rapp 1979). Part of this imbalance results not from native prejudices but from the gap between the interests of traditional peoples and the interests of those who study them. All traditional groups are interested in the economics of physical survival and in the problems associated with human reproduction. Yet these are areas in which, until very recently, social scientists have shown very little interest. In any standard anthropological text there is much more likely to be an entry under incest than under infancy or child-rearing and information on agricultural practices will almost invariably be swamped by descriptions of marriage rituals.

In contrast, demography is one social science which cannot in general terms be accused of neglecting women. In the central area of fertility studies the imbalance is in the other direction and it is men who are neglected (Ware 1981A; Chapter 8 below). Indeed, in many cases it would appear that women alone are being held responsible for the world's population problems resulting from their allegedly irrational breeding. Clearly, this view is as far from the truth as that which pays no attention to women. One aim in gathering the chapters for this book was to redress the balance by presenting women as whole

---

*To cite but one example, in John Cleave's otherwise admirable study of African farmers (1974), women are shown as often performing more productive work than men, yet they do not rate one single mention in the index, and there is no extended discussion of their role.

persons and not simply as reproductive agents serving the men of present and
future generations.

THE WEST AFRICAN FOCUS

Most discussions of household economics and of the economic aspects of
fertility behaviour float in an a-cultural limbo somewhere in mid-Atlantic.
Nevertheless there is also an often unstated assumption that the conditions to
be found in present day Chicago are also reproduced around the world. Any
discussion of familial decisions must be placed in a cultural context, for otherwise it is impossible even to define what constitutes a family or who may be
available to participate in decision-making. Concentrating upon a single
cultural area makes it possible to focus upon some of these issues and also to
show how cultural patterns may vary even within a single country or a single city.
The choice of West Africa was made partly on the pragmatic grounds of the availability of appropriate data. However there were further considerations. One
was that West African women are famed for an autonomy which is still very little
understood. It is also the case that West Africa provides innumerable
fascinating contrasts between the traditional and the modern and that traditional
ways are exhibiting remarkable powers of survival in some areas. In the area of
family studies there is a vast wealth of anthropological materials with varying
biases, a small group of studies of national elites (e.g.P.Lloyd 1967; Caldwell
1968; Oppong 1974 and Harrell-Bond 1975), and very little information on the
everyday lives of more commonplace individuals living within the modern sector
or on its fringes. Finally, if there is any region of the world where modern
developments are likely to result in increased fertility West Africa must be the
most likely area because of the broad extent of traditional sexual abstinence
(Nag 1979).

MODERNIZATION

Modernization is an awkward and elusive concept yet one that it is very
difficult to avoid in discussions of changes which are underway in Africa
(Rencontres Internationales de Bouaké 1965). An alternative term would be
development but this implies progress and there is no intention here to suggest
that the changes associated with modernization should necessarily be positively
evaluated.

Modernization of technology is easy to see and to define although modern
technology may be used as the means to a traditional goal, as when reinforced
concrete is used to build an Emir's palace. Modernization of the family is
much more difficult to recognise and to interpret, partly because so much depends
upon an understanding of the traditional situation. Thus, for example, depending
upon the ethnic group, the following practices may either be new developments

resulting from the impact of Western education and the market economy or be
long-standing traditional customs dating back beyond the group memory embedded
in folk-tales:

    (a)   the economic independence of wives (Yoruba):*

    (b)   the establishment of independent nuclear households at
           marriage (Basa);

    (c)   the delay of marriage until women are accounted
           to be responsible adults (Yoruba);

    (d)   the neglect of the elderly (Fulbe).

Just because a feature of family life seems familiar to the Western researcher
it does not necessarily follow that it reflects recent changes in family
structure consequent upon modernization.   Even where it is clear that a
practice does represent a new departure it is very difficult to produce any
kind of a valid measure of its adoption.   Residence patterns can fairly easily
be monitored once a baseline survey has established the pattern at a given point
in time, but no one has yet established a really satisfactory method of measuring
the economic nucleation of the family (Vercruijsse 1974).   Indeed the whole
issue of economic relationships within nuclear and extended families is one of
the highest priority areas for future research.

      This book does not directly address the issue as to whether it is possible
to have modernization of the family without Westernization.   Readers are left
to draw their own conclusions on the basis of the evidence presented in the
individual chapters, for so much depends upon the individual viewpoint and the
individual definitions.   Is the practice of polygyny invariably to be considered
traditional behaviour?   Is an increasing frequency of divorce to be considered
evidence of modernization, of Westernization, or of the adoption of a pattern
already common amongst a number of local ethnic groups?   When Nigerian university students are asked who they most trust, mothers were clearly most trusted
followed by fathers and then by wives (Beckett and O'Connell 1977: 59 + 84).
Is this evidence of clinging to traditional kin-based values or would American
or European students respond similarly?   Can a nuclear family in which there
are a minimum of interests in common between husband and wife be regarded as

*The ethnic groups named within brackets are examples of groups for whom these
practices are strictly traditional.   The Yoruba examples are discussed in
Chapters 2 and 3 of this book, the Basa example in Chapter 5.   The best discussion of traditional Fulbe neglect of the aged is in Hopen (1958: Chapter 13).

typically Western? It is much easier to pose such questions than to answer them. However, overall it would appear that the case for a distinctively African type of modern family adapted to living in an industrialized society has yet to be proved.

EDUCATION AND THE FAMILY

There are many issues related to the impact of education upon the family which can very profitably be examined in the West African context. One question relates to the contrast between the effects of education when it is restricted to a small elite group and the impact of education when it is provided for the masses as under the Nigerian Universal Primary Education (UPE) scheme introduced in the late 1970s. In a seminar paper Caldwell (1980) has argued that the real impact of education on the family is associated with mass education. When only a few are educated, education and the traditional extended family system are highly compatible. Relatives work together to support the education of gifted individuals, who, in turn, are expected to make a solid contribution to the education of the siblings, nieces and nephews and other relatives who come after them. At this stage education is essentially an excellent investment. The man who can get his child through secondary school knows that the financial returns to himself and his kin from a highly paid and grateful child should amply repay his expenditure. It should also help to start an overall move to- wards education for the extended family as a whole as a chain of educated individ- uals become available to assist others to follow in their footsteps.

Later, as education becomes much more widespread the situation changes radically. Firstly, the massive financial rewards to education become increas- ingly restricted to those with tertiary qualifications. Secondly, the number of children who are not in school and who are therefore making a significant early contribution to the family economy is drastically reduced. Thirdly, the content of formal education almost invariably serves to denigrate the importance of the extended family and to hold up Western middle-class values and that nuclear family as the ideal. Finally, educated parents find that, unlike their own illiterate parents, they have very little choice as to whether they should educate their children (in economists' terminology this decision refers to the quality rather than the quantity of children to be reared). Within the social context, parents are obliged to educate all of their children, almost irrespect- ive of talent, at least to the same level as they themselves have reached and preferably to a higher level in order to keep pace with the general spread of education with each succeeding generation. The overall result is that whereas having children once brought direct economic returns to the parents who benefited from their labours, children have become a drain upon the parents who have to pay their greatly increased costs. Thus each additional child instead of bringing its own reward simply creates extra costs which can no longer be recouped. This is the phenomenon which Caldwell (1978) refers to as the reversal of the intergenerational wealth flows. In traditional societies wealth flows from children to their parents but in modern societies the flow is from parents to children.

Clearly, this situation in which children are an economic burden on their parents can only be maintained where there are some surplus resources. In a subsistence economy with no surplus, parents are obliged to exploit their children in order to ensure the survival of the family, and, indeed, of the wider society. Parents need children for the children's current labour inputs and for support in old age. In contrast, in an industrialized economy, institutions take over many of the functions of children, and no one would choose to have children as a financial investment because the benefits go directly to the children themselves rather than returning to the parents who have to provide the expenditure.

The same transformation occurs with respect to the role of the extended family. In societies close to subsistence level, the sharing of resources within the extended family acts as a form of insurance against hard times (see Chapter 5). However, whilst food supplies can easily be redistributed, educational investments in children, once made, are fixed. It is difficult for the extended family to survive as an economic unit once education introduces a situation where investment in individuals can bring massive returns to those who choose to concentrate all their resources on their own children and where, once educated, individuals no longer need their extended families.

One survey of undergraduates in Nigeria asked: 'Does your education tend to reduce the understanding between you and your parents and other members of your immediate family?' (Beckett and O'Connell 1977). Despite the classic image of the educated African as cut off from the life of his or her own people only 11-17% of students answered in the affirmative. This finding is all the more striking since all of these students at Ibadan, ABU and Nsukka were being educated in a language other than their mother tongue. Whilst the children of farmers were slightly more likely to feel cut off, Moslem students felt less isolated than Christians and women felt less isolated than men. Certainly, one important factor in this lack of conflict between the family and the elite child is the ability to live in two worlds or to shift very rapidly from one world to another which is a common feature of the lives of the more cosmopolitan Africans. Similar adaptations are seen in a multiple ethnic context where

members of one ethnic group will converse in their own language when alone
but will shift without awkwardness to English or Pidgin when joined by someone
from another group.   In this sense a less rigid social ethos makes life much
easier for all those who do move within a range of different social spheres.

EDUCATION AND THE STATUS OF WOMEN WITHIN THE FAMILY

There have been very few attempts to investigate the relative impact of
education upon males and females. Caldwell (1980:248) maintains that 'female
illiteracy and an unquestioning total immersion in family morality enable the
patriarch to treat his wife (or wives) as one of the children and, through
dominance over her, to solidify his dominance over his schooled children. A
school child can falter in feeling part of a new, wider world if the father,
whether educated or not, maintains his patriarchal role and the mother remains
unwaveringly traditional.   In this case the wealth flow may not turn downward
until the second generation of mass education, when mothers as well as children
are educated, and may not turn down at all if only fathers are educated and
the tradition of illiterate wives persists.'

None of the studies of traditional societies in this book supports the
suggestion that the average husband is a patriarch who can treat his wife as one
of the children.   Instead the dominant image is of the strong woman whose
position is based upon solid foundations because of her control of her own
economic resources and because of her status as a mother.   Camara Laye's
mother presided over a polygynous household where traditional religious practices and the veneration of ancestors and snake-spirits were blended with conventional Muslim observances (see Chapter 4).   Her power stemmed from her own
personality and from her mystical status as the child born following the birth
of male twins, and her relationship with her husband was based upon mutual
respect.   Madame Laye was one of those exceptional but not uncommon women in
traditional West Africa who are powerful figures in their own right.

A patriarch's power stems not from his control over his wife (wives) but
from his control over his adult sons.   Where a polygynist has wives who are
young enough to be his children, they may well be treated like children. However,
in most cases, the senior wife will have been a partner to her husband since the
time when he himself was a young man under the control of his own patriarchal
father. She has the control of the women's side of the household and her status
stems from the respect given to her capabilities as an economic manager and as
a mother and mother-in-law.   Respect is strongly associated with age and a man
would not think of a wife who is his contemporary as being a child, rather she
is the mother of his children and it would belittle his own status if he were
not to grant her respect.   Concentration upon sex differences in social status
tends to obscure the importance of changes over the life-cycle.   One study in

Ibadan asked children whether they would rather be an older sister or a younger brother; the majority of both sexes chose to be an older sister (B.Lloyd 1967). For both sexes youth is associated with powerlessness and succeeding life-cycle stages bring increasing authority (Ware 1981 B).

Education serves to disturb the balance of power within the traditional family in which husbands and wives each hold power within their own spheres. Education dimishes the respect and authority given to older persons because of their greater wisdom and experience by providing a much more rapid route to the achievement of knowledge and practical skills. It may also create a division between men and women either because sons receive formal education whilst daughters do not, or because the content of formal education is specially modified for girls. This creation of a special form of formal education for females reflects Western, and especially missionary prejudices rather than local demands.

When an educated man marries an illiterate woman then a very unequal situation is created in which the two partners are often acting on different premises. Surprisingly, there would appear to have been no sociological or anthropological studies which specifically examine this type of mixed marriage in which two cultures meet. However, it would appear that the situation in which the West African wife is most likely to be at a disadvantage comes about not when she is illiterate but when she is educated but has no independent source of income. The idea of the wife as a dependant relying upon her husband for economic support is a European importation into West Africa. In traditional societies women are producers not hangers-on. Even in the urban context the illiterate woman can usually make some contribution to the family economy by petty trading or some handicraft or food-processing task. The problem for the educated wife of the educated husband is that she has to find an employment which does not lower her own status or reflect poorly on that of her husband. If her education and training are at a significantly lower level than his, or there is no work available for educated women, she may well find that she has become a dependant with very limited autonomy because she has no money of her own (see Chapters 1 and 3). For such women their status can become a prison and their hold upon the modern world depends upon their husbands. This newly vulnerable position of the educated wife who does not have a satisfactory career of her own has been well described for a matrilineal group in Ghana and for the Creoles of Sierra Leone (Oppong 1974: Harrell-Bond 1975).

Western discussions of family economies and of the context in which
economic decisions are made almost invariably assume that in traditional
settings the husband provides the major part of the income or resources and
that whatever contribution the wife makes is pooled in one common fund.   In
the traditional West African context, it is often the case that neither assumption is valid.   In many areas women make the major contribution to agricultural
production (Kaberry 1952; Meillassoux 1975), and the pooling of resources is
relatively uncommon.   Even where the husband is a farmer and the wife trades
in farm produce they often will not deal with each other because of the belief
that they will get fairer treatment elsewhere (Sudarkasa 1973: 119-20).   In
some Yoruba areas wives receive an annual sum of money from their husbands in
return for their work on the farm (Clarke 1979: 364, 371 quoted Eades 1980:68).
Evidence from Lagos (Chapter 3) shows that this economic separation between husbands and wives is still almost universally practised in cases where both
parties have incomes of their own.

In the individual chapters which follow the authors take up some of these
themes.   In all cases the emphasis is upon examining contemporary data to see
how far the theories are justified by the available information and how far the
application of theories developed elsewhere is inappropriate to the African
context.   Great stress is placed upon letting cultures and individuals appear
as they are rather than trying to mould them to fit a Western defined image of
what they should be.

THE INDIVIDUAL CHAPTERS

The book opens with a case study by Virginia DeLancey of women living on
a Cameroonian tea-plantation (Chapter 1).   Although the research was originally
designed to examine the possibility of incompatibility between the roles of
wage-earner and mother, the conclusion was that the most serious problems resulted rather from the incompatibility between the roles of wage-earner and
wife.   This researcher was sufficiently flexible and self-confident to appreciate and act upon the perception that the conventional questions raised about
the relationship between women's wage-employment and their fertility and family
lives were inappropriate to the cultural context.

Unfortunately in social science research it is very often the case that
theories developed in the United States of America or in Europe are imposed
upon cultures to which they have very little relevance.   The form in which
questions are framed very often determines the answers which are received.   In
this culture one reason why there was so little conflict between motherhood and
and wage-earning was because the definition of motherhood was divorced from the

twentieth century European concept which has been strongly influenced by psychological theories. The idea that a young child needs its own biological mother to be present twenty-four hours a day is foreign to the Tropical African context. Whereas motherhood in the West is an individual responsibility, in Tropical Africa there is much more acceptance of delegation and of child-rearing as a societal responsibility. In Cameroon the context of wage-earning has also been modified to make the setting more flexible for persons with dual responsibilities.

The definition of motherhood found on the plantation would be common to most of West Africa for only a tiny Western educated elite would understand the concept of maternal deprivation (Morgan 1975; P.Lloyd 1967; Weil 1976). However, conditions of women's employment in Cameroon would appear to be exceptionally favourable. Under national legislation women receive 14 weeks paid maternity leave (20 weeks if the birth results in maternal ill-health) as well as having the certainty of getting their jobs back and receiving maternity allowances almost equivalent to a month's wages for the average female plant-ation worker. For fifteen months after the birth women are allowed one hour of nursing break per day owing to a government measure intended to promote births and breast-feeding. On this plantation employees of both sexes and the wives of employees also receive free medical treatment; pickers have two breaks a day in which they can breast-feed and checkers can feed at almost any time through the day. Day care for children from birth to age five, when they can enter school, is also provided by the management. Very few women in the United States or Western Europe would enjoy such favourable working conditions for mothers. Both traditional attitudes concerning appropriate roles for women and governmental provisions vary widely across West Africa and any research must take these factors in the cultural context into account. Where governments wish to make female workforce participation compatible with high fertility levels they can certainly act very effectively.

Israel Olutunje Orubuloye examines the impact of education upon Western Nigerian society from the viewpoint of one who has lived through many of the changes which he describes (Chapter 2). Born in a polygynous household in a relatively remote traditional village he now has a doctorate in demography from an Australian university. For such pioneers, for whom even attending primary school involved leaving home, education obviously had a very dramatic impact. One question that inevitably arises in reading any discussion of current trends in Nigeria following the introduction of universal primary education relates to the effects of attempting to make the whole nation literate in a country

where literate persons do not expect to engage in farming or unskilled labour-
ing. Significantly, the standard text on the sociology of Nigerian education
examines the impact of the family upon education, but not the impact of
education upon the family (DuBey et al. 1979).

Orubuloye argues that the educated elite and their poor relatives are
linked in a dual symbiotic relationship. In the economic sphere the poor need
the assistance of the rich with securing education and finding employment, and
the rich need the services and clientage of the poor. In the cultural sphere
the elite act as guides to the modern world, and particularly its more bureaucratic aspects, but the poor and especially the rural poor provide the elite's
links with tradition. Whilst the economic exchange sees the elite in a position of power the balance is much more equal in the case of the cultural
exchange. The time has long past when the educated could see everything
Western as being superior. Now there is a great yearning to achieve some form
of development which is nevertheless distinctively African.

The Gambian Lenrie Peters' injunction to:

> Open the gate
> To East and West
> Bring in all
> That's good and best

now has the dated ring of the era when independence had just been won and a
brave new dawn seemed to be imminent. Much more in tune with today is the
Nigeria Mabel Imokhuende's plaint:

> Here we stand,
> Infants overblown
> Poised between two civilizations,
> Finding the balance irksome,
> Itching for something to happen
> To tip us one way or the other,
> Groping in the dark for a helping hand -

(Quoted by Beckett and O'Connell 1977: 62).

One problem in creating any kind of modern African life-style lies in
the diversity of traditions to be encompassed, and in the difficulty of defining
genuine traditional behaviour. Thus Orubuloye argues that polygyny only became
commonplace in Yorubaland after cocoa became a cash crop. On the other hand
late marriage for females, which has been interpreted as resulting from the
spread of education, was, in fact, the traditional pattern amongst the Yoruba
who expected a woman to be fully adult and self-sufficient at marriage.

Wambui Wa Karanja examines modern behaviour patterns in Lagos from the
standpoint of a Kenyan woman who is now married to a Nigerian and living and
working in the city. Lagos is one of the great cities of the world and one of
the factors which serves to make it such a vibrant metropolis is the survival of
traditional attitudes and behaviour patterns in the modern sector. An American

management degree will be of very little use to someone wishing to do business in Lagos where to succeed one must learn to think like a Lagotian and to use the pragmatic Nigerian logic which reaches its apogee in the capital.

One feature of this logic is that it does not require that all beliefs held by a single individual be consistent with each other. Rather individuals are able to choose the best in each sphere of life without feeling a need for a strict logical reconciliation. Thus individuals do not have to choose to believe either in modern or in traditional medicines, rather they make a series of trials of both varieties with the choice of the method to be tried first depending upon the social context of the malady (Maclean 1977). Equally a man who is a strict Catholic in private life may perform animist religious ceremonies in his public capacity as a traditional chief.

This ability to hold opposing beliefs without experiencing mental conflict appeared in the responses to the Lagos attitude survey. The majority of respondents (a) believed that leaving children in the care of nannies and house-maids has an adverse impact on them; (b) left their own children in the care of such hirelings; and (c) believed that the working of married women had no adverse effect on the children. For an outsider there is a great temptation to try and justify the incompatibility with some rationalization but that would be to falsify what individuals concerned believe. One reason why the position of women in Lagos remains relatively favourable is because inconsistency does not cause mental pain. Both husbands and wives can accept that the husband should be the head of the household and should provide for its needs even when the wife makes her own decisions and has a sizeable income of her own.

It is very clear that marriage in Lagos does not imply the pooling of assets. Even though some of the respondents came from areas where the husband traditionally controlled the family's resources almost all of the wives controlled their own incomes. None of the men or women kept joint accounts with their spouses, because it was agreed that men and women have different priorities which are less likely to cause conflicts if they do not have to be met from a common pool (cf. Chapter 3, Table 6). However, educated women who have no independent source of income find themselves in a new position of dependence upon their husbands. In this situation the educated woman's status relative to that of her husband is clearly less favourable than that of her illiterate cousins. Given the lack of interest in marriage as an economic partnership, it would have been very interesting to have had more information on the distinctively Lagotian view of the purpose of marriage.

Many of the most pessimistic denunciations of current developments in the Third World stem from ignorance of conditions which were widespread in

Europe and America less than a hundred years ago.   Paul Erlich's (1970)
horrified reaction to conditions in Calcutta as being worse than anything the
world had ever seen basically reveals his ignorance of conditions in nineteenth
century London.   Similarly those who discuss the power of witchcraft beliefs
in Africa rarely consider the European parallels.   Travellers' tales and
scientific anthropology alike appear to focus upon the strange and different
aspects of other cultures and not upon the remarkable similarities;   upon
rituals which vary enormously in their forms rather than upon emotions which
are much more constant.   Hence the strange debate as to the sorrow or lack
of sorrow felt by African women whose children die in infancy.

Susan Soyinka has reversed the customary procedure by taking accounts
of two apparently very dissimilar cultures in England and Guinea and looking
for the similarities (Chapter 4).   Apart from providing a valuable introduction to two very challenging autobiographical works, this examination shows
how many features regarded as typically European are only very recent developments for much of rural Europe.   So often in comparing Europe and Africa the
contrast is made between the great cities of Europe and the remoter rural areas
of Africa.   In many cases it would be much more revealing to contrast rural
Europe before the motor-car with rural Africa and thus to contrast one village
community with another.   It is often assumed that we know already how Europe
was developed.   Yet, in reality, there is surprisingly little information on
family structure prior to industrialization or the impact of the first village
primary schools.   There is a world vision which Europe has lost but very recently yet finds very difficult to recapture.   Autobiographies provide one of
the most direct links with this world.

Unfortunately autobiographies are almost by definition accounts of the
lives of individuals who have received sufficient education to write down their
experiences.   One remarkable exception is the life of Baba of Karo as recounted
to M.G.Smith (1954).   Before it is too late there is a great deal of scope for
the collection of oral histories of individuals who have lived through dramatic
social changes in Africa and can represent the views of those who are without a
voice because they are illiterate.   Women form the majority of this group and
they have not been well served by the few compilations which have appeared so
far (Andreski 1970).

It is now accepted that in pre-industrial Europe there were a very wide
range of family patterns ranging from the nuclear families of rural England to
the vast extended family households of the Yugoslav Zadruga (Laslett and Wall
1972).   Much less systematic attention has been devoted to the contrasts in the
dwelling patterns and economic inter-relationships within traditional African
families belonging to different ethnic groups.   Dolores Koenig (Chapter 5)

compares the family styles of the Basa of Cameroon and the Manding of Mali
and the factors which have allowed both groups, despite their very different
family patterns, to make a very successful adaptation to commercial farming.

The Basa live in the equatorial forests of coastal Cameroon and have no
traditional chiefs.   The basic economic unit is the wife and her children and
there is no pooling of resources between co-wives in polygynous households.
In many ways Basa nuclear families, with an average of six members, have a very
Western appearance.   However, the evidence quite clearly shows that this form
of family structure was the norm long before the introduction of cash crops and
Western education.   Houses were traditionally built in isolation rather than
in nucleated villages because of widespread distrust, even between full
brothers.

The Manding live in large stratified chiefdoms, in the Sahelian savannah,
which were formerly combined in sizeable kingdoms.   In formal kinship studies
the patrilineal Manding would appear to have a great deal in common with the
patrilineal Basa, but in actual practice the family lives of the two groups are
vastly dissimilar.   The basic economic unit of the Manding comprises the patriarch, his wives and children and the married sons' wives and children.   It
is the patriarch who controls the grain supplies of this large unit which are
produced in large communal fields and main meals are eaten by the males of this
extended family assembled together in one place.   Several village studies have
shown that the average number of persons living together and sharing food in
these extended family compounds is some 18 to 21 individuals.   It is argued
that the large size of these compound-dwelling households who pool their resources of labour and produce provides insurance against the harsh conditions
of the savannah.   For example, agricultural labour demands are very much concentrated within a few weeks of the year and a family with only one adult male
who was sick at this time would be in a very perilous position.   Equally seasonal migration is an important feature of the culture and the absence of young
males during the dry season is much less disruptive of the larger households.
In contrast, Basa agriculture makes fairly constant labour demands throughout
the two growing-cycle year and migration tends to be permanent rather than
seasonal.

Both cultures have proved to be very responsive to the opportunities associated with cash crops which are cocoa and palm oil for the Basa
and peanuts and cotton for the Manding.   Indeed it is tempting to ask
whether the crops were so readily cultivated because they were so admirably
fitted to the traditional social structures.   The individualistic Basa
cultivate or collect from trees without the need for any communal endeavours
and the co-operative Manding work together on both the traditional

grain crops and the newer cash crops.   Indeed it is the larger Manding
households which are most likely to be able to use new technology because
the pooled resources make it easier to afford the necessary inputs and the
young men who have the knowledge work together with the old men who control
the wealth that can be used to purchase inputs such as insecticides and
improved seeds.   It remains an open question as to how far the low fertility
of the Basa is the result of deliberate choice rather than involuntary infertility.   However it is clearly in the interests of Basa nuclear families
to have relatively few children, just as it is in the interests of Manding
extended families to maximize the size of the labour force by having as many
children as possible.   There is a great need for a range of similar studies
of the actual functioning of the family as the basic economic unit to be
carried out in a variety of cultural contexts in order to illuminate their
fertility strategies and to provide a base line for an examination of the
impact of various aspects of modernization.

The creation of an 'ideal type' of the traditional African extended
family, all of whose features are not found in any one culture, has often
served to obscure the diversified ways in which families actually function in
individual cultures (cf. Chapter 5).   Similarly, the tendency to regard
polygyny as a single institution has only served to obscure the relationship
between polygyny and family structure.   Oladele Arowolo (Chapter 6) endeavours
to unscramble the confusions which have arisen.   In this whole area of the
debate as to the impact of polygyny upon fertility it would often appear that
each researcher imposes his, or, very occasionally, her own definition of the
question which is at issue.   To give one example very few people who quote
Dorjahn's well known Sierra Leonian data appreciate that he deliberately reduced the fertility of wives in polygynous unions by omitting any children whom
he believed to have been born as the result of the women's infidelity (Dorjahn
1958).

Perhaps the major reason why researchers have had so many problems in
studying the relationship between polygyny and fertility is simply the fact
that they are trying to answer a question which has no meaning in the indigenous cultural context. Polygyny is intended to increase the number of children
born to or socially attributed to polygynous males and this aim is certainly
achieved.   The issue as to whether it increases or reduces the fertility of
the women involved is irrelevant to local concerns.   In one study in Western
Nigeria respondents were asked who had more children the wives of monogamists
or the wives of polygynists (Ware 1975).   Some 57% of polygynous husbands
and 45% of monogamous husbands responded that the question was without meaning
since the significant factor was the number of the husband's children.   A

A further 35% of men pointed out that there was no biological difference
between monogamously and polygynously married wives and that therefore their
fertility should be the same unless the distribution of barren wives was
socially determined.   Amongst the small proportion of men who believed that
the type of marriage does affect the fertility of the wives the majority felt
that polygynously married women have fewer children.   This was said to be
because they have less pressure upon them to produce many children; because
they observe traditional post-natal restrictions upon intercourse more strictly
and because they have more freedom of choice in childbearing (reasons given in
order of importance).   Interestingly, most of these explanations assume that
wives who have co-wives have more freedom of choice as to their sexual and reproductive behaviour than a monogamous wife who always fears that if she does
not satisfy her husband he will take another wife.   The very few men who felt
that polygynously married women would have more children argued that this was
because co-wives compete to have the largest number of children and thus the
largest share of the inheritance, and because polygynous husbands want to have
as many children as possible.

Arowolo's conclusion, drawn from an in-depth examination of his own
data for Ibadan, is that, after controlling for a wide range of other factors,
wives in polygynous unions do have a marginally greater number of children
ever born.   However, type of marriage is a very poor predictor of fertility,
poorer, for example, than birthplace within Western Nigeria.   Most of the
apparent association between marriage type and fertility is a simple reflection of the fact that women in polygynous unions tend to have very different
socio-economic characteristics from women who are in genuinely monogamous
unions.   Highly educated women are not found in polygynous unions (partly
because their husbands keep de facto 'outside wives' rather than officially
recognised co-wives living in the same compound), and many of the monogamously
married young illiterate wives will later be senior wives in polygynous unions.
For all but a tiny minority of elite wives in West Africa polygyny is both a
feature of their culture and an ever present possibility for their husbands.
All their decisions are therefore taken in a polygynous context, irrespective
of their current marital type (Ware 1979A).   Divorcing individuals and their
characteristics from their total cultural context is very rarely a rewarding
exercise.

Cameroonian women also live in a cultural context where polygyny is
an ever-present possibility (Chapter 7).   In this chapter the data for
Cameroon are drawn from three very small samples: (1) wage labourers on a

foreign-owned rubber and oil-palm plantation, (2) bank employees in Douala and Yaoundé and (3) an elite group of high-ranking women administrators. Owing to the small size of the samples, the interest of the findings lies less in the actual statistics than in the general indications of the survival of a society in which elite women have the greatest number of living children and still see no reason to control their fertility. The very low fertility of the women plantation workers is associated with the very high proportion who were widowed during the civil war of the late 1950s and early 1960s. However, it does not follow that widowed women are sexually inactive, but rather that the variety of their sexual partners exposes them to a high risk of sterility consequent upon venereal infections. It is also true that the plantation women have significantly fewer surviving full siblings, (with an average of only 1.4 as compared to the 4.4 of bank workers and the 4.5 surviving full-siblings of the elite). Thus it would appear that their mothers were also exposed to conditions in which low fertility and high mortality were common hazards. Overall the low fertility of the uneducated women who migrate to labour on plantations is but one more reflection of their general marginality. These plantation women average less than half a year of education apiece. In contrast the bank workers average 11 years and the elite fully 17 years. Although the bank workers marry later than the plantation workers there is no simple relationship between age at marriage and age at the commencement of childbearing for half of the unmarried bank workers already have children. Many of these were the results of schoolgirl pregnancies. Having learnt by their experiences these mothers then control their fertility until marriage, but the pregnancy has usually cut off their chance of pursuing higher educational aspirations which would eventually have allowed them to join the ranks of the elite women. At the other extreme, some of the unmarried bank workers have remained unmarried because of their inability to produce a pregnancy for men who would only accept the constraints of a legal marriage with a woman of proven fertility. Once married, bank workers would appear to exercise no deliberate control over the number of their children.

If direct economic constraints were the determining factor, then it would be expected that the bank workers rather than the much better paid elite women would be the first to limit family size. However, it is the elite women who are exercising some control although even they generally choose to have four or more children. The only woman who had deliberately had two or fewer children explained that her choice to have only one child came about because her husband had to support the fifteen children of his three unmarried sisters. Here the responsibilities associated with the extended family certainly resulted in controlled fertility. This is an extreme case, but it helps to pinpoint an experience common to most Cameroonians who are richer than their relatives. So long as both husbands and wives continue to acknowledge multiple economic responsibilities towards their less fortunate relatives there is little reason why they should limit the numbers of their biological children as an economy measure, for any surplus will still be used up in remittances to aged parents in the village, in the education of nephews and nieces or in supporting unemployed cousins who are determined to stay in the town until they can find work. In conditions of personal or political insecurity it is very difficult to resist such claims for help, for the man or woman who is in a position to give today may well become a supplicant in the near future. Continuing to help relatives provides both personal satisfaction to the giver and the only reliable long-term insurance.

When Western researchers deal with polygyny they are unequivocally aware that the institution is foreign to their own cultures and that they should tread warily if they wish to understand its workings where the practice is commonplace. In contrast, every academic researcher has, by definition, had a prolonged experience of formal education. There is thus an almost inescapable tendency to assume that they know what education is and that its workings will be the same in all cultures. This tendency is reinforced by forms of analysis in which the analysis precedes the formation of the hypotheses. Education is almost always one of the early factors to be examined and it is so rare for education not to be associated with significant differentials in behaviour and attitudes that where such differentials fail to appear there is usually good grounds for suspecting the quality of the data. The pursuit of the impact of formal education is unfortunately so easy that many researchers go no further and very few have stopped to investigate just why education should have such a dramatic impact upon traditional cultures (Caldwell 1980).

In one sense all of the chapters in this book are concerned with the impact of education upon people's lives whether it be in examining how formal education cuts children off from their traditional cultures (Chapter 4) or why it should be that educated women are not found in polygynous marriages (Chapter 6). The final chapter (Chapter 8) is not restricted to West Africa. It provides a very clear review of the evidence available from around the world on the relationship between education and fertility. As Susan Cochrane argues, many of the earlier generalisations which insisted upon the inverse relationship relied upon data in which the poorest, least literate societies and the rural areas of richer societies were very minimally represented.

West African data can be of great service in filling in some of these gaps. However it should be recognised that apart from the 'least developed' nature of many areas of West Africa, there are also cultural factors which make it especially likely that the relationship between education and fertility will be positive, at least in the first instance. In any very poor area education may be associated with higher fertility simply because the educated have higher incomes, better access to health facilities and knowledge of preventive medicine, and are generally more healthy than the poor whose fertility is limited by biological constraints consequent upon poverty and ill-health. In West Africa there is the additional factor that many traditional populations practice prolonged post-natal sexual abstinence as well as terminal abstinence once the woman is in a position to become (or has become) a grandmother (Caldwell and Caldwell 1977; Page and Lesthaeghe 1981). Where education is associated with the lesser observance of these traditional practices then there is very considerable scope for an association between education and higher fertility. Outside Africa there is comparatively little evidence on the traditional practice of sexual abstinence and this issue has been much less thoroughly explored (but see Hull and Hull 1977; Ware 1979B).

For anyone contemplating carrying out their own research on the relationship between education and fertility, Table 6 Chapter 8 sets out a comprehensive listing of the possible ways in which education may affect fertility through intervening variables such as age at marriage, cost of child-care substitutes or husband-wife communications on fertility regulation. For any individual culture it should be possible to assemble information on all of these demands, supply and fertility regulation factors which mediate the relationship between education and fertility and thus to see, at one level, how the linkages come about. Even after this research has been completed there will still remain very great scope for many in-depth studies with a sociological or anthropological approach. For example, such studies could compare and contrast the experiences of literate and illiterate siblings within a single family or of illiterate and literate wives married to men with similar educational and occupational experiences. The scope for innovative research is vast. What is lacking is the willingness to devote more attention to examining cultures from the points of view of those who participate in them rather than from the detached standpoint of the outsider who cannot empathise with the startled reactions of the first girl from an individual village who attends primary school.

The context in which policy oriented research is carried out often results in a very short-sighted approach to the examination of the factors

involved.   Such approaches are usually also based upon false premises concerning the ways in which governments make policy decisions.   Governments
are extremely unlikely to step up the provision of educational facilities
simply because they believe that this will serve in the long run to reduce
fertility.   Rather, the extension of education depends upon the strength of
popular demand and upon beliefs as to the need for a skilled workforce.
However, some governments, who are already interested in limiting their growth
rates, could be influenced to change their educational priorities if they
believed that more equal opportunities for girls or specific changes in
curricula would influence fertility trends.   At present data to prove such
contentions are not available.   Even where research focuses upon areas where
governments might reasonably be expected to be prepared to take action many
problems still remain.   For example even where there is a genuine political
will to improve the position of women in the modern sectors of Tropical
African countries there is no model of success which can be put forward for
other countries to emulate.

Much more attention still needs to be devoted to the examination of the
possibilities for the achievement of the modern African synthesis which would
be able to integrate many of the valuable features of the traditional cultures
into the culture of twentieth century society.   Both women and the educational
systems have very important roles to play in such re-assessments.   Western
education has done more than any other factor to destroy the traditional
cultures, and women have most to lose from the unthinking adoption of Western
ways.   Whilst it is easy to over-romanticize the independence of West African
women it is still true that they have a great deal to teach other women who
have yet to learn that the first element of independence is economic autonomy.

REFERENCES

Andreski, I. 1970. Old Wives Tales: Life Stories from Ibibioland, Routledge and Kegan Paul, London.

Beckett, P. and O'Connell, J. 1977. Education and Power in Nigeria: A Study of University Students, Hodder and Stoughton, London.

Caldwell, J. 1968. Population Growth and Family Change in Africa: The New Urban Elite in Ghana, ANU Press, Canberra.

Caldwell, J. and Caldwell, P. 1977. "The role of marital sexual abstinence in determining fertility: a study of the Yoruba in Nigeria", Population Studies, 31 (1): 193-217.

Caldwell, J. 1978. "A theory of fertility from high plateau to destabilization", Population and Development Review, 4 (4): 553-577.

Caldwell, J. 1980 "Mass education as a determinant of the timing of fertility decline", Population and Development Review, 6 (2): 225-255.

Clarke, R. 1979. "Agricultural Production in a Rural Yoruba Community", Ph.d. University of London.

Cleave, J. 1974 African Farmers: Labor Use in the Development of Smallholder Agriculture, Praeger, New York.

Dorjahn, V. 1958. "Fertility, polygyny and their interrelations in Temne society", American Anthropologist, 60: 838-60, cf. Ibid 61:893-895.

DuBey, D. et.al. 1979. An Introduction to the Sociology of Nigerian Education, MacMillan, Hong Kong.

Eades, J. 1980. The Yoruba Today, CUP, Cambridge.

Ehrlich, P. 1970 The Population Bomb, Ballantine, New York.

Harrell-Bond, B. 1975. Modern Marriage in Sierra Leone, Mouton, The Hague.

Hopen, C. 1958. The Pastoral Fulbe Family in Gwandu, OUP, London.

Hull, T. and Hull, V. 1977. "The relation of economic class and fertility: an analysis of some Indonesian data", Population Studies, 31 (1): 43-57.

Kaberry, P. 1952. Women of the Grassfields: A Study of the Economic Position of Women in Bamenda, British Cameroons, HMSO, London.

Laslett, P. and Wall, R. eds. 1972. Household and Family in Past Time, CUP, Cambridge.

Lloyd, B. 1967 " Indigenous Ibadan" in P. Lloyd et al. eds. The City of Ibadan, CUP, Cambridge.

Lloyd, P. 1967 " The elite" in P. Lloyd et al. Ibid.

Maclean, U. 1977. Magical Medicine: A Nigerian Case Study, Penguin, Harmondsworth.

Meillassoux, C. 1975. Femmes, Greniers et Capitaux, Maspero, Paris.

Morgan, P. 1975. Childcare: Sense and Fable, Temple Smith, London.

Nag, M. 1979. "How modernization can also increase fertility", Working Paper 49, Population Council, New York.

Oppong, C. 1974. Marriage among a Matrilineal Elite: A Family Study of Ghanaian Senior Civil Servants, CUP, Cambridge.

Page, H. and Lesthaeghe, R. 1981. Child-Spacing in Tropical Africa, Academic Press, London.

Quinn, N. 1977. "Anthropological studies on women's status", Annual Review of Anthropology, 6: 181-225.

Rapp, R. 1979. "Anthropology-review essay", Signs, 4 (3): 497-513.

Rencontres Internationales de Bouake 1965. Tradition et Modernisme en Afrique Noire, editions du Seuil, Paris.

Rogers, S. 1978. "Woman's place: a critical review of anthropological theory", Comparative Studies in Society and History, 20 (1): 123-173.

Smith, M. 1954 Baba of Karo A woman of the Muslim Hausa, Autobiography recorded by M. Smith, Faber and Faber, London.

Sudarkasa, N. 1973. Where Women Work: A Study of Yoruba Women in the Market Place and in the Home, Museum of Anthropology, University of Michegan, Ann Arbor.

Vercruijsse, E. 1974. "Composition of households in some Fante communities: a study of the frameworks of social integration", in C. Oppong ed. Domestic Rights and Duties in Southern Ghana, IAS, Legon, Accra.

Ware, H. 1975. Yoruba Social Structure: The Role of Polygyny, Demography Department, ANU, Canberra.

Ware, H. 1979A. "Polygyny: women's views in a transitional society", Journal of Marriage and the Family, 41 (1): 185-195.

Ware, H. 1979B. "The application of social science research to family planning programme needs and problems in the island communities of the South Pacific", in Fertility Control in the Pacific, WHO, Manila.

Ware, H. 1981A. Women, Development and Demography, ANU Press, Canberra.

Ware, H. 1981B. "The female life-cycle" in C. Oppong ed. Female and Male in West Africa, George Allen and Unwin, London.

Weil, P. 1976. "The staff of life: food and female fertility in a West African society", Africa, 46: 182-195.

CHAPTER 1

WAGE EARNER AND MOTHER:
COMPATIBILITY OF ROLES
ON A CAMEROON PLANTATION

Virginia DeLancey

CHAPTER 1

WAGE EARNER AND MOTHER : COMPATIBILITY OF
ROLES ON A CAMEROON PLANTATION*

Virginia DeLancey

Introduction

    Studies on the relationship between female labor force participation and
fertility in developing countries have shown both negative relationships
(Heer and Turner: 1965), as well as no relationship (Gendell: 1965; Stycos
and Weller: 1967) between the variables. One of the factors sometimes cited
as a cause of the lack of relationship is that of role compatibility. As
Stycos and Weller suggested from their studies in Turkey (1967), where the
roles of mother and worker are basically compatible, there should be no
relationship between employment and fertility. Role compatibility may exist
because of the type of work or because of the alternatives available for
child care. Thus, work on the family farm or in a cottage industry, petty
trading in the local market place, or various other types of self-employment
may be compatible with caring for one's children. This is because the mother
may be able to keep her child with her while she works or because she can
arrange her hours of work to suit the needs of caring for her child or to fit
a schedule which allows others to care for the child. Work for an employer
outside the home may also be compatible with the role of a mother if
'parental surrogates' such as relatives or friends are available to care for
the children or if suitable state, private, or employer-provided day care
facilities exist.

    Some studies have examined the factor of role compatibility in general
(Jaffe and Azumi: 1960: Hass: 1972). Studies carried out in Africa
sometimes question the lack of conflict (Boserup: 1970, pp.165-66), but more
often conclude that the work of women does not conflict with the role of
motherhood (Arowolo: 1976, p.33). In many instances, women do not have to
choose between the two roles; they work near the home and have family

* This paper is based upon field research in the United Republic of
   Cameroon from August 1975 to December 1976. Fieldwork was made possible
   through permission granted by ONAREST, Cameroon and by the Cameroon
   Development Corporation as well as through grants from the Social Science
   Research Council/American Council of Learned Societies, Fulbright-Hays
   Doctoral Dissertation Abroad program, and UNESCO. The author acknowledges
   with gratitude the assistance; however, she alone is responsible for the
   analysis and interpretation of the data.

members who can care for the children (Germain and Smock: 1974, p.39).
Women are often expected to work to support themselves even after marriage.
When doing so, they also tend to support their children, either partially or
totally (McCall: 1961, pp.288-291; Peil: 1972, pp.191, 202). It is not
uncommon for fertility to remain high in such situations, because of the
lack of role conflict, because children are viewed as performing positive
functions in life (providing a source of labor, serving as social and
economic security in old age, and building prestige for the parents), and
because the work generally does not offer rewards to compensate for having
few children. Most of the employment of women is of relatively low status
such as non-wage work in subsistence agriculture or in petty trading. Where
fertility has been found to be lower, it is more often among educated women
who hold prestigeful wage/salary jobs (Germain and Smock: 1974, pp.39-40).

Most studies of role conflict conducted in Africa have concentrated on
women in non-wage employment. Little work has been done among women
engaged in wage employment. One study which did investigate the topic
included women employed for wages in Ghana. It was found that such women
were twice as likely as men to say that in the future they planned to be
self-employed because they believed that it would be easier to combine such
work with maternal activities (Peil: 1972, p.109).

It is sometimes assumed that accepting the obligations of wage
employment such as having to go to work each day, to arrive at a regular
hour and to remain for a specified number of hours is incompatible with
carrying out the functions of a mother (See Arowolo: 1978). But, little
empirical work has been conducted to test the assumption. If role
incompatibility is found to exist, wage employement may affect fertility. If
role incompatibility is not found then there can be less expectation that
such employment will affect fertility except in the rare cases where the nature
of the employment is such that it biologically affects the ability to
reproduce. Any other relationship between labor force participation and
fertility would be in the opposite direction resulting from fertility
affecting the propensity to enter wage employment.

Women at the Cameroon Development Corporation, Tole Tea Estate

This study included questions specifically designed to determine
whether or not wage-employed women experience compatability or incompatibility
between their roles as wage employees and as mothers. Data for this study
were collected in 1975-76 from the population of 175 married women who were

living with their husbands, and who were employed for wages by the Cameroon Development Corporation at the Tole Tea Estates in the Southwest Province of Cameroon. Some data were also collected from the population of 53 non-wage-employed women who were married and living with their husbands in the same location.

Non-wage-employed women, in this study, refers to those women who are either self-employed or not employed for money. They may be traders in the market or at their homes. They may be farmers growing most of their own food requirements and possibly selling any excess farm products for cash. Some may even produce these or other products specifically for resale, although cash crops have more often been a male speciality, a few may have no source of income and may not even cultivate a garden for their own consumption purposes. They may utilise all of their time in caring for the house and tending the children. The common element among all of them is that they do any kind of work except work which provides a wage or a salary. Therefore, these women are grouped together for the analysis of the assumption that such non-wage work is more flexible, in general, than wage employment and thus potentially more compatible with the role of motherhood. This assumption is based upon the fact that these women have no employer who requires regular hours of work with few excuses for absence and with little patience for interruption of the schedule by children.

Most of the wage-employed women work in the fields at Tole Tea Estate, plucking tea leaves, although some are employed as headwomen in charge of a group of about 30 laborers, as checkers who weigh the plucked tea, or as overseers with three or more headwomen under them. A few work in the tea factory as packers, in the day care centre, in the office, or in the clinic as paramedic nurses or as the trained midwife. Such employment, manual labor for the majority of the female employees, cannot be expected to provide any reward or compensation for having fewer children other than a monetary reward. Cameroon Pidgin English proverbs reflect the possible ranking of importance of monetary rewards and children. There is one proverb which emphasises the importance of money, 'Soup i sweet, na money make am' (:If the soup is delicious, it is money which has made it so). However, there is another one which may be even more significant and which reveals that children may be even more important than money, "Pikin for hand de pass kobo for kwa". (:A child is more valuable/desirable than a purse full of money).

The influence of education on fertility should be minimal in this study because very few of the women are educated. Some 86% of the wage-employed and 53% of those not in wage employment have had no education. Only 4% of the wage-earners and 21% of the non-wage-earners have completed primary school, and only the midwife employed by the clinic has continued beyond primary school.   The wage-employed women ranged between 20 and 49 years and averaged 33 years old whereas the non-wage-employed women ranged from 14 to 44 years and averaged 27 years old.

Income data reveal that the wage-employed women who were interviewed earned an average of 9,767 CFA ($39) in wages or salary per women per month. Most of these women received additional income from sources such as a family allowance from the Cameroon National Social Insurance Fund (see below), earnings from petty trading or 'chop farm' produce, or in the form of the market value of food which they grow and consume. This additional income combined with wages and salaries brought average income to 17,354 CFA ($69) per woman per month. This is more than twice the average income of 8,250 CFA ($33) per month for each of the 51 out of 53 non-wage-earners who received an income.

A large proportion of the wage-employed women who were interviewed have been employed for many years, long enough to at least begin to show some relationship between labor force participation and fertility if it exists, and certainly long enough to show the individual employees whether or not they are personally experiencing role incompatability. Nearly four-fifths of them have been employed for five years or longer, often without interruption, and almost a quarter have similarly been employed for twelve years or longer. The average number of years of wage employment was 8.6, although two women have worked for twenty years.

Overall, the number of living children for wage-employed women ranged from 0 to 13, with an average of 4.1 children. The number for non-wage-employed women ranged from 0 to 9, with an average of 2.8 children. No conclusions should be drawn from this information at this point, however, because of the variations in ages and durations of marriage between the two groups of women.

Cameroon lies partially within the belt of sub-fertility which runs through Central Africa, but studies have shown that individual ethnic groups within Cameroon vary in their fertility performance (Azefor: 1972). The women interviewed have migrated from many ethnic homelands and represent thirty different ethnic groups from Cameroon as well as ethnic groups from Nigeria and Togo. Most, however, come from the Northwest and Southwest Provinces of Cameroon. Among the wage-employed women, only seven of the groups

contain more than 5% of the women, and only two groups include more than
10% of the women. There is equal variety amongst women with no wages.Thus,
it would be difficult to measure the effects of ethnicity upon fertility.

The Decision to Work for Wages and the Age of Youngest Child

In countries where studies indicate that a negative relationship
between female labor force participation and fertility exists, the
relationship sometimes persists because women with young children do not
work. It is often more difficult for a mother with young children to care
for them while working. Thus, for example, in the US, many women wait until
their children enter school, or at least a preschool, before they consider
entering or returning to wage/salary employment. To examine whether the age
of children affected the decision to work for wages, whether   age created
an unresolvable conflict or not, an attempt was made to obtain the age of
each women's youngest child. Table 1 shows the results.

TABLE 1 : NUMBER AND PER CENT OF WOMEN BY AGE OF YOUNGEST CHILD

Age of Youngest Child	Wage-Employed Women		Non-Wage-Employed Women	
	Number	Per Cent	Number	Per Cent
No children	8	4.6	10	18.9
0-3 months	14	8.0	6	11.3
4-6 months	14	8.0	5	9.4
7-11 months	12	6.9	7	13.2
Subtotal: 0-11 months	40	22.9	18	33.9
1 year	36	20.6	9	17.0
2 years	32	18.3	9	17.0
Subtotal: 0-2 years	108	61.7	36	67.9
3 years	12	6.9	0	0.0
4 years	10	5.7	0	0.0
5 years	8	4.6	2	3.8
Subtotal: 0-5 years, preschool age	138	78.9	38	71.7
6 years	2	1.1	3	5.7
7 years	5	2.9	0	0.0
8 years	3	1.7	0	0.0
9 years	0	0.0	0	0.0
10 years	3	1.7	0	0.0
11 years	0	0.0	0	0.0
12 years	3	1.7	0	0.0
Subtotal: 6-12 years, primary school age	16	9.1	3	5.7
13-18 years: secondary school age	9	5.1	2	3.8
19 years and older	4	2.3	0	0.0
TOTAL	175	100.0%	53	100.1%

As can be seen, only 8 (5%) of the wage-employed women had no living children and thus did not need to be concerned with any conflict between the roles of wage employee and mother. But 40 of the wage-employed women, nearly one-fourth, had children under one year of age. However, 12 of the 14 women with infants of two months of age or younger were still at home on official maternity leave provided under the Cameroon Social Insurance legislation and the Cameroon Labor Code. A total of 108 (62%) of the wage-employed women had children two years of age or younger. This is significant because two years is the time period during which many women continue to breastfeed their children and during which children are considered definitely too young to stay in the house alone. Finally, 79% of the women had children of age five or less, under the average age of entering primary school. It is apparent that very young children did not prohibit many of these women from entering wage employment or from re-entering it as soon as their maternity leave was over. In fact, if one compares the data from the wage-employed women with that of the non-wage-employed women, one can see that a greater percentage of non-wage-employed women than wage-employed women had no children and that a greater percentage of wage-employed women than non-wage-employed women had young, non-schoolage children, the reverse of what one would expect to find if role incompatibility were a serious problem.

Table 2 reveals another aspect of the effect of age of children upon entry or re-entry to the labor force. The women were asked for the age of their last child when they entered or returned to work. If the women had been employed and had taken maternity leave, the reply indicated the age of the last child when she returned to active employment. Once again it can be seen that the women entered or returned to active employment when their children were very young. Nearly 78% of the women claimed to have gone to work when their last child was less than one year old, and an additional 7% were still on official maternity leave at the time of interview. Such leave normally ends when the child is two months old. More than 87% had entered or returned before their last child was of primary school age. Only 3% of the women had waited until their children had reached school age.

State Support for Wage-Employed Mothers

One factor which has not very often been considered but which should affect the extent of role compatibility for female wage-earners with young children is the extent of support for mothers in national legislation.

TABLE 2 : NUMBER AND PER CENT OF WAGE-EMPLOYED WOMEN
BY AGE OF YOUNGEST CHILD AT TIME OF ENTRY OR
RE-ENTRY TO ACTIVE EMPLOYMENT

Age of Youngest Child	Number of Women	Per Cent of Women
No live births	3	1.7
Still on maternity leave	12	6.9
0-2 months	31	17.7
3-5 months	101	57.7
6-11 months	4	2.3
Subtotal: 0-11 months	136	77.7
1 year	4	2.3
2 years	6	3.4
Subtotal: 0-2 years	146	83.4
3 years	2	1.1
4 years	1	0.6
5 years	3	1.7
Subtotal: 0-5 years, preschool age	152	86.8
6 years	2	1.1
7 years	1	0.6
8 years	1	0.6
9 years	0	0.0
10 years	1	0.6
Over age 10	1	0.6
Subtotal: 6 years and older, primary school age and older	6	3.5
Unknown	2	1.1
TOTAL	175	100.0

Special provisions in labor codes as well as maternity and family benefits
provided by social insurance laws may help to reduce role incompatibility
for such women (see Peil, for example: 1972, p.109).

Several such legal factors make it easier for women in Cameroon to
work when their children are young. Wage-employed women must take
maternity leave at full pay beginning 4-6 weeks before delivery and ending
8-10 weeks after the child is born, a total of 14 weeks. If it is shown
that a mother is not well enough to return to work at the end of that time,
she is granted a six-week extension of the leave on full pay. During
maternity leave, a temporary replacement may be employed, but the woman's
job must await her at the end of her leave. Both wage-employed women and
wives of wage-employed men receive a maternity allowance of 6,300 CFA
($25.20) in two equal instalments prior to delivery and an additional 6,000
CFA ($24) at the time of delivery. Women employees of the Cameroon
Development Corporation (CDC) and wives of male employees receive free
medical care. Those working for other employers receive 200 CFA ($0.80) for
each office visit to the doctor for pregnancy-related reasons and 1,400 CFA

($5.60) for the delivery. From the time the child is born, the
wage-employed mother or father receives 700 CFA ($2.80) per month for each
child as a family allowance. However, if both the mother and her husband
are employed, the family allowance is paid to only one of them, normally to
the husband (Azeme Emile: personal interview, 1 December 1976 and Cameroon:
Law No.74/14 of 27 November 1974 Instituting the Labor Code). In addition,
the Labor Code provides that for 15 months following the birth of the child,
the woman is granted a nursing break of one hour per day (Cameroon: Law
No.74/14 of 27 November 1974 Instituting the Labor Code). One can see that
these benefits are consistent with the Cameroon policy of promoting
population growth, but they also make it easier for women to enter or
continue wage employment soon after giving birth to a child.

The Care of Young Children

If the women find it possible to enter or return to work when their
children are young, then one must look further to detect evidence of role
incompatibility. Once employed, what do the women do with their children?
Can they or do they bring them to work with them? Table 3 reveals that the
vast majority (94%) did not believe that they can bring their children to
work. However a few women stated that someone looking after the child can
bring the baby to the tea fields for a feed   if the baby insists. For
example, on two occasions during the day each woman brings the
leaves she has plucked to a central location to be weighed before the final
weighing of the day. The first time is about 9am and it is followed by a
break during which the women sit down near the weigh house and eat the
breakfast which they prepared before leaving home. It is not uncommon to
see young children delivering hungry babies to the resting mothers at this
time for mid-morning feeds.   The other women who said that it is possible
to bring their children to work were those employed, for example, as
checkers. These women sit in the weigh houses while the other women pluck
the tea, and three times a day they record the weight of green leaf which
each woman has plucked. The weigh houses in which they work are open on all
sides but are roofed for some protection against sun and light rain. There
is considerable waiting time for the checkers, so it is not too difficult
for them to care for their small child except during the weighing times.

Most of the women did not think that they can bring their children to
work with them or, for certain reasons, they do not bring them. What, then,
does each woman do with her children when she comes to work? A creche, or
day care nursery, is provided for care of children, free-of-charge, from

TABLE 3 : ABILITY OR WILLINGNESS TO BRING CHILDREN TO WORK
BY AGE OF YOUNGEST CHILD

(Number and Per Cent of Women Replying)

Age of Youngest Child in Years	Ability/Willingness to Bring Children to Work							
	Yes Can Bring Them to Work		No Cannot Bring Them to Work		Unknown/ No Reply		Total	
	No.	%	No.	%	No.	%	No.	%
No children	1	13	4	50	3	37	8	100
0	3	8	37	92	0	0	40	·100
1	1	3	35	97	0	0	36	100
2	0	0	32	100	0	0	32	100
3-5	0	0	30	100	0	0	30	100
6-12	1	6	14	8	1	6	16	100
12 and older	0	0	13	100	0	0	13	100
TOTAL	6	3	165	94	4	2	175	99

birth through the age of five, after which age they can enter school. Many
women in developed countries are still lobbying for the provision of such
day care. But Table 4A shows that only 7% of wage-employed women at Tole
were using the creche for their children. A count taken on one day showed
only 26 children at the creche, with two women attending them. This was at
the beginning of November, immediately after pay day, the day that primary
schools 'drive out' children who have failed to pay their school fees in
order to impress their parents that part of their pay must be allocated to
schooling. Many of these children automatically stopped by the nursery on
their way home from school and picked up their young charges. The records
of the women attendants of the creche showed that there were never many more
than 56 or 57 children on any day, and even less during the months when
school is not in session. But, looking at the tables above which show only
the age of the youngest child, one can see that there were 138 of those
children alone who were eligible to attend and that 79% of the
wage-employed women had preschool age children. Many of those mothers also
had one or even two other children who would have qualified for such care,
and that does not even consider the 352 women of all other marital
categories who were permanently employed, many of whom also had young
children. Many thought that the children do not receive enough individual
attention at the creche and that they are not picked up as soon as they
begin to cry. The latter is quite true; the attendant/child ratio is too
small to allow this. Some of the women also did not like the general
appearance of the creche. 'Na some wowo dirty place', (:What a terrible,

TABLE 4A : METHOD OF CHILD CARE USED BY WAGE-EMPLOYED WOMEN BY AGE OF YOUNGEST CHILD

(Number of Responses)

Age of Youngest Child in Years	Method of Child Care							Total Replies
	Left Children at Creche	Stay Alone, in School, Working, etc.	Siblings, Mbanyi, Other Relatives	Employed a Baby Nurse	Difficult to Provide Care	Other	Unknown/ No Reply	
No children*	2	4	0	0	0	0	3	9
0	2	4	33	5	1	1	0	46
1	4	0	29	2	0	1	0	36
2	2	5	24	1	0	1	1	34
3-5	1	7	24	1	0	1	0	34
6-12	1	11	7	0	0	0	0	19
12+	0	9	4	0	0	0	0	13
TOTAL WOMEN	12	40	121	9	1	4	4	191

Note: Multiple replies were listed.

* Women with no biological children of their own may still be responsible for other people's children.

dirty place) was a common opinion given by the women at the time of interviewing, although shortly after the management completely repainted it, was making attempts to refurbish it, and was thinking of ways to make it more desirable to the women.

TABLE 4B : METHOD OF CHILD CARE USED BY NON-WAGE-EMPLOYED
BY AGE OF YOUNGEST CHILD

(Number of Responses)

Age of Youngest Child in Years	Method of Child Care					
	Stay Alone, in School, Working, etc.	Siblings, Mbanyi, Other Relatives	Mother Works at Home; no Problem	Mother is Not Employed	Other	Total Replies
No child	0	0	0	9	1	10
0	0	1	7	10	2	20
1	0	3	1	3	2	9
2	0	1	2	6	0	9
3-5	1	1	0	0	0	2
6-12	1	0	1	1	0	3
12+	0	1	1	0	0	2
TOTAL WOMEN	2	7	12	29	5	55

Note: Multiple replies were listed.

Nearly a quarter of the women had at least some children who were old enough to remain by themselves, but many of these same women also had younger children who still needed care of some type. By far the most popular method of care for the children was by siblings, mbanyi (co-wives), or various other members of the family. Many families bring along a young relative from their ethnic homeland, specifically to help around the house or to care for the children. In return, the family generally maintains the young relative and eventually pays the child's school fees.

TABLE 5 : WAGE-EMPLOYED WOMEN WHO PAID OR DID NOT PAY FOR CHILD CARE

	Number of Women
Paid for child care	13
Did not pay for child care	158
Unknown/no reply	4
TOTAL	175

Very few women said that they have to pay cash for child care (see Table 5). However, if they bring a relative from home to live with them and to help around the house and care for the children, as mentioned above, they pay in kind by maintaining the relative, providing food, shelter, clothing, 'pocket money', and often school fees. This probably amounts to a larger total sum than if the mother simply employs someone to do the job, but it also gives more control over and greater flexibility of scheduling of the child-care duties. In addition, it is often expected that those who are earning money should try to help others in the extended family to better themselves by assisting them to obtain an education or occupational training or by providing them with the opportunity to find future employment. Therefore, many of these young relatives might be living with the women irrespective of whether or not they are asked to reciprocate for their maintenance.

In contrast to that of the wage-employed women, Table 4B indicates that non-wage-employed women care for their children in several different ways. Three-quarters of them stated that they had no difficulty caring for their children, either because they did not work (55% of the replies) or because they worked basically at home (22%) and that it was no trouble to care for the children while working in this manner.

In summary, neither non-wage-employed nor wage-employed women have experienced great difficulty in caring for their children. In fact, the wage-employed at this location have found it possible to work outside of their homes even while they have young children and even though they cannot take their children to work with them. Day care is provided at a convenient location for preschool children, but the women have preferred to use various family members to care for the young ones.

Care of Children Who are Sick or Who Need Extra Attention

The above picture seems to portray very little conflict between the role of female wage-earner and that of mother. However, further questions show that the women do not simply go off to work each day leaving the children to prearranged child care or sending them off to school without caring whether they are well or sick. When asked whether or not they have ever had to stay home from work because of their children, 63% of them stated that they have, some very often (18%) and some just occasionally (41%). Examination of Table 6 shows a tendency for the mothers with the youngest children to stay home more often than those with older children. Fortunately, the management of the tea estate is cognisant of the possible conflict between having to go to work and needing to care for a child who temporarily requires extra attention. If a child is very sick, a woman will not put work before her child; management has attempted to minimise the possible conflict by not penalising the women. Clinic hours are held each morning, and mothers will often bring a sick child to the clinic for treatment at that time. If the illness is not severe, the child will be treated, after which the woman must return to work with no excuse. However, if the child is very sick and requires the mother's attention, the mother will be given 'excused duty' and may stay home to care for the child while earning full pay. All of these provisions are in addition to the various types of sick leave given when the employee herself is sick (Elundu: personal interview, 4 November 1976).

In spite of the benevolent attitude of the management of the corporation toward employees and their medical problems, Table 7 shows that 12% of the women have had to formally quit work at some time in their career (although not always while working at the Tole Tea Estate) because of their children. Most often this occurred if the child had contracted an extended illness or if the child had been operated on and the woman had decided that it was necessary for her to remain at home with the child for an indefinite time period. Occasionally it was because she had been unable to find someone to care for the child in general, but it had not usually been because of the belief that it is better for a mother to remain at home with a young child.

The Importance of Attitudes

Attitudes, too, are important in determining whether or not there is any incompatibility in the roles which must be played. A positive attitude toward coping with potential difficulties can lessen conflicts which do occur. In Table 8, only 15% of the wage-employed women believed that it would be very difficult to leave home each day to go to work if they were to have another baby. Some 40% felt it would be a little difficult, and 44% thought that they would have no difficulty at all. In comparing this data to that of the non-wage-employed women in the same table, it is possible to see that, in general, more non-wage-employed than wage-employed women believed that it would be very difficult to work away from home if they had another baby and that fewer non-wage-employed than wage-employed women felt that they would experience no difficulty at all.

TABLE 6 : FREQUENCY OF INABILITY TO GO TO WORK FOR THE DAY BECAUSE NO ONE IS AVAILABLE
TO WATCH THE CHILDREN BY AGE OF YOUNGEST CHILD

Age of Youngest	Yes								No Never		Unknown/ No Reply		Total	
	Very Often		Occasionally		Frequency Unqualified		Subtotal							
	No.	%	No.	%	No.	%	No.	%	No.	%	No.	%	No.	%
No children *	0	0	3	38	0	0	3	38	2	25	3	38	8	100
0-1	11	28	17	43	2	5	30	75	10	25	0	0	40	100
1	8	22	20	55	0	0	28	78	8	22	0	0	36	100
2	3	9	14	44	0	0	17	53	14	44	1	0	32	100
3-5	4	13	11	37	1	3	16	53	14	47	0	0	30	100
6-12	4	25	5	31	2	13	11	69	5	31	0	0	16	100
12 and older	2	15	2	15	1	8	5	39	8	61	0	0	13	100
TOTAL	32	18	72	41	6	3	110	63	61	35	4	2	175	100

* These women may have had children who have since died or they may have other relatives whom they are caring for.

TABLE 7 : WOMEN WHO HAVE EVER QUIT WORK BECAUSE OF NO ONE TO CARE FOR THE CHILDREN

	Number of Women	Per Cent of Women
Have had to quit work for child	21	12
Have never quit work for child	147	84
Unknown/no reply	7	4
TOTAL	175	100

TABLE 8 : AMOUNT OF DIFFICULTY ANTICIPATED IN WORKING AWAY FROM HOME
IF THE WOMAN HAD ANOTHER BABY BY AGE OF YOUNGEST CHILD

Wage-Employed Women

	Amount of Difficulty Anticipated									
	Very Difficult		A Little Difficult		No Difficulty		Unknown/ No Reply		Total	
	No.	%	No.	%	No.	%	No.	%	No.	%
No children	0	0	4	50	4	50	0	0	8	100
0-1	7	18	17	43	16	40	0	0	40	100
1	6	17	18	50	12	33	0	0	36	100
2	6	19	10	31	15	47	1	3	32	100
3-5	5	17	13	43	12	40	0	0	30	100
6-12	1	6	5	31	10		0	0	16	100
12 and older	2	15	3	23	8	62	0	0	13	100
TOTAL	27	15	70	40	77	44	1	1	175	100

Non-Wage-Employed Women

	Amount of Difficulty Anticipated									
	Very Difficult		A Little Difficult		No Difficulty		Unknown/ No Reply		Total	
	No.	%	No.	%	No.	%	No.	%	No.	%
No children	2	20	6	60	1	10	1	10	10	100
0-1	6	33	7	39	4	22	1	6	18	100
1	5	56	2	22	2	22	0	0	9	100
2	4	44	2	22	3	33	0	0	9	99
3-5	0	0	1	50	1	50	0	0	2	100
6-12	3	100	0	0	0	0	0	0	3	100
12 and older	0	0	1	50	1	50	0	0	2	100
TOTAL	20	38	19	36	12	23	2	4	53	100

It is interesting to note in Table 8 that among the wage-employed women
it was those women whose youngest child was of primary school age or older
who were more likely to say that there would be no difficulty in continuing
to work if they had another baby and who were less likely to say that it would
be very difficult to do so. Have they learned to cope with the conflicts
which arise because they have had long experience dealing with them? Does it
mean that such women know that they have an older child who would be able to
help care for the new baby while the mother works? Or, does this indicate
that as one moves further away in time from the most difficult conflicts that
one forgets the problems which those with young children currently in the

home are continually experiencing and which lead them to give slightly less positive replies?

Reasons Why Some Women Do Not Work For Wages

The information analysed above was received mainly from women who were currently working for wages; they seemed to have a positive attitude toward their own ability to manage conflict situations which might arise, enough so that they were able to work even with young children in the home. However 21% of the 53 presently non-wage-employed women had previously worked for wages on a permanent basis at some time in their lives. Thus, one final test examined the question from the perspective of why the 53 non-wage-employed women who are wives of male employees of Tole Tea Estate were not working when so many of their fellow wives were. The results are displayed in Table 9. Because multiple replies were coded, the total exceeds 100%.

TABLE 9 : REASONS WHY WOMEN DO NOT WORK FOR WAGES

Reasons	Number of Women	Per Cent of Women
1. Does not like to work at any time or does not like to work at this time	12	22
2. Husband will not allow wife to work	12	23
3. Work is not available, at least not the kind that the woman would like to do	9	17
4. There is no one to watch the children	9	17
5. Has poor health and cannot work	8	15
6. Does not think that she has had sufficient training to secure a job	5	9
7. Prefers non-wage and 'chop farm' work	5	9
8. Believes women should remain at home – to care for husband and children	4	8
9. Other – including the response that the woman would like to work soon	5	9

Note: Multiple replies were coded.

As can be seen, a large proportion of the women replied that they do not like the difficult, scheduled, manual labor which is available at this

location, or they prefer non-wage labor. More relevant to the question of
role compatibility, only 4 of the women felt that women should remain at
home in order to care for their home, their husband, or their children.
However, a greater number of husbands thought that their wives should stay
home. Twelve of the women stated that their husbands do not allow them
or give them permission to work. Most often, these were the wives of the
male office employees or of higher-level field assistants or factory
managers whose husbands do not want to see their wives working as common
laborers in the fields when they themselves have managed to reach higher
positions through either education or long experience. Most significant
of the responses were those from the 9 women who indicated that they did
not work for wages because they had no one to watch the children. Thus, it
must be noted that the problem of role incompatibility does arise for at
least a small number of women and is apparently not resolvable to the
satisfaction of those women.

Conclusions

When confronted with the question of whether or not the women have to
grapple with a major problem of incompatibility between the roles of
wage-earner and mother, the manager of Tole Tea Estate suggested that
perhaps the women have greater difficulties dealing with the incompatibility
between their roles of wage-earner and wife. Many of the husbands do not
like their wives to work because they believe that they become too
'head-strong' and independent upon entering work and beginning to bring
home a regular pay cheque (see also Weekes-Vagliani: 1976, p.41). Due to
job categorization and overtime pay, the wife's total pay is often larger
than her husband's. That causes much greater conflict than determining how
to care for the children while the wife works; perhaps there are a greater
number of acceptable solutions to the child care conflict than to the pay
dilemma.

The data presented above gives strong support to the position that
under the relatively favourable conditions provided by the Cameroon
Development Corporation personnel policies and the government labor and
social insurance legislation, it is possible for female employees to work
for wages outside their homes and away from their families without having
unsolvable problems of role incompatibility. This is not to say that
conflicts do not arise, but that there are sufficient alternative solutions
available which allow most of the women who so desire to continue to work.

If most of the problems causing role incompatibility can be alleviated, can labor force participation affect fertility? More detailed analysis of the data would be necessary to confirm any relationship or lack of relationship, but a simple examination of the average number of living children per women did not reveal any consistently negative relationship, within each particular age group, between number of living children and the number of years of wage employment. Neither does the data show that the wage-earning women tend to have a smaller average number of children per age group compared to that of the non-wage-earning women (see Table 10). Note, however, that the wage-earners have been married longer, on the average. It is possible that other characteristics of wage employment may affect fertility in other places or under different conditions. Also it is possible that other conditions or places may produce incompatibility of roles between that of wage-earner and mother. This is a small, isolated case study, but it suggests that similar conclusions may be found elsewhere and may have important implications for the development of manpower and employment policies, for population policies, and for the inclusion of women in the economic development of their countries.

TABLE 10 : FREQUENCY OF NUMBER OF LIVING CHILDREN, AVERAGE NUMBER OF CHILDREN AND AVERAGE NUMBER OF YEARS OF MARRIAGE PER AGE GROUP FOR WAGE-EARNING AND NON-WAGE-EARNING WOMEN

Number of Living Children	Wage-Earners						Non-Wage-Earners						
	20-24	25-29	30-34	35-39	40-44	45-49	10-14	15-19	20-24	25-29	30-34	35-39	40-44
0	0	1	5	0	1	1	1	5	2	1			1
1	2	0	3	4	3	1		3	5	0			
2	5	2	3	4		0			5	3		2	
3	7	14	6	3		2			3	4	1		
4	1	11	16	7	1					1	1		
5		5	17	7	4					2	2		
6		1	5	9		1				2	4	1	2
7			3	8	4	1						1	1
8				3	1	1							
9													
10					1								
11													
12				1									
13													
Number of Women	15	34	58	46	15	7	1	8	15	13	8	4	4
Average Number of Children All Women	2.5	3.6	3.9	5.0	4.8	4.0	0.0	0.4	1.6	3.4	5.1	4.3	4.8
Average Number of Children Fecund Women	2.5	3.7	4.3	5.0	5.2	4.7	-	1.0	1.8	3.7	5.1	4.3	6.3
Average Number of Years of Marriage	6.8	12.1	15.2	19.7	25.5	27.1	3.0	1.3	4.6	9.5	12.9	21.0	24.8

Age in Years

BIBLIOGRAPHY

Arowolo, Oladele O. 1978. 'Female Labour Force Participation and Fertility: The Case of Ibadan City in the Western State of Nigeria', in C.Oppong et al.,(eds.), Marriage, Fertility and Parenthood in West Africa, Papers from the XVth Seminar of the International Sociological Association Committee on Family Research, Lomé, Togoland, January, 1976. Department of Demograpy, Australian National University, Canberra.

Azefor, M.A.N. 1972. 'Infertility and Subfertility in Cameroon', project report for M.Sc. Medical Demography 1971-72 (LSHTM University of London), pp.72.

Azeme, Emile, Chief of Office, Control and Matriculation of Employers, Cameroon National Social Insurance Fund, Bueam 1976. Personal interview, December 1.

Boserup, Esther, 1970. Woman's Role in Economic Development. New York: St Martin's Press, pp.283.

Cameroon, United Republic of, 1974. Law No. 74/14 of 27 November 1974 Instituting the Labour Code.

Elundu, Emmanuel, Manager, Tole Tea Estate, Cameroon Development Corporation. 1976. Personal interview, November 4.

Gendell, Murray, 1965. 'The Influence of Family Building Activity on Women's Rate of Economic Activity', 1965 United Nations World Population Conference, mimeo.

Germain, Adrienne and Audrey Smock, 1974. 'The Status and Roles of Ghanaian and Kenyan Women: Implications for Fertility Behaviour', paper presented at the annual meeting of the American Psychological Association, September 1 on 'Women's Status and Fertility Around the World', pp.46.

Hass, Paula H. 1972. 'Maternal Role Incompatibility and Fertility in Urban Latin America', Journal of Social Issues, Vol.28, No.2, 111-127.

Heer, David M. and Elsa S. Turner, 1965. 'Areal Differences in Latin American Fertility', Population Studies, XVIII, No.3, March, 279-292.

Jaffe, A.J. and K. Azumi, 1960. 'The Birth Rate and Cottage Industries in Underdeveloped Countries', Economic Development and Cultural Change. Vol.IX, N-.1, October, 52-63.

McCall, D. 1961. 'Trade and the Role of Wife in a Modern West African Town', in Aidan Southall, (ed.), Social Change in Modern Africa. Studies presented and discussed at the First International African Seminar, Makerere College, Kampala, January 1959. London, New York, Toronto: Oxford University Press, for the International African Institute, 286-299.

Peil, Margaret, 1972. The Ghanaian Factory Worker: Industrial Man in Africa. Cambridge: The University Press. pp.263.

Stycos, J. Mayone and Robert H. Weller, 1967. 'Female Working Roles and Fertility', Demography, Vol.4, No.1, 210-217.

Weekes-Vagliani, Winifred, 1976. Family Life and Structure in Southern Cameroon. In collaboration with Manga Bekombo and with the assistance of Lynn Wallisch. Paris: Development Centre of the O ganisation for Economic Co-operation and Development. pp.87.

EDUCATION AND SOCIO-DEMOGRAPHIC
CHANGE IN NIGERIA:
THE WESTERN NIGERIAN
EXPERIENCE

I.O.Orubuloye

CHAPTER 2

EDUCATION AND SOCIO-DEMOGRAPHIC CHANGE IN NIGERIA:
THE WESTERN NIGERIAN EXPERIENCE

I.O. Orubuloye

Introduction

By the turn of the 16th century, the Islamic religion had been well established in most of the northern parts of Nigeria thus making that part of the country the most thoroughly Islamised areas in tropical Africa. The religion was also making significant advances among the peoples of central and south - western Nigeria at that time (Coleman, 1958: 93).

The advent of this religion marked the beginning of written records, Moslem artistic culture, and trade links with the mediterannean countries. The development of trade links with these countries played an important role in the political, religious and commercial life of the people of Nigeria.

The first contact which Nigeria had with the Europeans was perhaps that of the Portuguese sailors who visited the country in the winter of 1472-73. It was not until 1553 however, when the first British ship landed on the Nigerian coast that significant changes began to occur (Nigeria, Ministry of Information, 1975: 18). Thereafter, the British gradually attained a dominant position in trade with the country. Although Roman Catholic missionaries arrived in Benin City as early as 1516, and remained there until 1688, their efforts failed to make any significant or lasting impression (Talbot, 1926: IV, 115). In 1861, Lagos was annexed as a British colony. Gradually the British extended their trading activities to the interior and greatly expanded their government's sphere of influence.

The 19th century witnessed a movement of development and western culture from the south to the north. European trading and missionary activities, and consequently western education had developed. By the turn of that century, Christianity and western education had spread to most of the coastal cities of Nigeria. By the first half of this century, the impact of Christianity and indeed western education had been felt in nearly all parts of southern Nigeria.

Prior to the introduction of western education, the family was the sole agent of socialization for its members, both old and young. The introduction of Christianity and consequently western education, therefore, are by far the most important changes which have taken place in Nigeria. At the onset, western education was closely associated with the Christian religion, and both were features of the major coastal cities.

The monopoly of education by the Christian Missionary Societies was described as follows:

> 'To all intents and purposes the school is the church. Right away in the bush or in the forest the two are one, and the village teacher is also the village evangelist. An appreciation of this fact is cardinal in all considerations of African education' (Murray, 1929: 65).

Until 1898 all education was under the direct control of the missionaries. In 1942, they still controlled 99% of the schools and 97% of the students in Nigeria were in mission schools (Nigeria, 1944: 3). Gradually, the idea of western education became part of the Islamic religion and traditional religion as well. Today, schools which were built and run by Christians operate side by side with those of the Muslims. It is now not uncommon to find Christian teachers teaching in Muslim schools and vice versa.

Although many parents, particularly in the rural areas refused to send even their sons to school when schooling was first introduced, the few who accepted the change saw this as an opportunity for the younger members of the family to learn alternative life-styles and for future employment opportunities in the non-traditional sector of the economy.

The advent of western education brought a new socio-economic order. The graduates of the earlier schools thus became the first school teachers, catechists and ministers of religion. This also marked the beginning of a partial emergence of a middle class in a society which was previously stratified into the class of the nobles and the commoners. The new class inevitably became an important force to reckon with in the society. Although the life-style of the new class was radically opposed to what existed in the traditional society, this was not seen as a threat to the system.

Secondary education was introduced in Lagos in the second half of the 19th century, and up till 1908, Lagos was the only resort for secondary education. Consequently, Lagos was until after 1908 the reservoir for clerical labour which was an important aspect of the administrative set up. By 1940, secondary education had spread to most parts of western Nigeria.

University and technical education was, however, not known in any part of
the country until the end of the first half of this century.

The spread and coverage of formal education varies from one region to
another. For example, universal free primary education had been established
in western Nigeria since 1955, whereas in the east, the Federal Capital
Territory, and in the city of Kano in the north, it was a fee paying
universal primary education. It was not until September 1976, that
Universal Free Primary Education (UPE) was established in other parts of the
country. This is expected to be compulsory as from the beginning of the
1979 school year.

The primary aim of this chapter is to examine the extent to which
education has influenced   family relationships and conjugal ties; and to
relate education to demographic changes in Nigeria, with special reference
to western Nigeria. The chapter will also examine the extent to which the
level of education attained can radically influence the life-style of the
recipients. Here, analysis will be based mainly on the observations made
by the writer. In relating education to demographic changes, evidence will
be drawn largely from Nigerian survey data.

Educational Trends in Nigeria, 1960-80

Since Independence in 1960, education has enjoyed a high priority in
Nigeria's development planning. In the first National Development Plan 1962-68,
it ranked fifth, and accounted for 10.3% of the gross public sector
investment. In the 1970-74 plan, education was second only to transport,
and 13.5% of total investment during the Plan period went to education.
During the third National Development Plan 1975-80, investment in education
is expected to increase from $78 million at the end of the second Plan to
$2.5 billion after the third Plan has been completely executed.

As shown in Tables 1 and 2, enrolment at various levels of educational
institutions (both National and western Nigeria) has been increasing
steadily. A substantial increase is expected between 1975-80, with
enrolment at the primary school level accounting for more than four-fifths
of all enrolments. Enrolment at the secondary school level is expected to
increase from 9.9% in 1973 to 14.2% at the end of the Plan in 1980; while
no percentage change is expected at the University level. In absolute terms,
enrolment at the University level is expected to increase from 23,000 in
1973 to 53,000 by 1980.

TABLE 1 : EDUCATION ENROLMENTS IN NIGERIA, 1960-80
YEAR AND NUMBER OF ENROLMENTS

Type of Institution	1960	1964	1971	1973	1975-80
Primary	2,912,618	2,849,488	3,894,539	4,746,808	11,521,500
Secondary	135,364	205,002	343,313	448,904	1,555,180
Technical and Vocational	5,037	7,702	15,590	22,588	117,686
Teacher Training	27,908	31,504	38,095	46,951	234,680
University	1,395	6,719	14,371	23,173	53,000
Total Enrolments	3,082,322	3,099,965	4,305,908	5,288,424	13,482,046

Percentage Enrolments at Various Levels of Education

Type of Institution and Percentage Enrolments

Year	Primary	Secondary, Technical Vocational and Teacher Training	University	Total
1960	94.5	5.5	0 (0.04)	100.0
1964	91.9	7.9	0.2	100.0
1971	90.4	9.3	0.3	100.0
1973	89.7	9.9	0.4	100.0
1975-80	85.4	14.2	0.4	100.0

Source: Nigeria, The Third National Development Plan 1975-80, Vol.I.

Until recently education was primarily under the control of the Regions. Most primary and secondary schools were built by the missionaries and private individuals, and there were only very few government sponsored schools. But the standards were set by the government. Primary school courses totalled six years in the south and seven years in the north. Under the Universal Free Primary Education Scheme (UPE), primary school courses are expected to last six years throughout the country. Secondary schools provide for five or seven years of education; while technical, vocational and teacher training schools vary from two to three years. University education lasts three years on the average; students in medical and related fields of study generally stay longer than three years in the university.

Since the Federal Government takeover of all educational expenses, primary, secondary and university education has been tuition free, while adult education, non-formal and special education for the handicapped has also been expanded and made free at all levels.

TABLE 2 : EDUCATION ENROLMENTS IN WESTERN NIGERIA, 1960-80
YEAR AND NUMBER OF ENROLMENTS

Type of Institution	1960[a]	1964	1971	1973	1975-80
Primary	1,124,788	733,170	869,765	980,000	2,096,700
Secondary	101,249	na	130.316	166,000	270,000
Technical and Vocational	194	815	1,863	2,450	3,541
Teacher Training	11,307	8,120	5,662	5,538	28,095
University[b]	1,136	2,943	3,989	8,623	15,745
Total Enrolments	1,238,674	745,048	1,011,595	1,162,611	2,414,081

Percentage Enrolments at Various Levels of Education

	Type of Institution and Percentage Enrolments			
Year	Primary	Secondary, Technical Vocational and Teacher Training	University	Total
1960	90.8	9.1	0.1	100.0
1964	98.4	1.2	0.4	100.0
1971	86.0	13.6	0.4	100.0
1973	84.3	15.0	0.7	100.0
1975-80	86.9	12.5	0.6	100.0

Notes: a. The 1960 figures include Mid-Western Nigeria (now Bendel State) which was created out of Western Nigeria in 1963.

b. Figures for university refer to all the universities located in Western Nigeria; however, 50-70% of students from these universities probably come from Western Nigeria.

na. Figure not available.

Source: Nigeria, The Third National Development Plan 1975-80, Vol.I, pp.238-243.

Education and Social Change

Much has been written and said about education being the main force in changing family relations and ultimately fertility, and that it was a powerful agent of Westernization in terms of family values. In a recent policy objective, the Nigerian Government has recognized 'education as a very powerful instrument for social change in process of dynamic national building' (Nigeria, 1975: 245). Despite the wide recognition of education as a major force in the process of change at both the individual and societal levels, a detailed analysis of how the school system was able (or expected) to bring about these changes has been given very little consideration.

In this section, the extent to which the individual life-style changes with the various levels of education, primary, secondary, and tertiary, will be examined in a greater detail.

In Nigeria, primary school education forms the lowest level of the formal school system. In 1973, 90% of students enrolled in formal schools were in the primary school. This proportion will be reduced to about 85% by 1980 (Nigeria, 1975: 238-234). One significant improvement in recent years is that most primary school students now attend schools located in their own town or village or in the village adjacent to theirs. When formal schooling was first introduced, most schools were first located in major administrative centres. Thus children in the villages or in places where there was no school were more frequently sent to relatives living in places where there were schools primarily for assistance with their education. In return, the children were also expected to work as assistants to such relatives. However, the first day in the school marks the beginning of a partial physical separation of most children from their parents and other members of their family. For the first time the children found themselves in an entirely different environment monitored by the school teacher. The children are made to learn new values that are in contrast to those obtained in traditional society. Their progress in the school is measured in relation to those of others who are in most cases non-relatives; and the authority of the school teacher is supreme. Respect due to age in traditional systems is greatly de-emphasised in the school, and the young may be placed above their elders in any competitive examination.

Those who cannot cope with the new changes automatically withdraw from the school system and very little effort is made to encourage them to stay at school. The drop-outs inevitably go back to the farm and continue to live under the authority of their parents. In contrast, those who were prepared to accept the changes remained at school and were exposed to a new set of values.

Although primary school education may socialise a person in a different way than did traditional society, many of the advantages of modernization and Westernization are still not properly assimilated at this level. Hence, most of the traditional values still predominate. In fact the attitudes and life-style of those who did not proceed beyond this level of education are very much similar to those of their counterparts who had not been to school. Most of the primary school graduates are, however, capable of reading and writing in their native language. The brighter ones may be able to read and write in the English language as well.

The male graduates of primary school are,even now, likely to marry more than one wife, while the female graduates may be absorbed into polygynous marriages. One significant effect of primary school education is that it prepares most rural recipients for city life. Most rural people who reached this level of education are aware of alternative life-styles in the city and are very much more likely to migrate to the city. On reaching the city most of them may end up learning a trade, while some earn wages. During their period of stay in the city, they are expected to learn the urban ways of life and behave differently on their return to the village. While in the city, they are expected to maintain close ties with their place of birth. Here, they visit frequently and even set up a trade after their period of apprenticeship in the city.

As shown in Tables 1 and 2, less than one-tenth of all school enrolments in Nigeria are at the secondary school level. Most rural children receive their secondary school education outside their birth place, where they are in most cases placed in a boarding house; while most of the urban children attend schools located in the city where they may stay in the boarding house or live with the parents. At this stage, children are placed under the authority of the school teacher and that of the senior students. Here, as in the case of primary school education, promotion is based on performance in the school examination. Seniority is measured in terms of the number of years already spent at school, in contrast to the traditional system where age was the only measure of seniority. At this stage, the children are exposed not only to the mass media but also to a large number

of other children with different backgrounds. Here most children select
their peer group and in many cases their life-long friends.

All secondary education in western Nigeria is in English. The students
inevitably learn about new sets of values that are in most cases quite opposed
to traditional values. As it has been rightly said 'Western ideas of
romantic love and companionate marriage are also disseminated through an
extensive study of nineteenth century English literature' (Ware, 1974: 141).
The school invariably carries messages about the nature of the western
family. The school teachers may even express western familial values in their
own lives although the family life of most of the indigenous school teachers
in the villages is markedly traditional. It is clear that the type of formal
education given to children even at this level reduces the children's
dependence upon parental authority. Although parents may spend more on
school children than they do on children who have never been to school, they
expect very little physical labour in return whilst the latter are hard at
work. Educated childre, however, are expected to translate all physical
obligations into monetary returns when it becomes feasible to do so.

Secondary school graduates are undoubtedly better equipped than their
age mates who did not proceed beyond the primary school level. Since the
traditional system has very little to offer them, they are motivated to search
for alternative life-styles in non-traditional sectors of the economy. Most
rural secondary school leavers migrate to the city in search of wage
employment. While in the city, they continue to maintain close ties with
their parents in the village. Frequently they send money home to pay for
the education of their younger siblings. Some younger siblings migrate to
the city to live with older family members for their education. Although
secondary school graduates working in the city are no longer under the
direct authority of their parents, the parents still expect to be consulted
when important decisions are made. Parents no longer chose marriage partners
for their educated children, but the children are under constant pressure
to select partners who will be acceptable to the parents. Usually both
partners have been to school and, as a result, often joint decisions will
be the rule rather than the exception.

Marriages of this type are far more likely to be monogamous. Children
born to those families have better chances of continuing at school. At this

stage children tend to become more expensive because parents   begin to think of continuing career advancement and of continuing education for the children. Here emphasis may be on quality rather than quantity. The chances that all the children will be successful in life are greater than in the case of those whose parents had not been to school. At this stage, parents may start to think of limiting their family size. They are more likely to achieve this by contraception rather than through the traditional methods of sexual abstinence. But all available demographic evidence indicates that not more than one-third of this group will limit their family size to fewer than four children (see Ware, 1974: 164-7).

University and other tertiary education is a recent phenomenon in Nigeria. The first institution of higher learning was established in 1948. The number of existing universities in Nigeria increased from six in 1973 to 13 in 1978. Similarly, enrolment in these universities rose from 23,000 to well over 50,000 during the same period. Although enrolment at university level has increased over the years, only 0.4% of all school enrolments is expected at this level of education by 1980 (see Table 1).

Most students attend universities located outside their birth place but still within their own cultural environment. Apart from the composition and nature of the student population, the programmes are strictly western oriented. Most students are economically independent of their parents because of the various government scholarships and assistance programmes designed to ease students' financial problems. Now that the Federal Government has taken over the control of university education in the country, all students have been granted   tuition-free university education.

The type of education received in these universities is completely western oriented. In fact most of the teachers were trained in western society. There is an emphasis on the individual and the students learn to think independently of the traditional values of the group. The system stresses the need to calculate costs and benefits in terms of the individual rather than that of the network of relations. The western type of family life inevitably becomes more acceptable to the group. Marriage at this stage tends to be monogamous and contracted under the English Marriage Ordinance. But such marriages are far less likely to be contracted without the knowledge of the relatives of both parties.

The life-style of this group differs significantly from the rest of the community. They are the class of people who live in various parts of the city in western-type homes, where a combination of European and Nigerian customs are practised. Their children are exposed to western values much earlier than those of the rest of the community. Much stress is placed on the nuclear family as a corporate group neglecting the extended family. Children born to this group have a greater chance of success in life than those of the less fortunate group in the community. Because of the high cost of bringing up children, and the little or no return expected from them, parents tend to idealise and have a smaller number of children. Education at this level does change relations between husbands and wives on the one hand and between parents and children on the other, and, in this way, relatively strengthens the nuclear family.

Although the life-style of the modern elite differs from that of the traditional group, it may be unreal to think that they have broken all ties with tradition. Most of them still identify themselves with their less fortunate relatives. Most wealthy people still spread their resources to cover the needs of a large number of immediate and less fortunate relatives. Children are still frequently sent from the rural areas to live with their relatives in urban areas for assistance with their education. Most urban elites of rural origin visit their birthplace regularly, here they may even build their first house. They are frequently called upon to contribute to the development programmes taking place in the rural areas. Among the Yoruba of western Nigeria, this type of flow of wealth from urban to rural areas has been well documented (Adepoju, 1974; Imoagene, 1976). The relationship between the poor and the rich is not only an economic one. The poor are the only link which the rich have with tradition. Similarly, the rich provide the poor with the only link with the modern world.

Education and Age at Marriage

One other important aspect of social change which came about as a result of the introduction of western education is that of a rising age at marriage. Age at marriage varies from one cultural area of Nigeria to another. Traditionally, it appeared that marriage was longer delayed among the Yoruba than among the other ethnic groups in Nigeria. Early in this century, Johnson observed that Yoruba girls seldom married until they were 20 years old (Johnson, 1937: 103). This evidence was later confirmed by Fadipe in 1939 (Fadipe, 1970: 65). A 1931 medical census of southern Nigeria gave the reason that Yoruba men traditionally thought that younger girls were unfit to be mothers (Nigeria, 1932-34: 5-7). The men

were not expected to marry until they were 30 years old. Tradition
demanded that they should serve their parents for a considerable length of
time, during which marriage was forbidden. Besides, they were also expected
to give their fathers ten heads of cowries (approximately £10 sterling in
those days) before they could get married (Johnson, 1937: 103).

It should thus be noted that delay of marriage in traditional Yoruba
society was partly based on economic considerations. Marriage marked the
beginning of economic independence for the children. Soon after marriage,
the father of the young man was expected to set aside a separate apartment
for him, as well as sufficient land for his exclusive use and equipment to
work the land. Parents with many sons were not able to meet these
traditional demands if their sons' marriages were too close together.
Marriage was also regulated so that the younger children do not marry before
their elder brothers or sisters. It was also expected that the Yoruba
wife will be an adult and capable of supporting herself at marriage, and
will have accumulated a sufficient stock of goods and experience to set up
her own household (Olusanya, 1969). Marriage inevitably reduced the type
of assistance given by children to that which they could perform during
their spare time.

In modern times, rising age at marriage appears to be closely
associated only with extended education. In fact, it is not generally being
observed that the younger illiterates and primary school graduates marry
earlier than the old illiterates (see Ohadike, 1967: 128, Table VI: 1;
Orubuloye, 1977: Table 5.13). In a 1964 survey of 596 currently married
African women in Lagos, it was found out that delayed marriage was closely
associated with extended education (Ohadike, 1967: 128). Similarly, in a
recent survey of Yoruba women, greater delay of marriage was found to be
closely associated with extended education on the one hand and town size
on the other (Ware, 1974: 142, see also Table 3). More recently, the
writer has observed in a study of rural Yoruba women, that delayed marriage
was closely associated with extended education. This was particularly so
in Ibadan Rural which was greatly being influenced by the developments
taking place in Ibadan City (see Table 3). With the expansion of education,
particularly female education, a continuous rise in age at marriage may be
expected.

Education and Polygyny

In traditional Yoruba society most marriages were monogamous. Polygyny

TABLE 3 : MEAN AGE AT FIRST MARRIAGE BY EDUCATION OF WOMEN
(LAGOS, 1964; EKITI RURAL AND IBADAN RURAL, 1975)

Education of Women	No. of Women	Mean Age at First Marriage	% Marrying Under 20 Years of Age	% Marrying at 20 or More Years of Age	Total
Lagos[a]	590	19.7	48	52	100
No schooling	278	19.5	50	50	100
Primary	222	18.9	56	44	100
Secondary	76	22.3	22	78	100
University/ Professional	14	23.8	7	93	100
Ekiti Rural[b]	600	20.4	34	66	100
No schooling	407	20.9	24	76	100
Primary	178	19.3	54	46	100
Secondary	15	20.5	47	53	100
Ibadan Rural[b]	497	20.0	36	64	100
No schooling	399	19.9	35	65	100
Primary	68	20.2	38	62	100
Secondary	30	21.4	17	83	100

Source: a. P.O. Ohadike, 1967 p.128.

b. I.O. Orubuloye, 1977c p.109.

was the prerogative of the rich (Johnson, 1937: 113). It has also been
noted that, among the Nupe of northern Nigeria, 'The number of wives a man
possessed was an infallible index of wealth and status; and that in the
houses of the talakazi, "the poor ones", monogamy was the rule' (Nadel,
1942: 151).

The high incidence of polygyny among the Yoruba is not unconnected with
the introduction of cash crops. Cocoa which has been cultivated since the
beginning of this century, is the major source of cash earnings. The
production, harvesting and marketing of cocoa requires a large pool of labour
which was not readily available in the labour market. Hence many farmers
must have married additional wives to cope with the problem of labour

shortage.   Wealthy farmers are far more likely to be successful in acquiring additional wives than the poor ones because of the high cost of marriage ceremonies in Yoruba society. Although relatives may assist the poor ones in defraying the cost of the first marriage, they are far less likely to succeed in securing the cooperation of their relatives in the case of additional wives. It should, however, be stressed that most men will be likely to marry a second wife if the first wife failed to have children or give birth to a son.

However, the incidence of polygyny now changes from one population to another, and varies with age and educational attainment. In a 1973 survey of Ibadan City women, for example, 46% of all married women were in polygynous marriages (CAFN1, 1974); compared to 53% and 56% found in a 1975 survey of Ibadan Rural and Ekiti Rural respectively. In the Ibadan City survey 71% of the illiterates over 38 years old were in polygynous marriages whereas, only 38% of those of that age who had ever been to school were in that type of marriage union (Sembajwe, 1977). In the Ibadan and Ekiti Rural Surveys, three-fifths of the married women who had not been to school were in polygynous marriages; compared to one-third of those who had only primary school education. Of those who had up to secondary education   only one-fifth were in polygynous unions (Orubuloye, 1977c).

Although education has influenced attitudes toward having more than one wife, it may be suggested that the increasing cost of raising children is by far the most important reason why polygyny may rapidly diminish. An overwhelming majority of parents, both rural and urban, have begun to express awareness   of the high cost of maintaining many children (Olusanya, 1971; Orubuloye, 1977a).

Education and Family Size

The debate about the relationship between education and fertility levels began in Nigeria about a decade ago. Okediji, in a 1965-66 survey of women in three areas of Ibadan City, produced evidence to show that improved education, advanced occupational prestige and higher incomes are all positively associated with decreased fertility (Okediji, 1969: 350). Ohadike has also shown that lowered fertility among Lagos women was only associated with the factor of education (Ohadike, 1967: 389).

In contrast, Olusanya (1967)   Farooq and Ekanem (1974) seem to hold

the view that extended education tends to increase fertility rather than to
depress it. Recently Ekanem (1974) has presented statistical evidence to
show that the fertility of the educated Ibo women was lower than that of
their illiterate counterparts. Further data gathered by a Lagos survey
(Lucas, 1976) and a survey of Ibadan City (Sembajwe, 1977) have shown that
women with secondary education or more had lower fertility than those with
primary or no formal education.

One general comment about the findings of the surveys reported is that
the number of women who proceeded beyond primary school level of education
was very small compared with the rest of the population. In Ohadike's
1964 survey of Lagos, for example, only 15% of the women had up to secondary
education or more. Even in Ibadan City where over 6,500 women were
interviewed, just over 1,000 of them (or 19%) proceeded beyond primary
school level of education. The data from the 1974-75 survey of Ekiti and
Ibadan villages also suffer from this limitation.

However, it is important to examine the position in the rural areas.
As shown in Table 4, the overall fertility of those who had been to school
was lower than that of women who had not. Differences within age groups
seem not to show any consistent fertility differential by education. Most
of the differences at younger ages were due to the differential in marriage
patterns among those groups. It has been suggested in the earlier part of
this chapter that delayed marriage and consequently late childbearing was
associated with extended education.

The impact of extended education on fertility is undoubtedly apparent
in the cities and large urban centres. The position in rural areas may be
very different. The constraints making a large number of children uneconomic
and perhaps disadvantageous are clearly active in the cities; while the
people in rural areas are yet to experience any significant changes in
their life-style. Although education may socialise a person in a different
way than did traditional society, these new values may be difficult to
translate into action if the recipients go back to live in traditional
society. It may be argued, therefore, that some element of non-traditional
environment has to come into being before education can significantly
depress fertility.

Education and Fertility Control

Fertility control through contraception is a new phenomenon in Nigeria.
But family size had been limited in a number of ways before the advent of

TABLE 4 : MEAN NUMBER OF CHILDREN EVER BORN BY AGE AND EDUCATION OF WOMEN
(EKITI RURAL AND IBADAN RURAL, 1975)

Age of Women	No Schooling		Primary		Secondary		All Literates	
	No. of Women	Mean No. of Children Ever Born	No. of Women	Mean No. of Children Ever Born	No. of Women	Mean No. of Children Ever Born	No. of Women	Mean No. of Children Ever Born
Ekiti Rural	409	4.50	185	2.49	25	1.72	210	2.40
15-24	37	1.38	67	1.18	13	0.62	80	1.09
25-34	116	3.38	91	2.90	9	2.67	100	2.88
35-44	132	5.29	25	4.16	3	3.67	28	4.11
45-59	124	5.63	2	6.50	-	-	2	6.50
Ibadan Rural	419	4.23	81	2.68	88	1.51	169	2.07
15-24	50	0.98	21	0.62	57	0.04	78	0.19
25-34	122	3.16	43	2.93	16	3.13	59	2.98
35-44	150	4.97	13	4.46	14	5.43	27	4.96
45-59	97	6.09	4	5.00	1	5.00	5	5.00

Source: I.O. Orubuloye op.cit., Table 6.13, p.151.

modern methods of contraception, the chief method being extended post-partum
abstinence. The impact of prolonged sexual abstinence has been examined
recently (Caldwell and Caldwell, 1977; Orubuloye, 1977c: Ch.7). Many of
the findings revealed that the length of such abstinence varies from one
place to another and from one group to another. Significant variations
were observed between rural and urban areas; and between educated and
non-educated women. Although the traditional emphasis on prolonged periods
of post-partum abstinence (lasting for about three years) has diminished,
it is significant to note that the practice is still an important aspect
of Yoruba culture.

However, fertility control through contraception is gradually
emerging in the society. The pattern of acceptance is very much the same as
that of other changes which have taken place in the society. Evidence
from available literature suggests a considerable range in the levels of
contraceptive knowledge and usage between different sizes of centres. The
levels also vary significantly between one educational group and another.

Although contraceptive revolution is underway in the cities, the
question has been raised whether the revolution is aimed at reducing the
overall fertility. It has been suggested that it may merely replace
abstinence (Ware, 1974: 144). Evidence from my survey of rural Yoruba
women seems to suggest that contraception within marriage was not aimed at
reducing the overall fertility but to space births and for extended sexual
relations. There was also the indication that unmarried school girls were
also contracepting merely to guarantee pregnancy-free pre-marital sexual
relations; while some married women were using it to guarantee
pregnancy-free extra-marital sexual relations (Orubuloye, 1977c; Ch.9).
Recent investigations in Ibadan City have proved the high incidence of
contraceptives being used to guarantee pregnancy-free pre-marital sex
(Caldwell, 1976; Caldwell and Ware, 1977).

One major reason why contraceptive usage may not necessarily be aimed
at reducing fertility is the apparent lack of individual and community
pressures making large families uneconomic or inconvenient. There is the
general belief in Nigeria, that it is not so disadvantageous, at least in
the present state of development in the society, to have large families.
The reasons usually given in support of large families are partly economic
but mostly socio-cultural.

There are many indications to show that advancement in education and

increasing level of urbanization, particularly urbanization due to
industrialization, are necessary pre-requisites for a dramatic decline in
fertility. Expansion of primary school education without a corresponding
increase in the number of secondary school intakes may not bring about
radical changes that could lead to fertility decline. It is now generally
being observed that the fertility of women who had primary education only
is higher than those who had not been to school, and very much higher than
that of women who had been to secondary school (see Olusanya, 1967; Lucas,
1976).

Future Prospects

It has been widely recognised that education has brought about
important changes in Nigeria's socio-economic organisation. The advent of
western education brought about the emergence of a middle class in a
society which was traditionally separated into the class of the commoners
and that of the nobles. Although the new class has accepted many of the
western values which are in many cases opposed to traditional values, the
family is still very much regarded as the pillar of the society.

Education has opened the door to wage employment in the modern sector
of the economy. The society is witnessing a juxtaposition of modern and
traditional values. This has produced relatively little conflict in
the system.

Spectacular demographic changes have also taken place in Nigeria. One
of these   changes is the dramatic decline in infant and child mortality.
This decline has been associated with an improvement in public health
services and personal hygiene. It has been observed that child mortality
generally varies with educational attainment (Orubuloye and Caldwell, 1975;
Sembajwe, 1981; and Orubuloye, 1981). Similarly, in a survey of the
relationship between nutritional and intellectual deficiencies, education
of the parents was found to be significantly associated with better
nutritional standards and high intellectual development (US Department of
Health, Education and Welfare, 1967).

All KAP surveys conducted in Nigeria to date have indicated that
knowledge and practice of contraception is closely associated with
urbanization and education. There is also the evidence that fertility
decline among the educated urban women is underway (Lucas, 1976; Sembajwe,
1977). Education will therefore continue to play an important role in the
diffusion of western family values. This may be a significant step to

future fertility decline. Many of these changes, however, will depend upon the size of school intakes at both the secondary school and tertiary levels of education, and the acceptance of effective methods of contraception. Be that as it may, it is very unlikely that the completed family size, even among the highly educated Yoruba women, will significantly fall below that of four children in the immediate future.

BIBLIOGRAPHY

Adepoju, A. 'Migration and Socio-economic Links Between Urban Migrants and Their Home Communities in Nigeria', Africa, XLIV, 4, Oct. 1974, pp.385-395.

Caldwell, J.C. The Socio-economic Explanation of High Fertility, Changing African Family Project Monograph Series, No.1., Department of Demography, Australian National University, Canberra.

Caldwell, J.C. and Pat Caldwell. 'The Role of Marital Sexual Abstinence in Determining Fertility: A Study of Yoruba in Nigeria', Population Studies, Vol.XXXI,No.2.July,1977. pp.193-217.

Caldwell, J.C. and H. Ware. 'The Evolution of Family Planning in an African City: Ibadan, Nigeria', Population Studies, Vol.XXXI,No.3.November 1977, pp. 487-507.

Changing African Family, Nigerian Segment Project I, Department of Demography, Australian National University, 1974.

Coleman, J.S. Nigeria: Background to Nationalism. Berkeley, University of California Press, 1958.

Ekanem, I.I. 'Correlates of Fertility in Eastern Nigeria', The Nigerian Journal of Economics and Social Studies, Vol.16, No.1, 1974, pp.115-127.

Fadipe, N.A. The Sociology of the Yoruba edited by F.O. Okediji and O.O. Okediji, Ibadan University Press, Ibadan, Nigeria, 1970.

Farooq, G.M. and I.I. Ekanem. 'Early Demographic Transition: The Case of South-Western Nigeria', Paper Presented at the Inaugural Conference of the Population Association of Africa, Ibadan, Nigeria, 1974.

Imoagene, S.O. Social Mobility in Emergent Society: A Study of the New Elite in Western Nigeria. Changing African Family Project Monograph Series, No.2. Department of Demography, Australian National University, Canberra.

Johnson, Rev. S. History of the Yoruba (From the Earliest Times to the Beginning of the British Protectorate) edited by O. Johnson, CMS Bookshop, Lagos, Nigeria, 1937.

Lucas, D. The Participation of Women in the Nigerian Labour Force Since the 1950's with Particular Reference to Lagos. Ph.D. Thesis, London School of Economics and Political Science, 1976.

Murray, A.V. The School in the Bush. London, 1929.

Nadel, S.F. A Black Byzantium: The Kingdom of Nupe in Nigeria. Oxford University Press, London, 1942.

Nigeria, Census of Nigeria, 1931. London: Crown Agents for the Colonies, 1932-34.

Nigeria, Ten-Year Educational Plan. Sessional Paper No.6, Lagos, 1944.

Nigeria, Handbook 1975-76, Federal Ministry of Information, Lagos, 1975.

Nigeria, Third National Development Plan, 1975-80. Federal Ministry of
   Economic Development, Lagos, Nigeria, 1975.

Ohadike, P. Patterns and Variations in Fertility and Family Formation:
   A Study of Urban Africans in Lagos, Nigeria. Ph.D. Thesis, Department
   of Demography, Australian National University, 1967.

Okediji, F.O. 'Socio-economic Status and Differential Fertility in an
   African City', Journal of Developing Areas, 3, April 1969. pp.339-354.

Olusanya, P.O. 'The Educational Factor in Human Fertility: A Case Study of
   the Residents of a Suburban Area in Ibadan, Western Nigeria', The Nigerian
   Journal of Economics and Social Studies, Vol.10, No.3, Nov. 1967,
   pp.351-375.

Olusanya, P.O. 'Rural-Urban Fertility Differentials in Western Nigeria',
   Population Studies, Vol.XXXIII,No.3. Nov.1969, pp.363-378.

Olusanya, P.O. 'Status Differentials in the Fertility Attitudes of Western
   Nigeria', Economic Development and Cultural Change, Vol.19, No.4, July
   1971, pp.641.651.

Orubuloye, I.O. 'High Fertility and Rural Economy: A Study of Yoruba Society
   in Western Nigeria', in J.C. Caldwell (ed.), The Persistence of High
   Fertility: Population Prospects in the Third World, 1977, Department
   of Demography, Australian National University, Canberra.
Orubuloye, I.O. Abstinence as a Method of Birth Control: Fertility and child-
   spacing practices among rural Yoruba women of Nigeria, Changing African
   Family Monograph Series No.8, Department of Demography, Australian National
   University, Canberra. (Forthcoming)

Orubuloye, I.O. and J.C. Caldwell. 'The Impact of Public Health Services
   on Mortality: A Study of Mortality Differentials in a Rural Area of
   Nigeria', Population Studies, Vol.19, No.2, July 1975, pp.259-272.

Sembajwe, I.S.L. Fertility and Infant Mortality Amongst the Yoruba in Western
   Nigeria,1981, Changing African Family Project Monograph No.6, Department of
   Demography, Australian National University, Canberra.

Talbot, P.A. The Peoples of Southern Nigeria. Vol.IV, London, 1926.

US Department of Health, Education and Welfare. Republic of Nigeria:
   Nutrition Survey, February-April 1965. A Report by the Nutrition
   Section Office of International Research Institutes of Health, 1967.

Ware, H. 'Educational Differentials in Family Building Aspirations and
   Practice in Rural Nigeria', Rural Demography, Vol.1, No.2, 1974,
   pp.129-171.

CHAPTER 3

WOMEN AND WORK: A STUDY
OF FEMALE AND MALE ATTITUDES
IN THE MODERN SECTOR OF AN
AFRICAN METROPOLIS

Wambui Wa Karanja

CHAPTER 3

WOMEN AND WORK : A STUDY OF FEMALE AND MALE ATTITUDES IN THE
MODERN SECTOR OF AN AFRICAN METROPOLIS

Wambui Wa Karanja

Introduction

The important contribution that women's work can make to socio-economic
development has been extensively discussed by Boserup (1970) amongst others.
Its significance for the status of women has also been emphasised (Largui
1975). The importance of a study of women and work therefore [1] hardly
needs to be justified.

This paper describes an investigation of female and male attitudes to
women and work in the metropolis of Lagos, Nigeria. With an estimated
population of about 4 million people in 1980, Lagos is the largest urban
centre in tropical Africa. It is not only the capital of the Federal
Republic of Nigeria - Africa's most populous nation - but is also the
centre for much of Nigeria's recent rapid development.

As women are playing, and are expected to play an increasing role in
Nigeria's development, it is important to understand their attitude to this
involvement in the world of work - an aspect ignored in most of the previous
anthropological and sociological investigations of African and other
societies (E. Ardener and S. Ardener, 1975). However, since males play
dominant roles as employers, bosses, and supervisors in the work place, as
well as husbands and fathers in the home, an understanding of male
attitudes towards women and work is also vital to the evaluation of women's
participation. Finally, a comparative study of female and male opinions on
the issues raised has important implications for harmony or conflict with
the family.

My study is focussed on employees in the modern sector of metropolitan
Lagos. It should, however, be remembered that these modern urban workers
have a regular interaction with workers in the more traditional sectors of
Lagos, as well as with the rural population outside. Since the employees

---

[1] This study is part of a larger study of female and male attitudes
towards marriage, family and work in Lagos, Nigeria. Financial
assistance from the University of Lagos, the Ford Foundation, and the
Wenner Gren Foundation is gratefully acknowledged. An earlier version
of this paper was read at the Conference on Rural Development and Women
in Development held at the University of Benin in 1980.

under consideration have had a western-type education, either in Nigeria or
in the western countries, they are expected to have adopted western ideas
and values on a wide range of issues. We shall examine the extent to which
male attitudes on women and work in metropolitan Lagos are based on
traditional African or western values, and the extent to which totally new
ideas are emerging.

Methodology

The data analysed here are based on a stratified sample of 300 male
and female respondents, randomly selected from a list of Nigerian federal
civil service workers in Lagos, including workers at the University of
Lagos. Stratification is by broad income groups. Until recently these
groups corresponded roughly with senior, intermediate, and junior categories
of work divisions, which, in turn, tended to reflect educational attainment.
The research was carried out during 1978 and 1979, most of the
questionnaires being administered during the months of June-August 1979.

Through a simple random sample, I selected 150 males - 50 senior, 50
intermediate and 50 junior staff - as well as 150 females, also distributed
equally in the above three categories. This resulted in different sampling
fractions in the three categories, since in actuality the different
sub-groups are not equally distributed. For example, there are more males
than females in the various strata, and of course the proportion of workers
in the junior and intermediate categories, especially the former, exceeds
that in senior staff categories.

Previous surveys in 1975 and 1977, together with other pilot studies,
clearly demonstrated that it takes much longer to locate and to interview
junior and intermediate than senior staff. For example, junior staff are
four times more likely to interrupt the interviewer by asking him/her to go
and 'come back later'. They also ask more frequently than either intermediate
or senior staff for questions to be repeated. In addition, junior staff are
more likely to comment on questions and elaborate their answers, than are
those in the other two categories. An explanation for this attitude might
be the fact that junior workers particularly and intermediate workers to some
extent, do not fully appreciate the usefulness of survey research. It is
thus significantly more expensive to interview intermediate and junior staff,
especially the latter, and the cost factor is one of the main reasons for the
decision to sample disproportionately. A proportionate sample would have
meant reducing the number of senior staff, or increasing the number of
intermediate and junior staff. Financial constraints militated against this

latter option, while the former - that is, decreasing the number of senior staff interviewed - was also unacceptable on the grounds that this sub-sample was already quite small, and further reductions might significantly alter generalisations. In order to compensate for this shortcoming, there is a separate analysis for each category, which prevents the totals from being too heavily weighted in favour of senior male and female respondents.

The interviewers were all university undergraduates, male and female, except for three who had just completed their degree courses. Most were recruited from the Social Science Faculty of the University of Lagos, where all students are required to take a year's course in either research methodology, or statistics, or both. Despite the high educational background of the interviewers, a good deal of time was spent coaching them on interviewing methods and procedures before they presented the questionnaires. In addition, frequent meetings were held to discuss issues arising from field experience.

I personally interviewed all the female senior civil servants who were beyond the Principal Assistant Secretary grade. This was done for three reasons. In the first place, I believed that women at this level might feel they were too busy in the office to give time to an interviewer whom they considered their junior. Secondly, my interviews enabled me to check the responses I got against those obtained by my assistants. Thirdly, I wished to set the pace for my helpers. My interviews were mostly conducted at home, either on a Saturday afternoon or in the evening when interruptions were at a minimum. At my request, we talked in the absence of the women's spouses, because I suspected that the women might be inhibited by their husband's presence and also because I wanted to avoid the husbands volunteering their opinions. The other respondents were interviewed at their places of work.

Since the survey covered a much wider area than just decision-making, it was important to gain the confidence of the respondents by assuring them that the survey had nothing to do with any government agency. We explained that the research was being conducted by a sociologist from the University of Lagos and that the results would be used purely for teaching purposes and statistical analyses. No names were recorded on the questionnaire.

'Work' as used in this paper refers to employment outside the household. A wide variety of questions could be raised on the issue of women and work. However, I decided to focus on five of the major areas which I considered to be of the greatest concern: (i) the desirability of married women's involvement in the world of work; (ii) considerations affecting the choice of work undertaken by women; (iii) determinants of women's progress and mobility at work; (iv) the control and use of women's income; and (v) the impact family stability of women's participation in work.

(i) The Desirability of Married Women's Involvement in the World of Work

A review of the literature shows that attitudes vary considerably on the question of whether married women should work. In the west, married women, particularly in the middle and upper classes, play the role of full-time housewives (Rohrlich - Leavitt, 1975). While attitudes and practice are changing, it appears that most men and women in the west support the current practice. In the Soviet Union, however, married women are actively involved in work (Rosenthal, 1975). In some developing African societies, some men are opposed to the idea of women seeking employment outside the home (Southall, 1961). In some Asian countries, too, Boserup (1970) has shown that men are against women working.

The first question asked in Lagos was, 'Should a married woman go out of the house/home to work?' 88% of junior male workers and 92% and 100% of the intermediate and senior workers respectively, were of the opinion that a married woman should be allowed to go out to work. Female workers (86% of the juniors and 92% of the seniors) also overwhelmingly agreed with this view. Opposition to women working, on the part of both men and women, ranged between 4% and 10%. Less than 5% of the respondents failed to give either a 'Yes' or 'No' answer.

Asked whether their husbands approved of working wives, 82% of the junior females, 88% of the intermediates, and 96% of the seniors said that their husbands were not opposed to the idea. The conclusion must therefore be that the vast majority of females and males of all educational and income classes in modern Lagos agree that married women should be allowed to go out to work. It is clear that these attitudes in the modern sector of Lagos are in sharp contrast with those in the west and in the societies reported by Southall and Boserup, where it is not considered desirable that married women should work.

Despite the almost unaminous approval of women going out to work, there is considerable difference of opinion on the right time for them to do so. To the question 'What do you think is the right time for a married woman to go out of the home to work?' there was a wide diversity of answers. 80% of the senior male workers felt the women could work whenever they were ready to do so; but only 4% of the junior male workers and 8% of the intermediate

group took this view. On the female side, 4% of the juniors, 20% of the
intermediate, and 30% of the seniors thought the women could work any time
they were ready to do so.

TABLE 1

Question 4	Percentage Response					
	Male			Female		
What do you think is the proper or right time for a woman to go out of home to start work?	Jnr	Int	Snr	Jnr	Int	Snr
1. Any time she is ready	4	16	80	4	20	30
2. When all the children are grown up	20	32	2	40	60	56
3. When her husband allows	76	40	–	52	12	8
4. When she needs the money	–	–	18	4	8	6
5. D.K., N.R.,etc.	–	–	–	–	–	–
Total	100	100	100	100	100	100

A high proportion (40% of the junior females, 60% of intermediates, and
56% of seniors) felt that women should not go out to work until the children
had grown up. Among male workers, 60% of the juniors, 54% of intermediates,
and 25% of seniors felt women with small children should not go out to work.
Both junior male (78%) and female (52%) workers thought that the woman
should have her husband's approval before going out to work.

Surprisingly, the consideration of money turned out to be relatively
insignificant as a motive for work. Less than 10% of all female workers, none
of the junior and intermediate male workers, and 18% of senior male workers felt
that women should only work if they needed the money. A majority of the
women – 80% intermediate and 76% senior – said they would go to work even
if their husbands had enough money for the family's needs and could give
the wife pocket-money equal to her salary from work. The main factor
seemed to be less the money itself than the economic independence it
brought.

It might have been expected that senior male workers who had imbibed
western attitudes would either oppose married women working or would support
working only after the children had grown up. That this was not the case
could be explained as follows. Firstly, senior male workers are able to
hire or secure household help to take care of the children while the wives

are out to work. Secondly, males typically give very little help with the
care of young children whether their wives work or not. Thirdly, as
discussed in an earlier study (Karanja - Diejomaoh 1978), and as shown later
in this study, the income of the wife is not central to the maintenance of
the household. Thus, the senior males may be indifferent as to whether or
when their wives choose to work. Female workers, however, even when they
have household help, still shoulder a heavy responsibility for the care of
young children while they are working. This explains their opinion that
married women should go to work only when the children are grown up. The
support of junior and intermediate male workers for this idea is probably
related to the fact that, owing to their lower incomes, they would find it
very difficult to hire household help to replace their wives.

It can be argued that the approval given to the idea of women working
is based more on traditional values that have persisted in the metropolis
than on current western values such as the women's liberation movement.
This would explain why junior male and female workers, who are least
educated and least likely to fully appreciate the ideas on women's
liberation, support the concept of working wives.

Although the vast majority of females feel that married women should
be allowed to work, only a minority would be ready to do so if their
husbands opposed the idea. 54% of junior female workers, 58% of
intermediate female workers, and 70% of senior female workers said they
would not defy their husbands in this regard. However, a significant
proportion of the women (responses ranged from 20% for seniors to 40% for
juniors) would be ready to work even if their husbands were against the
idea, which suggests that there is some potential for conflict between
husbands and wives on this issue. In practice, however, the likelihood of
such conflict is minimised by the fact that between 84% and 96% of the
working women did have their husbands' approval. Only 4% of the intermediate
and senior working women did not have their husbands' approval.

(ii)   Considerations Affecting the Choice of Work Undertaken by Women

Having established that both females and males agree that women should
be allowed to go out to work, what kind of work is considered best suited
for them? 60% of junior male workers, 50% of intermediates, and 20% of
seniors thought that teaching was the best job for a woman. The female
workers, however, did not think so highly of teaching (only 18% of juniors,
20% of intermediates and 16% of seniors were in favour of it). Most of the
female respondents (70% of juniors, 76% of intermediates, and 80% of

seniors) felt that married women should do any job for which they were
qualified. A notable number of the males (32% of juniors, 40% of
intermediates, and 58% of seniors) supported this view. A small proportion
of both female and male respondents favoured nursing and housework.

TABLE 2

| Question 11 | Percentage Response | | | | | |
| | Male | | | Female | | |
What kind of job would you say is best for a woman?	Jnr	Int	Snr	Jnr	Int	Snr
1. Teaching	60	50	20	18	20	16
2. Nursing	-	2	20	4	-	-
3. Any job for which she is qualified	32	40	58	60	76	80
4. Housework	4	4	2	8	-	-
5. Other (specify)						
6. D.K., N.R.,etc.	4	4	-	10	4	4
Total	100	100	100	100	100	100

Several studies (Boserup 1970, Amon-Nikoi 1978, Fapohunda 1978) have
shown, however, that the type of education received by Nigerian women still
restricts them to a narrow range of jobs, so that even if women were free to
move into whatever jobs they were qualified for, they would probably still
end up doing a narrow range of women's jobs. It is therefore necessary to
broaden the scope of women's education as well as the aspirations of
younger women and girls.

Although most women and some men favour a wider range of jobs for women,
between 80% and 92% of all female and male respondents felt that the job
best suited to a married woman was one that did not involve long hours at
work, was not too exhausting, and did not necessitate frequent transfers.
Only 8% - 20% of both male and female respondents felt that a married woman
should do 'any work for which she is qualified'. This pattern of response
reflects the concern of both females and males that a married woman should
have time for family responsibilities after work, and that the working wife
should not be separated from her family through being transferred. There
was an almost unanimous belief (94% - 100%) that a married woman with small
children should not have a very demanding job.

These findings clearly indicate the limits to the job opportunities
and prospects of working wives compared with those of their male
counterparts. Attitudes in modern Lagos about married women's work undermine
prospects for equalising jobs and incomes between working males and females.
Analysts have drawn attention to the large gap between the incomes and job
conditions of males and females, and suggested substantial reduction or
elimination of the differentials (MacKinnon 1979, Rohrlich-Leavitt 1975).

(iii) <u>Determinants of Women's Progress and Mobility at Work</u>

Ideally, the objective criteria for getting employment and making
progress within a job are qualifications, experience, seniority, and
efficiency. These criteria should apply to both females and males. Several
studies have shown that females tend to have lower qualifications, shorter
experience, less seniority, and thus are adjudged to be less efficient than
male workers (Boserup 1970, Rohrlich-Leavitt 1975, Amon-Nikol 1978, Fapohunda
1978, MacKinnon 1979, Diejomaoh 1979). This study explores other questions.
What, for example, is the extent of discrimination against women on the grounds
of sex? What is the nature and magnitude of sexual harassment of working
women? What is considered the ideal family size for working women? How
adequate are the institutional supports for working mothers? Such questions
have important consequences for the progress of women at work.

Asked about discrimination against women in job selection, most women
maintained that they were discriminated against. (The percentages were 66%
of juniors, 72% of intermediates, and 82% of seniors). On the male side,
80% of juniors, 58% of intermediates, and 50% of seniors agreed that there was
discrimination against women in job selection. Among the intermediate and
senior males, who are usually responsible for job selection, there was a
strong feeling (50% of seniors and 42% of intermediates) that there was no
discrimination against women when selecting people for work. Only 18% of
junior males, 30% of junior females, 26% of intermediate females, and 12% of
senior females denied that there was discrimination against women in job
selection. On the whole, it is fair to conclude that there is a very strong
feeling, particularly among female workers, that women are discriminated
against when trying to obtain employment.

Apart from the feeling that women in general were discriminated against
in job selection, there was also a very strong belief (about 80% of all
respondents except the senior males) that women were discriminated against in
job selection simply because they were married. Only 50% of senior males

agreed with this, however, the remaining 50% denying there was any such discrimination. Discrimination against married women is probably linked to fairly generous laws which allow married women paid maternity leave for about three months.

Discrimination against women in general is attributable to a strong feeling that there are inadequate employment opportunities for women. Among male workers, 40% of juniors, 50% of intermediates and 76% of seniors felt that female job opportunities were inadequate. On the female side, 56% of juniors, 64% of intermediates and 32% of seniors took this view. The lower percentage response on the part of senior females probably reflected their perception of employment opportunities at this level. There is a shortage of high-level manpower generally (National Manpower Board 1976) so that female senior workers are likely to experience little or no difficulty in securing employment. Unemployment tends to be a problem mostly for those at an unskilled or low level, whether they are male or female workers (Diejomaoh 1978).

Although there was a strong feeling that job opportunities for females were inadequate, the extent of the contrary response should also be noted. Of the males, 78% of juniors, 46% of intermediates and 24% of seniors and, of the females, 44% of juniors, 36% of intermediates and 64% of seniors, believed that there were adequate job opportunities for females. Apart from the senior females, who were probably reflecting on their own not unfavourable situation, the other respondents were probably not well enough informed to know the extent of the availability of jobs for females. One would expect senior males, who are the main employers, to be most informed about job opportunities; hence we should attach greater weight to the fact that only 24% of these respondents felt that female employment opportunities were adequate. In fact 92% of senior male respondents felt that there were not enough jobs for either male or female workers in Lagos.

Given the strong desire of work to work, and the inadequacy of employment opportunities for them, it might be expected that women would be rather vulnerable in their search for employment and job advancement. We therefore asked whether women are subject to sexual pressures or harassment before they are offered employment or business contracts. 96% of senior males, the decision makers, agreed that women are put under sexual pressures before employment is offered to them; 88% of junior females and 80% of intermediate females took the same view. However, only 36% of senior females thought that females were sexually harassed before being offered employment, 56% believing that it depended on the type of job sought and the qualifications of the job seeker. On further detailed interviews of senior females, they tended to reply that senior females were not subject to sexual harassment.

A detailed breakdown of the categories of women who might be subject to sexual harassment revealed the following pattern. About 25% - 30% of both male and female respondents thought that females without training or secondary education were most likely to be subject to sexual pressures. 36% - 40% of both males and females specified typists and secretaries as the females most vulnerable. About 30% of male and senior female respondents and about 20% of junior and intermediate females thought female petty contractors were also likely to be sexually harassed. Less than 10% of all respondents felt that housemaids, nannies, and cleaners were sexually harassed. Only about 5% of all male respondents and 8% of junior female respondents thought professional women, such as doctors, lawyers, senior civil servants, and the like, were subjected to sexual harassment. Almost no intermediate or senior females (less than 5% of respondents) felt that professional women were harassed sexually.

There was virtual unanimity among male workers of all categories (100% of juniors, 92% of intermediates, and 100% of seniors) that women submitted to sexual pressures in order to secure employment. Among the women, 60% of juniors and 76% of intermediates agreed that women submitted to sexual pressures, while only 8% of senior females held this view. The sexual demands made by males and the submission of females probably accounts for the belief that 88% - 96% of the male workers who thought that women had special advantages over them in the search for work, despite the fact that they were generally agreed to have lower qualifications and less experience than the males. 84% of junior female and 70% of intermediate females agreed. However, only 14% of senior female workers, who do not consider sexual harassment as a factor, thought women had special advantages over men. There was a strong feeling that married women do not have any special advantages over men, which indicates that it is the single girls who are most subject to sexual harassment. However, 40% of junior female workers thought married women did have special advantages. This suggests that junior married female workers are also harassed to a significant extent.

Sexual harassment is a major factor in the life of working women in metropolitan Lagos. Some commentators have suggested that modern African males desire sexual access to several women because of the tradition of polygamy (Southall, 1961). While the tradition of polygamy could be a factor,

TABLE 3

Question 29	Percentage Response					
	Male			Female		
Of the following categories of women, please tell us who in your opinion is the most subject to sexual pressures in seeking and maintaining employment?	Jnr	Int	Snr	Jnr	Int	Snr
1. Housemaids, nannies and cleaners	6	8	2	–	–	2
2. Those without WAEC or 0 levels and no training	24	20	24	40	36	24
3. Teachers and nurses	4	6	4	–	2	–
4. Typists and secretaries	28	30	28	32	40	42
5. Women professionals, such as doctors, lawyers, senior civil servants, university lecturers, accountants, etc.	4	6	6	8	–	2
6. Women petty contractors	28	26	30	18	22	28
7. Other specify	6	4	6	2	–	2
Total	100	100	100	100	100	100

it cannot be regarded as the complete explanation. MacKinnon has shown that there is pervasive sexual harassment of working women in the United States. In fact the extent, pattern and structure of sexual harassment that we discovered in Lagos, was remarkably similar to MacKinnon's findings (MacKinnon, 1979). It appears probable that the incidence of sexual harassment of working women in Lagos is due to the special features of modern sector employment for women.

If working women suffer disabilities such as sex discrimination and sexual harassment, factors outside their control, one might expect them to attempt to control personal factors impeding their progress at work. Accordingly we asked several questions on the attitudes of females and males to the ideal family size for working women and the affect of childbearing on women's work. 81% of senior females, 70% of intermediate females, and 40% of junior females felt that childbearing adversely affected women's advancement and promotion at work; 70% of junior males, 50% of senior, and 36% of intermediates agreed.

But when we asked what constituted the ideal number of children for a

woman seeking rapid promotion and success at work, we had a wide range of
answers. For the females, the ideal number of children in these circumstances
averaged four   (60% of juniors, 70% of intermediates and 64% of seniors
specified this number). The number of children advocated by male workers also
averaged four, although the proportion of males giving this response (40% - 50%)
was lower than that of females. One striking aspect of this response is that
there is little or no difference in the ideal number of children favoured by
women and men in the different grades. Demographers have usually posited an
inverse ratio between the number of children desired and the level of
education and income of the individual (Arowolo, 1978). Another noteworthy
aspect of the female responses was that about 20% gave the ideal number of
children for a woman desiring success at work as five or more. Only about 10%
of the females gave two or three children as the ideal. On the male side,
however, only about 10% of the respondents specified five or more children as
the ideal, while 20% specified less than four. The men therefore tended to
have a preference for fewer children than the females. This was particularly
clear in the contrast between senior males and females. While 32% of senior
males regarded three children as ideal only 9% of senior females named this
number.

TABLE 4A

Question 18	Percentage Response					
	Male			Female		
What is the ideal number of children for a working mother?	Jnr	Int	Snr	Jnr	Int	Snr
1. One						
2. Two						
3. Three	12	4	30	–	2	12
4. Four	50	56	50	48	58	70
5. Five	20	24	14	32	18	12
6. Six and above	10	8	–	6	12	2
7. As many as God gives	6	4	–	10	8	–
8. Other specify	2	4	6	4	2	4
Total	100	100	100	100	100	100

Our findings in Lagos are similar to Arowolo's findings (Arowolo, 1978)
for Ibadan, the second largest city in Nigeria. This desire of all classes of
females for four or more children is in sharp contrast to the much smaller

family size desired in the West (two or three children). Traditional
considerations, such as the availability of family or hired household help
with children while mothers are at work and the desire of wives to strengthen
their marital position by having many children, have so far outweighed fears
of the negative effects of a large number of children on the women's career
prospects.

TABLE 4B

Question 34	Percentage Response					
	Male			Female		
The ideal number of children for a woman aiming for rapid promotion and major success at work is	Jnr	Int	Snr	Jnr	Int	Snr
1. One child	10	–	–	–	2	–
2. Two children	–	–	2	8	6	6
3. Three children	10	22	32	4	4	8
4. Four children	40	46	48	60	70	64
5. Five children	22	4	14	4	4	10
6. Six children	8	16	4	20	8	–
7. As many as God gives	10	10	–	4	6	12
8. D.K., N.R., etc.	–	2	–	–	–	–
Total	100	100	100	100	100	100

This view of family size is little affected by a decrease in the
availability of family or household help as a result of rising labour costs
and increased educational opportunities. Only about 10% of all male and
female respondents thought women should have fewer children if the
availability of household help declined. However, both male and female
respondents thought that, with less help available, women should space
children better, demand more day-care centres, or have jobs more compatible
with motherhood. The latter requirement will be difficult to fulfil and
better spacing of children will not completely eliminate the burden of
child-care for working mothers in the future. Accordingly, as the supply of
household help decreases, the prospects for job mobility for married women
will largely depend on the availability of day-care centres, nurseries, play
schools, and the like.

TABLE 5A

| Question 53 | Percentage Response | | | | | |
| | Male | | | Female | | |
As the supply of house-girls in Lagos is becoming very short what do you think should be done by working mothers?	Jnr	Int	Snr	Jnr	Int	Snr
1. Have less children	6	10	12	6	40	14
2. Space children better	8	34	16	56	42	16
3. Demand more day care centres and nursery schools that are reasonably priced from the government	34	40	28	12	–	32
4. Get more support from their husbands in caring for the children	4	–	–	6	–	–
5. Get jobs that are compatible with motherhood	42	12	42	16	16	30
6. Other, specify	–	–	–	–	–	–
7. D.K., N.R.,etc.	6	4	2	4	2	8
Total	100	100	100	100	100	100

TABLE 5B

| Question 52 | Percentage Response | | | | | |
| | Male | | | Female | | |
What measures do you think government could take to protect the rights of working mothers?	Jnr	Int	Snr	Jnr	Int	Snr
1. Provide more day care centres and nursery schools	58	74	72	50	74	60
2. Longer maternity leave with pay	36	20	26	42	22	30
3. Better pensions and gratuities	–	–	–	2	4	–
4. Other, specify	2	–	–	–	–	–
5. D.K., N.R.,etc.	4	6	2	6	–	10
Total	100	100	100	100	100	100

About 90% of our respondents, both male and female, felt that present institutional supports (such as day-care centres or nurseries for working mothers) were very inadequate or virtually non-existent. On the whole, less than 10% of respondents felt that institutional support for working mothers was adequate. Since resources are limited, the government does not provide or intend to provide day-care centres or nursery schools, although it is willing to regulate the institutions operated by private enterprise. Unless the government provides a vast number of day-care centres - which is unlikely, despite considerable support for such centres - working women's preference for a large number of children is likely to have an increasingly adverse effect on their job prospects as family and household help dwindles. If women are to progress in their careers there is therefore a need to increase the scale of the public enlightenment in general and for the working women in particular to be made aware of the need to reduce the size of their families. Despite the provision of State child-care Russian working women have adjusted to their combined working and maternal functions by drastically reducing their desired number of children to one (Rohrlich - Leavitt 1975).

Although our respondents were generally dissatisfied with the supply of day-care centres, opinion was more divided on the adequacy of the present maternity leave arrangements. The current practice in the public sector is that women are given three months' maternity leave and nursing mothers are allowed to go home one hour before closing time. The private sector has less generous provisions. About 60% of both junior and intermediate females and males, and about 30% of the senior females and males, thought the present maternity leave arrangements were adequate. 70% of the senior males, 60% of the senior females, and about 30% of the junior and intermediate males and females thought the present arrangements were inadequate. About 10% of the junior males and females, and the same percentage of the intermediate females thought the maternity leave arrangements very inadequate. The broad implication of our results is that there is a strong feeling that current maternity leave arrangements should be made more liberal. Since the public sector arrangements are already fairly liberal it is in the private sector that there is more urgent need for improvement. If this does not happen, women may find themselves confined mainly to the public sector where arrangements are more liberal but where the wages and salaries are generally lower. This will further depress their incomes relative to men.

(iv) <u>The Control and Use of Women's Income</u>

When asked who controlled their incomes, 84% of junior female workers, 96% of intermediates, and 94% of seniors replied that they, and not their husbands, controlled their incomes. Only 10% of junior females, 4% of intermediates, and 4% of seniors replied that their incomes were controlled by their husbands. There is virtual unanimity among all classes or working women that the woman controls her own income.

In traditional society, however, the practice was more varied. Most of the male respondents (50% junior, 70% intermediate, and 54% senior) said that in their areas women did traditionally control their incomes. 34% of junior females, 54% of intermediates, and 56% of seniors agreed. However, about 60% of junior females and about 40% of intermediate and senior females replied that in their areas, husbands traditionally controlled women's incomes and this view was supported by 22% of senior males, 10% of juniors, and 4% of intermediates. About 25%-40% of males either expressed ignorance of the traditional practices or gave no answer; but only about 4%-8% of female respondents fell into the 'don't know' or 'no reply' category. What is clear from the above is that women's control of their incomes has strong traditional foundations. However, the current support for women's control of their incomes is more pervasive than it used to be and, to that extent, attitudes have shifted more in favour of women controlling their own incomes.

There was virtual unanimity among males and females that both husbands and wives should keep separate bank accounts; only 5% of female and 10% of male respondents advocated joint bank accounts. These attitudes are translated into action. No respondent reported keeping a joint account with their spouse.

There was general agreement between the males and females that the keeping of separate bank accounts was conducive to greater marital harmony. The bulk of the females felt that bank accounts should be kept separate because husbands and wives have different expenditure patterns,and also because husbands spent too much money on girl friends and 'outside wives'. 10% of the females felt husbands spent too much money on their relations. On the male side, about 40% of the junior and intermediate workers thought that wives complained too much about money spent on husbands relations and this favoured the separation of accounts. However, only about 8% of senior males attached importance to this point. 20% junior and 30% intermediate males agreed that accounts should be kept separate because husbands spent too much money on girl friends and 'outside wives'.

TABLE 6

Question 45	Percentage Response					
	Male			Female		
Husbands and wives prefer to keep their income separate because.	Jnr	Int	Snr	Jnr	Int	Snr
1. Husband and wives have different ways of spending their money.	6	20	2	60	52	42
2. Wives complain too much about money spent on husbands relatives.	40	44	8	10	8	8
3. Some husbands spend too much money on girlfriends and outside wives.	30	28	20	24	12	10
4. It makes homes more peaceful.	22	8	70	6	26	40
5. Husbands complain too much about money spent on wives relatives.	-	-	-	-	-	-
6. D. K., N. R. etc.	2	-	-		2	-
TOTAL	100	100	100	100	100	100

It is clear that there is general agreement amongst males and females that the woman should control the income from her work, and keep it in her own separate bank account. Furthermore, there is the expectation that the

woman should keep her income for her own use or should contribute to the
family budget in whatever way she sees fit. The husband is expected to
provide all the money for household expenditure and even pocket-money for
their working wives, as well as money for clothing, holiday expenses, and
the like. Asked why this should be so, most of the female and male respondents
attributed it to the fact that the husband was the head of the household.
About 80% of males and about 60% of females felt husbands should bear the burden
of expenditure because they earn more. Approximately 8% of females felt that
wives must keep their earnings in case the marriage should break up; another
8% felt that wives might not inherit the husband's wealth and so they should
put their incomes aside; while about 5% thought women needed more money for
clothing and jewelry.

The current practice in Lagos whereby working women keep or put aside
their incomes, is contrary to the practice both in traditional Yoruba society and
in Western society. In traditional Yoruba society married women work but they
are responsible for feeding themselves, their children, and their husbands out of
the proceeds of their work. Some of the women also contribute to the clothing
and education of their children. In Western society, when married women work,
their incomes are usually put with their husband's in joint bank accounts and
spent on household needs jointly determined by both spouses. The working
married woman in modern Lagos who keeps her income essentially for her own use
is therefore in a privileged economic position compared to her counterpart
either in the traditional Yoruba or Western society.

We have shown elsewhere (Karanja-Diejomaoh 1978) that married working
women in Lagos, even though they keep their incomes separately, do in fact
contribute to household expenditure, contrary to popular belief and
expectations. However, their contributions are made voluntarily and are
usually aimed at supplementing the efforts of the husbands who are still
expected to shoulder all the responsibilities. The expectation that the
husband should be responsible for all household expenditure probably derives
from the practice in the West, where, however, the wife is expected to be a
full-time housewife. The current attitudes in Lagos have therefore been
copied out of context. However, the males do not mind the burdens imposed
on them, because they think their authority over their wives is strengthened
when, to the best of their abilities, they undertake the entire household
expenditure. Moreover, they experience a greater sense of freedom, as they
do not have to account to their wives for their expenditure, since the

TABLE 7

Question 47	Percentage Response					
	Male			Female		
Why is it that many married women including those earning high salaries require their husbands to provide all the money for house keeping and education of the children while the wives keep all the income to themselves and even expect their husbands to provide them with pocket money, clothing, holiday expenses etc?	Jnr	Int	Snr	Jnr	Int	Snr
1. Because husbands are the heads of families.	80	78	72	60	60	50
2. Because husbands earn more money than their wives.				4	2	14
3. Because wives must have savings in case their marriages break.				8	6	12
4. Because women need extra money for clothing and jewellery.	16	10	20	10	4	2
5. Because women may not inherit their husbands property.	–	4	–	6	16	2
6. Other (specify)						
7. D. K. N.R. etc.	4	8	8	12	12	20
TOTAL	100	100	100	100	100	100

wives themselves are controlling their own incomes. The women, on the
other hand, seem content to accept the weaker marital positions which
result from their contributing little or nothing to household expenditure
in exchange for the privilege of keeping most or all of their incomes
for their own use. The women, however, feel a greater sense of economic
independence compared with full-time housewives who depend on their husbands
for all their money. Their economic independence is, however, less than
that of the traditional African women who were economically independent of
their husbands once they received the initial trading capital or farm land
from them.

(v)   The Impact on Family Stability of Women's Participation in the World
      of Work.

There has been increasing concern that the family might suffer as a
result of married women's involvement in work. However, our study showed
that there is considerable division of opinion amongst males and females
on the adverse results of married women working. Some 64% of senior females,
58% of intermediates, and 60% of juniors thought marriages were in fact more
stable because married women were allowed to work. About 20% and 36% of females
felt work had no impact of any kind on the stability of marriage and only about
10% of females thought marriage was made less stable. While 56% of senior males
felt that women's work made marriage more stable, only 28% of junior males felt
so. 36% of juniors felt that the stability of marriages was adversely affected
but only about 10% of male intermediate and senior staff agreed. The bulk of the
male staff (40%-50%) felt that the marriage was not affected one way or the
other by women working.

The general view that marriage was unaffected or even made more stable
by women working is consistent with the strong support given to the idea that
married women should be allowed to work. Similarly, the belief of some of the
junior male staff that marriages were made more unstable reflects their feeling
that married women should not work until the children have grown up.

Most of the female and male respondents (about 70% and 80%) thought the
position of a working woman in her extended family was enhanced, because she
would have more money for family obligations. About 20% of the respondents
did not think the position or working women in their extended family was
affected in any way by their working.

There was virtual unanimity amongst females and males (80% - 100%) that sexual pressures put on women in their search for work adversely affects their families and marriage. However, we have shown that sexual harassment of married women is not pervasive and is limited mainly to junior and to a lesser extent intermediate workers.

While males generally support the idea of women working, they do have some misgivings about women who are ambitious and successful at work. 92% of senior male workers felt that successful female workers do not perform their roles as wives and mothers very well. 76% of senior males felt that women who have many children and also are very ambitious at work tend to have unstable marriages; 94% of senior males felt that the children of such women tend to be disturbed. Junior and intermediate male workers gave varying support to these views, but tended to feel less strongly. About 50% of female workers felt that the struggle for promotion at work is likely to affect the marriage, family, and children adversely; the remaining 50% did not think so. The female workers generally thought (about 60% - 80% response) that women who were successful at work performed their roles as wives and mothers very well. Between 64% and 86% of female workers of all classes also disagreed with the males' belief that professionally ambitious women were likely to have unstable marriages and disoriented children. This disagreement between males and females points to an area of potential marital conflict.

While there was disagreement between males and females on the affect of women's ambition at work on their marriages and families, there was general agreement that leaving children in the care of nannies and housemaids has an adverse impact on them. Yet most males and females responded that they left the care of their children to nannies and housemaids while the mothers of the children were out at work. This response seems inconsistent with the views of both males and females that the working of married women has no adverse effect on the children. However, it is felt that the adverse effect on children caused because they are left in the care of nannies or housemaids, is not great enough to diminish support for the idea that married women, even with children, should be allowed to work.

TABLE 8

Question 48	Percentage Response					
	Male			Female		
Who takes care of your children while you are at work?	Jnr	Int	Snr	Jnr	Int	Snr
1. Nanny/House girl.	50	60	80	28	56	82
2. My relatives.	20	12	14	28	12	6
3. My husband's relatives				24	20	6
4. My wife's relatives	14	20	4			
5. D. K., N.R. etc.	16	8	2	20	12	4
TOTAL	100	100	100	100	100	100

Question 49	Percentage Response					
	Male			Female		
Do you think there is any adverse impact on children left to the care of nannies and housegirls?	Jnr	Int	Snr	Jnr	Int	Snr
1. Yes, there is adverse effect.	58	44	60	68	74	50
2. No adverse effect	22	52	32	20	18	40
3. Other (specify)	–	–	–	–	–	–
4. D. K., N.R. etc.	20	4	8	12	8	10
TOTAL	100	100	100	100	100	100

Conclusions

In this paper, we have shown that in the modern sector of Lagos, in contrast to past experience in the West, both males and females fully approve of married women going out to work. However, there is a strong feeling among all classes of females, as well as junior and intermediate males, that married women with small children should not work until the children are grown up. On the choice of work for women, we found that generally women felt they should be allowed to do whatever job they were qualified for. Male workers tended to prefer women working in the traditional 'women's' jobs of teaching, nursing, office work, etc. Both males and females felt that married women, especially those with small children, should not have jobs that are too demanding, especially in terms of hours and changes in location.

In analysing the deterrents to working women, we found that sexual harassment of single girls and married juniors pervasive. There was agreement between males and females that sex discrimination against females was common in job selection. In spite of agreement that a large number of children adversely affects women's progress at work, both males and females of all income categories thought the ideal number of children for a working mother was four. Rather than consider reducing the number of children as the supply of nannies and housemaids dwindles, female workers are demanding more day-care centres and nurseries.

On the issue of women's incomes we found full agreement among males and females that women should control their own incomes and that husbands and wives should keep separate bank accounts. There was also general agreement that the husband should be responsible for all household expenditure and that the woman should keep her income to spend as she likes, although she often supplements the husband's housekeeping allowance of her own volition.

We also found that there is general agreement between males and females that the phenomenon of working wives does not adversely affect marriage, family, or children. While males feel that ambitious and successful women at work do not perform well as wives or mothers, females reject this view.

On the whole, our study showed a considerable harmony between the
attitudes of men and women towards women's participation in paid employment.
The pattern of the responses often reflects attitudes very different from
those found in Western societies even though one might have expected
similarities,   as the respondents have been schooled in Western ideas
and are operating in a modernising Western-type economy. It appears
that women working in the modern sector in Lagos retain much of the
economic freedom which characterises rural African women in many ethnic
traditions.   A striking difference however is that the woman working in
the modern sector in Lagos actually contributes proportionately less than
her traditional African or Western counterpart to household expenditure.
where there is any surplus.

Yet, in spite of the economic freedom enjoyed by many modern working
African women in white collar employment in Lagos, their position vis-a-vis
their male counterparts in the modern sector has weakened considerably.
This is evident in sexual discrimination, sexual harassment, and the
disadvantages consequent upon their continuing preference for a large number
of children.   In order to strengthen their relatively weak position, there
must be increased efforts to improve the higher education of women and to
ensure that such education is of practical utility.   There is also a need
to point out the apparent conflict between the large families desired by
these women workers and their career aspirations.

BIBLIOGRAPHY

Amon-Nikol, G. 1978. "Women and Work in Africa", in U.G.Damachi and
V.P.Diejomaoh (eds.), Human Resources and African Development.
Praeger, New York.

Ardener, E. 1975. "Belief and the Problem of Women" in Ardener S., (ed.),
Perceiving Women, Malaby, London.

Ardener, S. 1975. (ed.),"Introductory Chapter", Perceiving Women. Malaby,
London.

Arowolo, O.O. 1978. "Female Labour Force Participation and Fertility: The
Case of Ibadan City in the Western State of Nigeria" in C.Oppong et al.,
Marriage, Fertility and Parenthood in West Africa, Department of
Demography, Australian National University, Canberra.

Boserup, E. 1970. Woman's Role in Economic Development. George Allen &
Unwin, London.

Diejomaoh, V.P. 1978. "Nigeria's Human Resources: A Preliminary Assessment"
in U.G.Damachi and V.P.Diejomaoh. Human Resources & African Development,
Praeger, New York.

Diejomaoh, V.P. 1981. "Education and Income Distribution in Nigeria", in
H.Bienen and V.P.Diejomaoh (eds.), The Political Economy of Income
Distribution in Nigeria. Holmes and Myers, New York, in press.

Fapohunda, E. 1978. "Women at Work in Nigeria: Factors affecting Modern
Sector Employment" in U.G.Damachi and V.P.Diejomaoh. Ibid.

Hafkin, N.J. and Bay, E.G. 1976. Women in Africa: Studies in Social and
Economic Change. Stanford University Press, Stanford.

Karanja-Diejomaoh, W.M. 1978. "Disposition of Incomes by Husbands and Wives:
An Exploratory Study of Families in Lagos", in C.Oppong et al. Ibid.

Wambi Wa Karanja, "Aspects of Juvenile Delinquency in Nigeria: A Preliminary
Report". West African J. of Soc. and Pol. Science, forthcoming.

Larguia, I. 1975. "The Economic Basis of the Status of Women" in Rohrlich-Leavitt,
(ed.), Women Cross-Culturally Change and Challenge. Mouton, The Hague.

MacKinnon, C. 1979. Sexual Harassment of Working Women. Yale University Press,
New Haven, Conn.

Remy, D. 1975. "Underdevelopment and the Experience of Women: A Nigerian
Case Study" in Reiter, R.R., (ed.), Towards an Anthropology of Women,
Monthly Review Press, New York.

Rosenthal, B.G. 1975. "The Role and Status of Women in the Soviet Union:
1917 to the Present", in Rohrlich-Leavitt, R. (ed.), Ibid.

Southall, A. 1961. Social Change in Modern Africa. Oxford University Press,
London.

Sudarkasa, N. 1973. Where Women Work: A Study of Yoruba Women in the Market
Place and in the Home. Museum of Anthropology, University of Michigan,
Ann Arbor.

CHAPTER 4

WORLDS APART?

Susan Soyinka

CHAPTER 4

WORLDS APART?

Susan Soyinka

A comparative study of European and African traditional
family life as depicted in the novels of Laurie Lee and
Camara Laye.

This chapter compares two autobiographical novels, to demonstrate
that literature can be a rich source of sociological information. More
specifically, it concentrates on the type of family life each novel portrays,
in particular the relationship between various members of the family, and
between the family and the community at large. It also discusses the ways
in which traditional family life has changed, and the causes of such change.

In using literature in this way, it is not intended to rob these works
of their artistic merit. Both novels are highly evocative and poetic
descriptions of a particular era, and convey to readers an atmosphere which
they certainly would not find in any scientific journal. They therefore
afford knowledge beyond that of facts and figures, and it is precisely for
this reason that a reading of such novels is highly valuable to the sociologist.
Indeed, the contribution of these two novels to sociology lies not so much in
the sociological facts which can be elicited from them, but in the world view[1]
which each of them conveys.

The two novels are Cider with Rosie by Laurie Lee.[2] and The African
Child by Camara Laye.[3] The former describes the author's childhood
experiences in a Cotswold village, Slad, in England, during the period
immediately following the First World War, and the second, also a description
of the author's childhood experiences, is set in the small town of Kouroussa
in Upper Guinea during the nineteen thirties.

In Cider with Rosie, Laurie Lee gives us a wealth of detail about his
family background. His father's first wife had eight children before she
died, of whom five survived. Of these, the first was a boy, who later went
to live with his grandmother, and the remaining four were made up of three
girls and a boy. The author's father subsequently married his housekeeper
(Laurie's mother) who was herself an only sister to five brothers. She

herself gave birth to a girl and three boys (Laurie being the middle of
the three), but the little girl died, and Mrs. Lee always regretted her
lack of sisters and daughters. Laurie's mother had four children within
four years, and would presumably have continued having children had not
her husband deserted her at this point. She continued to look after her
husband's two families, four of the five children by his first marriage,
and her own three surviving children. This she did with apparently no
bitterness or resentment, her only hope being that her husband would one
day return to her. It is this hope which gave her life, for when her
husband died in London some thirty five years later, having still not
returned, the news of his death killed her, her reason for living having
been extinguished. The father's place was, for the children, largely filled
by the presence of no less than five maternal uncles, and one paternal uncle,
to all of whom Lee was devoted. In spite of the absence of husband and
father, the family lived in a state of happy-go-lucky confusion, the memory
of which obviously gave the author very great pleasure. Each chapter of
the book is like a vivid snapshot of some aspect or other of his childhood
experiences, thrown together in a somewhat loose fashion.

Camara Laye was born into a more conventional family. He was the first
child of his father's first wife, and though he does not state specifically
how many younger brothers and sisters he had, there were evidently quite
a number of them, probably about twelve. He makes only one reference to
the fact that his father, a strict Muslim, had a second wife. The whole
family, parents and children, together with a number of the father's
apprentices, lived in the father's compound, in a number of different huts.
The family was obviously a very close one, and Laye must have had a
particularly strong attachment for his parents, both of whom were prominent
members of the society, since he describes them much more vividly than any
of his brothers and sisters, of whom we do not even know the names. He also
had a close relationship with his maternal grandmother, and like Lee, with
his uncles, both maternal and paternal, all of whom he went to visit at
different points in his life. As can be seen from the lack of detailed
information about his close family, Laye's account is more impressionistic
and nostalgic than factual, but like Lee, he remembers his childhood with a
great sense of pleasure, even joy. Each chapter describes some facet of his
childhood, or some incident he remembers particularly vividly, and although
there is no chronological link between each chapter, there is a definite

movement throughout the book from childhood to adolescence. Both authors
devote separate chapters to their mother, life at the village school, a
description of village festivals, and to a sensitive portrayal of first
contact with the opposite sex.

Though these two novels have such widely different geographical and
cultural settings, they do have certain things in common, and it is indeed
their similarities which are emphasized here. Both depict rural life in
communities which were then relatively isolated, and where tradtions had
not changed for hundreds of years. Both, however, are on the verge of
sudden and dramatic change. This sense of tradition, and of interrupted
tradition, is so striking in both novels that it suggests that the very
profound changes which have taken place in African society cannot simply
be explained in terms of westernisation, although the influence of the West
has been very powerful. It appears from a reading of the two novels that
Western society, as represented by Lee's novel, has changed almost as profoundly as
African society, as portrayed in The African Child, and that change is not therefore so much due to the influence of one on the other, as to the impact on both
of education and technology. Each author as a young boy began to feel the
impact of the outside world, first of all through his education in the village
school, and later through modern technology, which resulted in each of them
being carried away physically from his home environment.

In Camara Laye's novel, the link with the past is still a very strong one.
Not only were ancient customs and rituals still performed during his childhood,
but also the history of his people was carefully preserved by the 'griots':

> "The praise-singer would install himself in the work-shop, tune
> up his cora, which is our harp, and would begin to sing my
> father's praises. This was always a great event for me. I
> would hear recalled the lofty deeds of my father's ancestors,
> and the names of these ancestors from the earliest times; as the
> couplets were reeled off, it was like watching the growth of a
> great genealogical tree that spread its branches far and wide
> and flourished its boughs and twigs before my mind's eye." (4)

For Laurie Lee, the link with the past is a much more tenuous one,
nonetheless he is deeply aware of his ancestral connections, and of the
fact that he was witnessing the close of an era, "the end of a thousand
years' life."[5] This is sensitively conveyed in the following passage:

"The village in fact was like a deep-running cave still linked
to its antic past, a cave whose shadows were cluttered by
spirits and laws still vaguely ancestral. This cave that we
inhabited looked backwards through chambers that led to our
ghostly beginnings; and had not, as yet, been tidied up, or
scrubbed clean by electric light, or suburbanized by a
Victorian church, or papered by cinema screens.

It was something we just had time to inherit, to inherit
and dimly know - the blood and beliefs of generations who
had been in this valley since the Stone Age. That continuous
contact has at last been broken, the deeper caves sealed off
forever. But arriving, as I did, at the end of that age, I
caught whiffs of something old as the glaciers." (6)

Even Laye, steeped as he is in tradition, is aware that some of the
customs performed by his people are mere echoes of the past:

"Sometimes only the spirit of a tradition survives, and so it
happens that the merest ghost of an outward ceremony remains." (7)

What were the dominant characteristics of these traditional societies
to which Laye and Lee were so closely bound? And in what way did traditional
lore affect family life? The answers to these questions were provided by
Camara Laye himself on one of the few occasions when he decided to discuss his
work. (8)   He maintained that the two factors which largely distinguish the
old civilisation from the new are Mystery and Love. The Africa of old was
permeated with mysterious forces which were all pervading, and which bound all
members of the society one to another, and gave each individual his place in
the universe. These mysterious forces binding society were mysterious
precisely because they were unseen, only dimly understood even by those who
believed in them, and because they defied rational explanation. "Is there
nothing to the world except what we can see at a casual glance?" (9)   asks
Laye, presumably of the sceptic.

Closely tied up with the idea of mystery is that of love:

"I am talking now of the love which unites us so closely to each
other; the love that made our families and tribes -- our very
large tribes - into those compact groups which made our country
villages so friendly, so peaceable and so united ... It was
through that love that we remained within the mystery, ...
for there is no mystery in the absence of beings and things,
any more than the mystery can be clearly or intimately
apprehended without at least a beginning of love for beings and
things, without some kind of almost mystical union between them." (10)

It is interesting that Laye is not making a case for Africa being different from Europe. He even admits that Europe, too, has her mystery, though, as he puts it, he felt its presence more strongly in Africa. He does moreover make the suggestion that the European rationalist in his attempt to explain everything in logical, scientific terms, may have stifled the true soul of Europe:

> "What is truly deep and genuine in Europe is the message of her writers and artists, her scientists, moralists, musicians and revolutionaries. That is Europe's soul and the message is not one of rationalism. It is a message coming from the soul and nowhere else." (12)

The idea that Africa and Europe are not so very different in essence, though they may be in degree, is pursued here, because it is borne out in the two novels under discussion. Whilst there can be no doubt about the presence of the elements of mystery and love in The African Child, it will not be difficult to demonstrate that they are almost as strongly, though less consciously, felt in Cider with Rosie.

To make our comparison viable, let us take first of all the concept of mystery in The African Child.

Both of Camara Laye's parents possessed inherited magical powers, and in both cases it was the possession of these powers which determined their role in society and their relationship with other members of society, both within and outside the family. His father was a blacksmith, but worked with a number of mediums including gold. His creative activity did not depend simply on his skill, but also on the presence of spirits which guided him in his work. Readers are confronted with the supernatural at the very beginning of the novel when they learn that the little black snake which frequently entered the workshop was his guiding spirit. It is not even sufficient for Laye's father to use his skill, under the guidance of the spirit in the form of the snake. The spirits have to be invoked, and hence the services of the praise-singer are required. The act of creation becomes then, not the work of a solitary artist, but a communal activity.

Laye's father's powers were inherited, and Laye, as his father's eldest son would have learned their secret too, had he not been physically removed from his environment in order to go to school.

Laye's mother had been born after male twins, and this, according to
tradition, meant that she too was endowed with mysterious powers. She
could for example, go and draw water from a crocodile-infested river. The
dignity with which she used her powers caused her to be both feared and
respected in society, and was one of the main reasons why she wielded an
unusual amount of authority in her own home. As Laye points out, the African
woman is generally thought to play a subservient role, but he feels that
a woman who commands respect will get it:

> "(My father) had the greatest respect for her, and so did our
> friends and neighbours. That was due, I am sure, to my mother's
> character, which was impressive; it was also due to the strange
> powers she possessed." (13)

Mysterious forces linked the individual who possessed them with the
society of which he was part. Likewise all members of the society were
enclosed in a network of such forces, since most activities in traditional
African society were communal, and since such communal activities could only
reach a successful conclusion with the goodwill of the spirits concerned.
This is seen clearly during the time of the rice harvest at Tindican, when
the ripening of the rice depended on "the goodwill of the spirits of the soil,
whose influence could not be ignored." (14) It is seen even more clearly at
the circumcizion ceremony when Laye and his age mates were initiated into manhood
During the course of this ceremony, a number of mysterious things occurred,
the secret of which was only known to initiated men, since women and children were
deliberately kept in the dark. Laye makes the interesting observation that this
secret is necessary if the ceremony is to achieve its objective which is that
"there is given to every boy the opportunity to overcome his own baser nature."
(15) As he points out, "it is obvious that if the secret was given away, the
ceremony would lose much of its power." (16)

Laye is making here a distinction between mystery and mystification or
"false mystery". (17) whereby an apparent mystery, the secret of which is fully
understood by certain members of the society, is imposed on other members of
the society in order to encourage them to conform to the accepted standard of
behaviour.

Laurie Lee's childhood world was also peopled by unknown, unseen, and
greatly feared forces. There were still in the village of Slad at that time
a number of supernatural phenomena, such as ghostly apparitions (18), which
continued to inspire awe and fear. What is interesting about these occurrences

is that "it was the women who were clearly affected".[19]   and one is
reminded that in Laye's Kouroussa, the men deliberately created an
atmosphere of fear "so as not to give the show away to the women and
children". [20] One wonders whether there may not have been, at some time,
similar constraints on women in Lee's corner of England.

Lee analyses his own perception of these mysterious events in the
following way:

> "The yard and village manifested themselves at first through
> magic and fear. Projections of their spirits and of my
> hallucinations sketched in the first blanks with demons."[21]

One sees here that he is one step removed from the type of magic which
binds Laye's world, as he is not quite sure of the dividing line between magic
and hallucinations. The mysterious forces are there, they are dimly
comprehended, but they have lost the cohesive power which they must once
have had. Lee makes frequent use of the words "magic", and "mystery", and
uses the descriptive terms "tribal", "tropic", "jungle", "primitive",
"shrine". He refers to water as that "substance of magic".[22] He talks
of the time when he was on the point of death, but recovered "aided by unknown
forces"[23]   convinced that his little sister who died had given him life.[24]
On another occasion he mentions that the church clock stopped "so that both
time and the winds were stilled; nothing, we thought could be more exciting
than this; interference by a hand unknown, the winter's No to routine and laws –
sinister, awesome, welcome".[25]

The power of these mysterious forces is still felt, but they have lost
their grip, since they are no longer so all-pervasive. They are no longer
able to mould society, to insist on conformity, to define and determine
relationships. However, the presence of these forces, dimly felt as they
were, clearly shows that Lee's world had much more in common with African
traditional society than with the modern technological era. In the following
passage from Cider with Rosie there is a description of what can only be
understood as a traditional world view, which bears an uncanny resemblence
to African traditional religion. Rationalists might indeed be inclined to
disbelieve that this passage refers to twentieth century Europe.

"There were ghosts in the stones, in the trees, and the walls,
and each field and hill had several. The elder people knew
about these things and would refer to them in personal terms,
and there were certain landmarks about the valley - tree-clumps,
corners in woods - that bore separate, antique, half-muttered
names which were certainly older than Christian. The women in
their talk still used these names which are not used now any
more. There was also a frank and unfearful attitude to death, and an
acceptance of violence as a kind of ritual which no one accused
or pardoned." (26)

Love, according to Laye's own definition, is one of the most powerful
cohesive forces at work in any given community. It not only binds together
the individual members of the family, it also provides the basic motivation
for co-operation between the family and the rest of society, and hence is
the basis of unity, unity of thought, belief and action. The concept of
love is examined by analysing the relationship of each author with different
members of his family and the rest of the community.

Laye's father represented for him authority, tradition, and wisdom.
Ironically it was his wisdom and foresight which led to his son _not_ following
in his footsteps, for he it was who forecast that his country would be needing
men educated in a new kind of way. From an early stage he had stoically
accepted that his son's destiny was to go to school and lead a very different
kind of life from his own. But even though Camara Laye was to lead a very different
life from that of his father, there can be no doubt that he was profoundly
influenced by him, both in terms of his art and in terms of his philosophy of
life. Camara Laye's father provided him with an exceptionally strong link
with both past and future.

Laurie Lee knew very little of his father. What is perhaps astonishing
in the modern western context is his natural acceptance of his father's
absence. It indeed seems from Lee's analysis that it was because his father belong
to a different world, the modern world of "tidy laws", that he was unable to
accept his wife's naturalness, her closeness to nature:

"She was, after all, a country girl; disordered, hysterical, loving.
She was muddled and mischievous as a chimney-jackdaw, and she made
her nest of rags and jewels, was happy in the sunlight, squawked
loudly at danger, pried and was insatiably curious, forgot when
to eat or ate all day, and sang when sunsets were red. She lived
by the easy laws of the hedgerow, loved the world, and made no plans,
had a quick holy eye for natural wonders and couldn't have kept a
neat house for her life. What my father wished for was something
quite different, something she could never give him - the protective

order of an unimpeachable suburbia, which was what he got
in the end." (27)

The striking difference between these two people was that whereas
Lee's mother was a woman overflowing with love, his father was a
"frightened, remote man". It is very significant that by removing
himself geographically from his wife's influence, he in effect passed from
one era to another.

A father figure was supplied for Lee and his brothers and sisters by
five maternal uncles "whom we loved and who were the kings of our youth".[28]
Just as Laye's father had done for him, these five heroes of Lee's
childhood represented an ancient order which he regarded with awe and
affection, and to which he only reluctantly bid farewell.

"They were bards and oracles each, like a ring of squat megaliths
on some local hill, bruised by weather and scarred with old
glories. They were the horsemen and brawlers of another age,
and their lives spoke its long farewell. Spoke, too, of
campaigns on desert marches, of Kruger's cannon, and Flander's
mud; of a world that still moved at the same pace as Caesar's,
and of that Empire greater than his - through which they had
fought, sharp-eyed and anonymous, and seen the first outposts
crumble ..." (29)

Both Laye and Lee had an extremely deep attachment to and strong
affection for their mothers which was reciprocated.

Laye's mother was a very traditional person, both in terms of her
beliefs and in terms of her powers. Her authoritarian attitudes did however
mark her as somewhat different. Like her husband, she provided her son with
a very strong anchor in traditional society, and it was with very great
reluctance that she let him go into another world. Her concept of motherhood
obviously embraced physical closeness, and she bitterly resented those
(presumably the French) who had snatched her son away from her. The
accusation she made on hearing that her son was to go to France is one of
the only direct criticisms of the French in the whole novel:

"Your place is here. What are they thinking about at the school?
Do they imagine I'm going to live my whole life apart from my
son? Die with him far away? Have they no mother, those people?
But they can't have mothers, of course. They would not have gone
so far away from home if they'd had mothers." (30)

Laye's mother was rigid and authoritarian, Lee's mother muddle-headed
and disorganized, but what they both had in common was their great
capacity to love. What is quite extraordinary about Lee's mother is her calm
acceptance of her fate - deserted by her husband she was left to care alone
for seven children, four of them not even her own. [31] Few modern
western women would tolerate such a situation. Her acceptance can in fact
only be understood in terms of the great love she had for her husband and
her children, both her own and her step-children. She lived by the laws of
nature. She had inherited her boundless love from the very countryside
in which she was born and bred. "She loved this world and saw it with fresh
hopes that never clouded. She was an artist, a light-giver, and an original,
and she never for a moment knew it ..." [32]

It is interesting that both Laye and Lee experienced a physical
separation from their mother which marked for them the beginning of adulthood.

Laye had, until the time of the initiation ceremony which occurred
during his adolescence, slept in his mother's hut. The initiation ceremony
marked a turning point in his life, and he knew that he would return to
occupy a separate hut in his father's compound. After his circumcision,
and before he returned home, his mother visited him in the hut he was
occupying with the other newly circumcized boys. Laye is told of his mother's
arrival:

> "With a few swift strides I covered the few yards that separated
> me from the gate, and suddenly I saw my mother. She was
> standing in the dusty road a few steps away from the fence;
> she, too, was forbidden to come any closer.
>
> "Mother!" I cried. "Mother!"
>
> And all at once I felt a lump in my throat. Was it because I
> could go no closer, because I could not hug my mother? Was it
> because we had already been separated so long, because we were
> still to be separated a long time? I do not know. All I know
> is that I could only say "Mother!" and that after my joy in seeing her
> I suddenly felt a strange depression. Ought I to attribute this
> emotional instability to the transformation that had been worked
> in me? When I had left my mother, I was still a child. Now ... But
> was I really a man now? Was I already a grown man? ... I was a man!
> Yes, I was a grown man. And now this manhood had already begun to
> stand between my mother and myself. It kept us infinitely further
> apart than the few yards that separated us now." [33]

As a small boy, Laurie Lee, alone of all the family slept in his mother's bed. This he felt was his right, and, it seemed to him "life's whole purpose".(34)   He vividly remembers this early physical closeness:

"So in the ample night and the thickness of her hair I consumed my fattened sleep, drowsed and nuzzling to her warmth of flesh, blessed by her bed and safety. From the width of the house and the separation of the day, we two then lay joined alone. That darkness to me was like the fruit of sloes, heavy and ripe to the touch. It was a darkness of bliss and simple langour, when all edges seemed rounded, apt and fitting; and the presence for whom one had moaned and hungered was found not to have fled after all." (35)

After some time he began to hear rumours that he was to be replaced by his small brother Tony.

"When I first heard whispers of moving me to the boys' room, I simply couldn't believe it. Surely my Mother would never agree? How could she face the night without me?" (36)

Laurie was, however, eventually ousted from his privileged position, and this was his first step away from childhood.

"I was never recalled to my Mother's bed again. It was my first betrayal, my first dose of ageing hardness, my first lesson in the gently, merciless rejection of women. Nothing more was said, and I accepted it. I grew a little tougher, a little colder, and turned my attention more towards the outside world, which by now was emerging visibly through the mist ..." (37)

The physical separation which accompanies the first step into adulthood is remarkably similar in both cases, except that for Laye, the transition was a more formalized one, accompanied by ritual and ceremony.

In spite of the all-consuming nature of their mother's love, both Laye and Lee were indulged and petted by other mother figures, the grandmother in Laye's case, three much older half-sisters in Lee's.

Laye frequently visited his maternal grandmother in Tindican, and the sheer joy they both experienced in each other's company is conveyed in the following passage:

"Before we even reached the outskirts of Tindican, I would
see my grandmother coming to meet us. I would drop my
mother's hand and run shouting towards her. She would lift
me high in the air, then press me to her bosom, and I used
to squeeze her as hard as I could, flinging my arms around her,
overcome with happiness."

     "How are you, my little man?" she would say
     "I'm fine!" I would cry
     "Now is that so?" (38)

A strikingly similar scene is protrayed on the very first page of Lee's
novel. His family had just moved to the village of Slad where he was to
spend the rest of his childhood, and on arrival he found, to his terror,
that he had been inadvertently dumped in a patch of grass taller than himself:

"From this daylight nightmare I was awakened, as from many another, by
the appearance of my sisters. They came scrambling and calling up
the steep rough bark, and parting the long grass found me. Faces
of rose, familiar, living; huge shining faces hung up like shields
between me and the sky; faces with grins and white teeth (some
broken) to be conjured up like genii with a howl, brushing off terror
with their broad scoldings and affection. They leaned over me -
one, two, three - their mouths smeared with red currants and their
hands dripping with juice.

'There, there, it's all right, don't you wail any more. Come down
'ome and we'll stuff you with currants.'" (39)

It is evident from this analysis that Camara Laye and Laurie Lee were
both the focal point of a great deal of love and attention as children. At
the same time this love was not only directed towards them, but was, as has
been intimated, part and parcel of the society in which they lived. Every
individual was, so to speak, the centre of a network of social and emotional
relationships. For a child, the network was at its strongest at the heart
of the family, but it spread its tentacles outwards, so that all members
of the society were bound one to another.

Activities such as eating were confined largely to the home, but even
here it was largely a communal affair. For Laurie Lee, for example, the
kitchen was the focal point of family life.

"But our waking life, and our growing years, were for the most
part spent in the kitchen, and until we married, or ran away,
it was the common room we shared. Here we lived and fed in a
family fug, not minding the little space, trod on each other like
birds in a hole, elbowed our way without spite, all talking at

once or all silent at once, or crying against each other, but
never I think feeling overcrowded, being as separate as notes
in a scale " (40)

Likewise for Camara Laye, meal times were largely a communal activity
involving not only his very large family, but also his father's
apprentices, and anyone else who happened to be present:

"In the morning, when, after some persuasion, we rose, we would
find the breakfast all ready. My mother used to get up at
dawn to prepare it. We all would squat round the steaming
platters: my parents, sisters, brothers, and the apprentices,
those who shared my bed as well as those who had their own
hut. There would be one dish for the men, and another for
my mother and sisters." (41)

It was also an extremely ritual affair, and everyone present was
expected to observe the rules of hygiene and silence, largely imposed by
Laye's mother.

Movement was outwards from communal activity within the home to activities
within the community. Village life was a largely seasonal affair, being
predetermined to a great extent by the regular recurrance of festivals
of one kind or another. This was as much true for Laurie Lee as it was
for Camara Laye; as the following extract from Cider with Rosie shows:

"The year revolved around the village, the festivals round the
year, the Church round the festivals, the Squire round the
Church, and the village round the Squire." (42)

When a particular festival occurred, everyone was expected to participate
indeed it would not have occurred to anyone to refuse:

"No one in the village stayed away without reason, and no one
yet wished to do so. We had come to the Church because it was
Sunday, just as we washed our clothes on Monday." (43)

For Laye, the villagers did not participate in a communal activity merely
out of a sense of duty, they did for the pleasure it afforded them, as for
example during the harvesting of rice:

"Our husbandmen were singing, and as they sang, they reaped;
they were singing in chorus, and reaping in unison: their
voices and their gestures were all harmonious, and in harmony
they were one! - united by the same task, united by the same
song. They were bound to one another, united by the same soul:
each and every one was tasting the delight, savouring the
common pleasure of accomplishing a common task." [44]

A further example in The African Child of communal activity is that of
the initiation ceremony. A group of young boys were to be circumcized, but
the whole village was involved in the celebration:

"At this point young girls and women joined the circle and
began to dance: young men and adolescents, stepping out of
the crowd, moved into the circle too and began to dance
facing the women. The men sang, the women clapped their
hands. Soon the only ones left to form the circle were the
uncircumcized boys. They, too, began to sing - they were not
allowed to dance - and as they sang, sang in unison, they
forgot their anxiety; I, too, mingled my voice with theirs." [45]

Evidently, the experience is a shared one. The importance to the
village of this ceremony was that it was about to welcome into its midst
a group of young men (who up to then had been mere boys) who would from that
time on assume their rightful place in the community.

The sense of belonging is so pronounced that in Lee's village of Slad
even wrongdoers were protected from the outside world, for "they belonged
to the village and the village looked after them." [46] "transgressors
were dealt with by local opinion, by silence, lampoons, or nicknames." [47]
"Sometimes our sinners were given hell, taunted, and pilloried, but their
crimes were absorbed in the local scene and their punishment confined to
the parish." [48]   There was never any question of reporting such wrongdoers to 'appropriate' authorities.

This study demonstrates the close network of family and social relationships
in two different environments in the inter-war years, and shows that rural
life in countries as far apart as Guinea, West Africa, and England, Europe
was similar in many ways, although there were also vast differences.
Communities such as these bore more resemblance to each other than to the
modern technological age in the Western world.

What were the factors which caused these two authors to move away from their traditional environment? Since both of them have very evidently such a strong attachment to their childhood memories, one can only assume that the pressures on them must have been very great.

For Laye, there can be no doubt that the chief contributing factor was western education in the form, first of all, of the village school, later the technical school in Guinea's capital, Conakry, and finally college in France. He makes constant reference to this fact, obviously with some regret. For example, when he is on the verge of learning some of his father's secrets, his father says to him:

> "I fear, I very much fear, little one, that you are not often
> enough in my company. You are all day at school, and one
> day you shall depart from that school to a greater one. You
> will leave me, little one ..." (49)

The child's reaction is confusion:

> "And I was no longer sure whether I ought to continue to
> attend school or whether I ought to remain in the workshop:
> I felt unutterably confused." (50)

He longs to be able to converse with the little black snake, as does his father, but knows this will not be possible:

> "Would I, too, converse like that one day? No: I was still
> attending the school." (51)

At a later stage in his life, immediately after his circumcision, his companions go on to be initiated into the secrets of manhood, but he has to return to school. School, in spite of what it represented in terms of opportunity in the future, was an alien world, uprooting him from the environment he knew and loved, and transporting him into a totally different one:

> "Young though we were, we all regarded our schoolwork as something
> deadly serious. Everything we learned was strange and unexpected;
> it was as if we were learning about life on another planet; and
> we never grew tired of listening." (52)

All hardships, and there were many of them, were tolerated for the ultimate achievement:

"Naturally we could hardly wait for our schooling to be over, for the day when we should receive our famous proficiency certificates that would proclaim to the world that we were 'educated'" (53)

For Laurie Lee, too, school was an alien world which removed the country children from the fields and farms, and crammed them with irrelevent facts:

"Every child in the valley crowding there, remained till he was fourteen years old, then was presented to the working field or factory with nothing in his head more burdensome than a few memories, a jumbled list of wars, and a dreamy image of the world's geography." (54)

But it was modern technology which physically carried Laye away from his home: he travelled by train from Kouroussa to Conakry, and later by plane from Guinea to France, where he was to complete his studies. In the very last paragraph of the novel Laye, at that point on the plane heading for France, put his hand in his pocket and felt something hard - a map of the Metro. The Metro, one of the innovations of technology and here a very appropriate symbol of the changes Laye was to experience in his life henceforth.

Laurie Lee attributes the changes largely to the advent of technology. He was a first-hand witness of the passing of an era:

"the last days of my childhood were also the last days of the village. I belonged to that generation which saw, by chance, the end of a thousand years' life. The change came late to our Cotswold valley, didn't really show itself till the late 1920's; I was twelve by then, but during that handful of years I witnessed the whole thing happen.

"Myself, my family, my generation, were born in a world of silence; a world of hard work and necessary patience, of backs bent to the ground, hands massaging the crops, of waiting on weather and growth; of villages like ships in the empty landscapes and the long walking distances between them; of white narrow roads, rutted by hooves and cartwheels, innocent of oil or petrol, down which people passed rarely, and almost never for pleasure, and the horse was the fastest thing moving. Man and horse were all the power we had - abetted by levers and pulleys. But the horse was King, and almost everything we knew grew around him: fodder, smithies,

stables, paddocks, distances and the rythm of our days. His eight
miles an hour was the limit of our movements, as it had been since
the days of the Romans. That eight miles an hour was life and
death, the size of our world, our prison.

"This was what we were born to, and all we knew at first. Then, to
the scream of the horse, the change began. The brass-lamped motor-car
came coughing up the road, followed by the clamorous charabanc; the
solid-tyred bus climbed the dusty hills and more people came and went.
Chickens and dogs were the early sacrifices, falling demented beneath
the wheels. The old folks, too, had strokes and seizures, faced
by speeds beyond comprehension. Then scarlet motor bikes, the size
of five-barred gates, began to appear in the village ...

"These appearances did not immediately alter our lives ... most of
us still did the journey on foot, heads down to the wet Welsh winds ...

"But the car-shying horses with their rolling eyes gave signs of
the hysteria to come. Soon the village would break, dissolve, and
scatter, become no more than a place for pensioners. It had a few
years left, the last of its thousand, and they passed almost
without knowing." (55)

There can be no doubt that technology made a profound impact on rural
English society. And yet, the reverberations of this impact have, from all
accounts, been felt even more deeply in the continent of Africa. In England,
the impetus of change came largely, though by no means entirely, from within.
In Africa, western education and technology came from without and prised
open an extremely closely-knit society, shaking it to the very foundations.

From these two novels, it is certain that life in both Africa and
Europe has changed beyond recognition, within a short space of time. It is
easy to assume that change is synonymous with progress, and that progress is
always for the better, that life in the old days was hard and intolerable.
Hardships there certainly were, sickness, and death at an early age, were
rampant, as both novelists acknowledge. But neither would agree that life was
intolerable, on the contrary, it was a sense of mourning for what had been
lost that urged both men to record their experiences in writing, so that at least
some small part could be salvaged.

With regard to family life, it is often assumed that the move from the
extended family to the nuclear family has resulted in a greater concentration
of love between members of the nuclear family, since, it is believed, the
same amount of love was formerly more spread around. It appears from this
analysis of these two novels that this may not necessarily be the case.

Quite evidently, there is no lack of love between individual members of
Laye's and Lee's families. Rather love was more open, and directed outwards,
first to the members of the family, and then beyond to the community at
large. Modern man has been seized by a form of "hysteria" to use Lee's word,
and is constantly in fear of losing not only his material possessions, but
also his family. In modern urban society love is directed inwards and is
absorbed into the self. True, modern technology has brought with it many
advantages and conveniences. But it has only been with us for a short while,
and we are not yet certain of all its implications. Traditions which were
established and maintained over hundreds of years had a firm basis in
knowledge and experience, and we would be unwise to ignore the lessons which
this accumulated knowledge and experience can teach us.

85

REFERENCE NOTES

1.   The concept of "world view", or "world vision" has been developed by a
     number of writers interested in the sociology of literature.   cf. in par-
     ticular: Diana Laurenson and Alan Swingewood, The Sociology of Literature,
     (London: Paladin 1972) and also Wole Soyinka, Myth, Literature and the
     African World, (Cambridge University Press, 1976).

     My own conception of world view is that the vision that an author has of
     society is in itself an important sociological phenomenon and must be con-
     sidered along with other sociological data, more susceptible to objective
     analysis, if a fuller understanding of society is to be achieved.

2.   Laurie Lee, Cider with Rosie, (London: Penguin, 1962).   All subsequent
     quotations are taken from this edition.

3.   Camara Laye, The African Child, translated from L'Enfant Moir by James
     Kirkup, (London: Fontant, 1959).   All subsequent quotations are taken
     from this edition.

4.   Ibid., p.23

5.   Laurie Lee, Cider with Rosie, p.216

6.   Ibid., p.104-105

7.   Camara Laye, The African Child, p.46

8.   This was at a seminar held at the University of Dakar, 1963, entitled
     "African Literature and the University Curriculum".   Part of the proceeds
     of this seminar, together with a subsequent one held at Fourah Bay College,
     the University College of Sierra Leone, were published in a volume entitled
     African Literature and the Universities, edited by Gerald Moore.   (Ibadan
     University Press, 1965).

9.   Camara Laye, "The Soul of Africa in Guinea", in Gerald Moore (ed.,), African
     Literature and the Universities.   (Ibadan University Press, 1965), p.69.

10. Ibid., p.67-68

11. Ibid., p.67

12. Ibid., p.69

13. Camara Laye, The African Child, p.58

14. Ibid., p.45

15. Ibid., p.92

16. Ibid., p.92

17. Camara Laye, "The Soul of Africa in Guinea", p.67

18. Laurie Lee, Cider with Rosie, p.28-34

19. Ibid., p.29

20. Camara Laye, The African Child, p.91

21. Laurie Lee, Cider with Rosie, p.28

22. Ibid., p.15

23. Ibid., p.156

24. Ibid., p.157

25. Ibid., p.138-139

26. Ibid., p.105

27. Ibid., p.121

28. Ibid., p.169

29. Ibid., p.183

30. Camara Laye, The African Child, p.156

31. It is not at all clear in the novel how Mrs.Lee coped financially, apart from a few pounds sent from time to time by her husband, which certainly could not have been adequate. Her three step-daughters went out to work by the time she was left alone, and that contributed towards housekeeping.

32. Laurie Lee, Cider with Rosie, p.126

33. Camara Laye, The African Child, p.109

34. Laurie Lee, Cider with Rosie, p.25

35. Ibid., p.27

36. Ibid., p.27

37. Ibid., p.28

38. Camara Laye, The African Child, p.35-36

39. Laurie Lee, Cider with Rosie, p.9-10

40. Ibid., p.64

41. Camara Laye, The African Child, p.56-57

42. Laurie Lee, Cider with Rosie, p.184

43. Ibid., p.219

44. Camara Laye, The African Child, p.51

45. Ibid., p.81

46. Laurie Lee, Cider with Rosie, p.98

47. Ibid., p.205

48. Ibid., p.206

49. Camara Laye, The African Child, p.20

50. Ibid., p.20

51. Ibid., p.21

52. Ibid., p.65

53. Ibid., p.68

54. Laurie Lee, Cider with Rosie, p.42

55. Ibid., p.216-217

BIBLIOGRAPHY

Lee, L., Cider with Rosie, London: Penguin, 1962.

Laye, C., The African Child, translated from French by James Kirkup, London: Fontana, 1959.

Laye, C., "The Soul of Africa in Guinea" in Gerald Moore, (ed.), African Literature and the Universities, Ibadan University Press, 1965.

Laurenson, D. and Swingewood, A.   The Sociology of Literature. London: Paladin, 1972.

Soyinka, W., Myth, Literature, and the African World, Cambridge University Press, 1976.

CHAPTER 5

THE STABLE AFRICAN FAMILY: TRADITIONAL AND MODERN FAMILY STRUCTURES IN TWO AFRICAN SOCIETIES

Dolores B. Koenig

CHAPTER 5

THE STABLE AFRICAN FAMILY:
TRADITIONAL AND MODERN FAMILY STRUCTURES IN
TWO AFRICAN SOCIETIES

Dolores B. Koenig

There is no doubt that the double processes of Westernization and
industrialization have affected almost all individuals in third world
countries in one way or another. Small scale economies and states have
become part of large nation-states which in turn are part of a worldwide
economy. These changes have meant new constraints on individual and family
decisions. Yet differential patterns of adaptation are found, and this may
be particularly true in regard to family structures. While customs change
to some degree everywhere, neither the direction of change nor the rate of
change is constant throughout one continent, much less throughout the entire
third world.

Many have argued that differential rates of change of family and fertility
structures are related to the differential rates of involvement of individuals
in modern or Western institutions and cultural values (Caldwell, 1976). Those
with more involvement in modern societal institutions are likely to show more
Westernized family structures and fertility patterns. While this may indeed
be true, particularly in the long term, it is proposed in this paper that this
model does not explain all the variety found among present day family
structures. Although the contemporary socio-economic structures and values of
a society will constrain the actions of individuals in some directions, their
actions will also be constrained by the traditional structures and values of
their society. Thus we would expect to find different contemporary patterns of
family structure and fertility among people coming from widely differing
traditional cultures, although they may today live in similarly structured
societies, or even with one nation state.

This paper looks at traditional and contemporary rural family structures
of two African societies to compare the effects of modernization and
Westernization versus traditional social structures in influencing contemporary
rural family patterns. The two societies to be investigated, the Basa of

Southern Cameroon and the Manding of Mali, differ along some significant parameters (including family organization), yet are similar along others.

Both Basa and Manding (primarily Bambara and Malinke) are West African agricultural societies.[1] The most significant differences between the two are the ecological zones in which they live and their degree of political centralization. While the Basa are a society without chiefs in the equatorial forest, the Manding live in stratified chiefdoms, and formerly lived in large states, in the savannah. These striking differences in ecology and political centralization are strongly related to the differences in family structure discussed in detail below. In light of the relationship of these variables, a comparison that controlled for these two variables, as well as the subsistence base of agriculture would be very difficult.

There are moreover significant similarities between these two societies in terms of their colonial history and their contemporary integration into national economies. In regard to colonial history, neither society remained isolated from European contact, yet neither experienced the long intense contact found among societies on the Guinea Coast. The colonial presence was established among both groups in the late 19th century. Malian Manding were already going to Senegal and the Gambia in the 1920's to seek agricultural wage labour, and many of the famous "tirailleurs senegalais" of the early 20th century were Bambara or other Manding. The Dakar-Bamako railroad was built through Malinke country in the early 20th century. In the early 1900's, the Basa were furnishing forced labour for a number of projects in Cameroon, were providing food for many of these labourers, and were also working on the railraod from Douala to Yaoundé which passed directly through their territory.

Today both societies are relatively highly integrated into their respective national economies, primarily through the production of agricultural crops for cash. The Manding of Mali are heavily involved in peanut and cotton production, while the Basa produce and sell palm oil products and cocoa. Not only the household heads, but also other family members within both household groups expect to have some kind of cash income, although remaining in the rural area. Thus although there are some

important differences between these two societies, the similarities are
sufficient to provide some basis of commonality, and thus of comparison.

The Literature: Changing Family Structures and Fertility of Modern Africa

Writers on changing family structure and fertility in the third world
have tended to stress the dichotomy between the structure of third world
families and industrialized families, and also between the fertility patterns
found in these two major groups. De-emphasizing the differences among
traditional family structures and fertility patterns (and also among
different classes of industrialized families), they have focused instead
on the larger causes and variables which correlate with the overall
differences between these two ideal types of family - "traditional" and
"industrialized". They are interested in accounting for differential rates
and directions of change, believing that societies starting with different
kinds of traditional family structure will of necessity take different
paths to reach a single end point. However, the main interest remains the
single end point and the constraints barring the way to it.

The hypotheses as to how traditional family structures change in
response to modernization can stress either structural or attitudinal changes.
For example, Goode (1963:6) says that when the economic system expands and
changes through industrialization, family patterns change and there is
generally a trend toward some form of conjugal family. He stresses the
industrial values of unversalistic achievement, individualism and social
mobility that have led to a "fit" between the conjugal family and a
predominantly urban bureaucratic technology (Goode, 1963:12,17,24).
Alternatively, Handwerker (1977) stresses structural correlates in his
discussion of the co-variation of different kinds of technologies with
family and fertility patterns. Although the technology does not directly
determine family structure, particular types of family units will be
maintained only if they permit acceptable levels of subsistence within the
constraints of the given technology (Handwerker, 1977:261). Others stress
the joint attitudinal and structural changes that accompany industrialization
and modernization; Leibenstein (1974:459) lists eleven different structural
(e.g., female labour force participation, reductions in infant mortality)
and attitudinal (e.g., decline in religious beliefs promoting high fertility)

variables presumed to lead to structural changes resulting in lower
fertility and birth rates in industrializing populations.

While the above have stressed the adoption of industrial technology
as the major precipitating factor in family change, others have focused
on the Westernization that accompanies industrial development. Caldwell
(1976:344) pinpoints the critical factor in familial nucleation, and the
accompanying drop in fertility, as the change in net flow of wealth. In
traditional societies, the net flow of wealth tends to be from children
to parents; thus it is to the parents' benefit to have large families.
But in modernizing societies, the wealth flow is reversed and parents invest
more in their children than they receive in return. However, he also finds
that the emotional nucleation of the family at times precedes the actual
economic circumstances that lead to this nucleation (Caldwell, 1976:347), and
that this emotional nucleation appears as a result of the adoption of
Western values, most commonly through schooling and/or Church influences
(Caldwell, 1976:352).

This is not the place to discuss which of these theories is the most
accurate model of the general demographic changes that occur. Rather more
important for this paper are the similarities in these models in contrast to
the approaches which stress more strongly the variability of responses to
the processes of industrialization and modernization. To reiterate, a common
assumption behind all these models is that the similarities among both
"traditional" and "modern" societies are more important than their differences,
at least for the purposes of understanding those variables leading to long
term demographic change. Furthermore, the different types of family
patterns within modernizing societies are related to varying levels of
exposure to the most industrialized or Westernized section of the society.
Differential exposure of groups of individuals to industrialization and
Westernization can come about through membership in different social classes
(Goode, 1963:12,13), through urban versus rural residence, or through the
differential impact of direct Western influences such as education.
Differences in traditional social structures (one component of what is commonly
called ethnicity) or differences in the historical experiences of different
groups are rarely considered among the variables affecting changes in family
structure.

Yet in spite of these large scale theories those social scientists who have dealt more particularly with data from one region or one society have often pointed out the differences which correlate with family structures. Most notably, LeVine (1966) found a relationship between different personality types and different social structures. He found variations in achievement motivation, especially with regard to the adoption of entrepreneurial roles among the three major ethnic groups of Nigeria. Achievement motivation was especially strong in those societies where child rearing laid particular stress on characteristics of excellence and autonomy. In the realm of general family structure, Clignet (1970:286-294) notes that the responses of the patrilineal Bete of the Ivory Coast to urbanization were different than those of the matrilineal Aboure. Furthermore, the reaction of Bete and Aboure wives to increased income was of different intensity (Clignet, 1970:326). Concerning fertility, Page (1975:51) notes that marital instability, which is often correlated with ethnic (e.g., among the Fulbe) or historical (e.g., among the Bakweri of Cameroon) differences, can reduce fertility. Ware (1977:37) also discusses the importance of analyzing Cameroonian fertility data with regard to ethnic differences, since "no Cameroonian survey to date has failed to find marked ethnic fertility differentials."

How does one reconcile these two different approaches to the problem? And which approach is more fruitful? Two considerations seem relevant. First, is the aim to understand similarities in the processes of fertility and family change through the third world or is it to understand the differentials in routes and rates of change? This is related in turn to the goals of research; is the researcher trying to build a general model for long term demographic change, or is he or she more interested in the formulation of particular population programmes in specific countries? An interest in creating a general model will likely lead to a stress on the broad lines of change occurring everywhere, with more emphasis on the similarities than the differences. In turn the population planner is more likely to be concerned with micro-level data which seeks to show why some people in his country are doing one thing and others something else. The interest in this paper lies with the planners rather than with the theoreticians. However, planners cannot be content with uncovering simple correlations between family structure and ethnic variables. Rather one wants to know why these correlations exist. The purpose of this paper is, therefore, to point out some of the salient differences in traditional

African family structure that may contribute to differences observed in contemporary family structure and to suggest some of the mechanisms by which this occurs.[2]

Traditional Differences among the Basa and Manding

Ethnicity is not an uniquivocal category; rather many different parameters can be used to constitute ethnic differences. Among those parameters most commonly used to constitute ethnicity are social structural, cultural, historical and language differences. In light of the concerns of this paper, social structural differences, in particular those most clearly related to family structure, will be stressed.

Although few, if any, researchers would characterize all African family structures as similar, one result of extended research on African families has been the construction of an ideal type of the traditional African family which stresses the similarities among different societies. Within the perspective of this paper, the following characteristics are most salient. In general, Africans get their familial identification from a kin based unit larger than the nuclear family. The effective familial unit is ideally polygynous, and often comprises three generations, married adult sons commonly remaining in their father's compound. These two characteristics lead to relatively large family units.

Kinship provided one of the major organizational principles of traditional society. Marriages were viewed as the union of two kinship groups, not two individuals. One's natal kin identity was often inalienable; even in patrilineal societies, women were likely to keep a high degree of identification with their natal kinship unit, although living with their husband's kinship group. Political power, too, except in some of the largest states, was usually acquired through kinship ties; small scale societies were often governed by lineage heads, the nominal head of the lineage usually being the most senior (non-senile) male.

In spite of (or perhaps because of) the importance of kinship in allocating many important societal resources, such as land and authority, sociologically defined kin ties tended to be stressed more than direct lines of biological kinship. For example, brothers "of the family" (often cousins) are often simply referred to as "brother" and have the same rights and duties as a biological brother if they go and live in the family as "brother". Lines of clientage or adoption are often phrased in the kin idiom and again have rights and duties similar to those of these biological kin. The societies thus avoided too rigid distinctions based on a single parameter of kinship, and individuals often had a number of different lines of kin ties they could mobilize even in formally unilineal societies.

Many would accept this description as a relatively accurate representation of traditional family structure in most African societies (including both Basa and Manding). Yet very few African societies would show each characteristic of this ideal type, and more importantly, there is an even greater variety in the family structures found when one looks at the actual functioning of families instead of stressing ideal relationships. In particular, in traditional societies, household sizes may be relatively large or relatively small, and the degree of extended family co-operation may range from relatively high to relatively low, and may be formally instituted or remain rather informal. African societies form a continuum, ranging from those with relatively small families with limited informal networks between nuclear families to those with large households and more reciprocity of networks, some formally organized, among the component nuclear families. The two societies discussed in this paper fall near the opposite ends of this continuum. The Manding of Mali have rather large households with a high degree of formalized inter and intra-family reciprocity. The Basa of Cameroon, alternatively, have small households with relatively little, mostly informal, reciprocity between them. As will be discussed below, these characteristics of family structure do not seem to be independent but seem to be related to the ecological zone in which the society is found and also to its degree of political centralization.

Traditional Manding Social Structure

The Manding are a large group of people inhabiting the West African savannah; they number some 1.5 million in Mali (Republique du Mali, 1961), some 125,000 in the Gambia (Weil, 1976:182) and are also found in Senegal, Guinea, Guinea Bissau and the Ivory Coast. They are patrilineal, and seniority in the patrilineage is one of the major means of access to power and resource control. It is the head of the compound or canton who, having

gained his position through lineage seniority, controls access to land
and to stocked grain. Individual compounds or cantons in turn combined
into centralized, stratified chiefdoms that were often part of great
empires. Some Bambara, for example, were found in the kingdom of Segou,
which reached its height in the 18th century (Meillassoux, 1968:42), while
the Malinke were founders of the great Malian empire of Sundiata Keita,
at its height in the 14th century (Cisse, 1970:20).

The basic economic unit of the society was the large extended family:
an older man, his wives, his adult sons, their wives and their children.
Younger brothers of the head and their sons, wives and children might also
be members of the unit, as were other clients and slaves in the pre-colonial
days. The number of these other individuals depended on the wealth of the
household, since wealthier households attracted more people. The head of
the household organized the work of all the household members on the large
communal fields (foro ba) where the majority of the subsistence grain,
usually millet or sorghum, was grown (Paques, 1954:28). At harvest time,
the household head stocked the grain in the household granary and he was
in charge of the redistribution of the stocks for feeding the household
throughout the rest of the year. Although other adult men in the household
owed the household head a certain amount of work on the communal fields,
they also had individual fields where they had rights to produce. Women
also had gardens and raised other crops, commonly rice and cotton, on
lands flooded during the rainy season (Paques, 1954:28; Weil, 1976:182-3).

The head of the household was responsible for apportioning labour of
the members within that unit, but other formalized means of apportioning
labour between households also existed. A son-in-law (usually from a
different household since marriages were exogamous and patrilocal) owed
his father-in-law specified periods of work as a part of the bride payment.
Other communal work groups would be formed by the age sets commonly found
in these societies; these were most often used for those tasks of the
agricultural season, such as weeding, which required intensive work over a
short period of time (Paques, 1954:56,57). Women, who had often married in
from different villages, formed community based work groups which cut across
lines of both kinship and age (Weil, 1973:28). Since people were usually
provided with food in return for their work, these cross-household work
groups provided a means of apportioning produce as well as labour, tying

the various households within the village together in a whole series of reciprocity networks. In fact, it has been argued that the primary decision making unit within the village is some unit larger even than the large extended family that forms one household, and is rather at the quarter, lineage or village level (Lewis, 1977).

What maintains these networks of both intra and inter-household reciprocity? One reason commonly suggested has to do with the minimization of the effects of a year of bad rainfall in these savannah regions where rainfall is not abundant, and is furthermore, relatively unpredictable from year to year (Caldwell, 1975:48ff,57). Average annual rainfall ranges from 800 mm. near Segou to 1300 mm. near Sikasso in southern Mali, and actual rainfall may vary widely from the average over any 10 year period. The short rainy season (3-4 months long) moreover, means that certain agricultural tasks must be done fairly quickly within a short period of time; for example, sowing must be done as soon as the rains begin. Large households, i.e., those with a large number of economically active adults, are less affected by the sickness or inability to work of one member and thus are less likely to be affected by the exigencies of the savannah agricultural season. Inter-household reciprocity, furthermore, minimizes risk for the whole village during the bad years. Although no one household becomes very rich during the good years (due to its obligations to give grain to other households), neither are the poorer households likely to suffer significantly more in the bad years (Lewis, 1977).

These reciprocity networks are in turn controlled by the central authorities of the society. No matter what the reasons for the institution of these practices, it is clearly in the political interests of the elders (heads of households as well as heads of quarters, lineages and villages) to maintain their control over the household granary, for it is through the control of this undoubtedly strategic resource that they maintain their control over their own household. Young men accepted the system, for although they did not control it, they got immediate benefit from the reciprocity networks insofar as they were given wives, as well as land to farm and food, through the head of the household. They also saw long term advantages since as they grew older they would themselves become elders and gain political power (Meillassoux, 1975).

Although a social structure based on the economic unit of large
extended households, with much interhousehold reciprocity of both labour
and produce is not the only possible successful adaptation to the
exigencies of the savannah climate, it has clearly provided a successful
adaptation to these ecological constraints, that has, moreover, been
successful over a long (i.e., centuries) period of time.

Traditional Basa Social Structure

The Basa are a small ethnic group, numbering about 195,000, who inhabit
the Cameroonian forest between Yaounde and Douala (LeVine, 1964:12).[3] A
description of the general framework of family organization of the Basa of
Southern Cameroon would make them sound much like the Manding of Mali.
They are also patrilineal, and seniority is the primary means of apportioning
control in the society. The ideal family unit is the father, several wives
and children, and sometimes other dependents (Nkomha Nkomha, 1974:12) adult
sons are not truly independent while the father still lives as the son depends on
his father to get land to farm and bridewealth for his wife. In spite of this
similar framework, an actual look at how these units functioned shows that
the major economic unit is much smaller than the household unit found among the
Manding and is, in fact, very similar to a nuclear family unit. Furthermore,
even in traditional circumstances, there was little co-operation between these
household units.

As just noted, the major difference between the Manding and Basa is in the
size and extension of the major economic unit. Among the Basa, the major
economic unit was a small household similar to a nuclear family: a man, his
wife or wives, and their children. Moreover, a woman and her children had a
certain degree of autonomy as an economic unit since each wife produced the
major subsistence crops in her own fields, and she, in turn, had control over
this produce. In the savannah families, control over produce resided in
the head of the household. Each day, he allotted grain from the common store
to a woman household member (or a group of women, in larger households) who
then prepared one meal which was consumed by the whole extended family. Among
the Basa, in contrast, each woman provided a meal for herself and her children
from the produce of her own fields; in a polygymous family, the husband would
take turns eating with his various wives during the week. Since he did not
control the produce, the Basa household head did not have the degree of control

over his household that the savannah household did. In sum, the
effective productive and consumption unit was oriented around each of the
wives and her children in the Basa household, while in the savannah
household it was oriented around the male head and included all of his
wives and children.

Although his part was much less, the male Basa household head was not
totally peripheral and did act as a unifying force over these female centered
agricultural units. Traditionally and today, he was responsible for
clearing and providing land for all his wives' fields. A woman could clear
her own land if necessary, but her fields were usually much smaller in that
case. Traditionally, he also hunted, providing a good deal of game, and
the protein needed to balance the otherwise largely carbohydrate diet. Today
he also cultivates cash crops (commonly cocoa or oil palm), and controls the
cash this brings to the household unit. In general however, there was much
less extended co-operation between individuals within the household unit
among Basa than among the Manding, and success depended much more on
individual initiative. In turn the control exercised by the Basa household
head was much less than that exercised by Manding heads of households.

There was, moreover, less co-operation between Basa households,
particularly at an institutionalized level. Some co-operative work groups
did exist, but not at the formalized level that they did in savannah
agriculture.[4] Data on other forms of reciprocity between household units,
especially in traditional circumstances, is very scanty, but in general,
circumstantial evidence indicates that inter-household reciprocity was quite
low, particularly in comparison with that found between Manding household
units. The Basa have a reputation among Southern Cameroonians for being
individualistic and egotistical, and the ecological forces that might
encourage various kinds of inter-household co-operation do not exist.
Rainfall is abundant, ranging from 1500 mm. to over 2000 mm., and comes
regularly throughout the year. Even if it is a "bad year", there is
virtually always enough rain to have a decent harvest. Population density
is low, ranging from 3.52 to 4.86 persons per square kilometer (Franqueville,
1971:42.45), and there is enough empty land to move on to if one does not
get along with one's neighbours or relatives. Another symptom of the lack

of co-operation between households is the dispersed settlement pattern;
Basa did not even live in nucleated villages under traditional circumstances,
but rather in homesteads dispersed throughout the countryside. As one Basa
has himself noted, the dispersed habitat of the Basa is explained not only
by their extensive itinerant agriculture but also by a spirit of independence
which sometimes makes it impossible for two brothers to remain on decent
terms unless they move apart (Mboui, 1971:706). Since land is abundant
and the ecology permits, they often do so.

The general lack of co-operation and reciprocity in Basa society is also
reflected in their political institutions, which Melone (1972:19) has
characterized as "anarcho-democratic". The chief could make no decisions
without prior consultation with family elders (Melone, 1972:20), but in light
of his relatively low degree of control over production, even the power of the
head of the household was somewhat fragile. The Manding household head
controlled land, its produce, and the labour that worked it. The Basa household
head also controlled land, but, as seen above, only a small portion of its
produce and little of its labour.[5] Moreover, even his control of land was
somewhat tenuous, seeing the ease with which a younger brother or adult son could go
out and create his own farm in the bush.

The Manding and Basa, thus, exemplify two extremes in regard to traditional
familial organization within Africa. Should we expect that these different kinds
of families would be similarly influenced (particularly over the short term)
by the double processes of industrialization and Westernization? Is it not more
likely that these two different ethnic groups will show very different short
term familial adaptations in reaction to these processes which planners must
take into account in formulating population programmes?[6]

Contemporary Rural Social Structure

In both cases, Manding and Basa, the traditional family structures have
remained remarkably viable, in spite of relatively great involvement by both
ethnic groups in their new nation states through the medium of cash crop
agriculture. Where there was much extended family co-operation in the
traditional arena, as among the Manding, this remains.[7] Where there was
traditionally little extended family co-operation, as in Basa country, small
nuclear units remain important.

This section will look at the present day family structure among the
Malinke in the region of Kita, Mali, and among the Basa of Southern
Cameroon. It must be emphasized that one cannot argue that the differences
discussed below are simply the result of different levels of involvement in
modern state structures, particularly involvement in export crop markets.
Neither the Malinke or Kita nor the Basa are isolated from production for
cash markets. The region of Kita is the biggest peanut producer in Mali (CRED,
1976) and the Basa produce oil palm products and some cocoa for the market
(Champaud, 1973:24).

Household size continues to be a major difference between these two groups
as Basa households prove to be considerably smaller and less "extended" than
those found among the Manding. In one study the average Basa household size
was found to be 5.7 persons per family., for 109 families in a relatively
large village (Champaud, 1973:22). Among six non-randomly selected families
in another village, the average household size was 6.1 (Nkomha Nkomha, 1974:47).
Although a widowed mother or an unmarried sister might remain with her brother
who was a household head, Champaud (1973:22) rarely found two adult brothers living
together, and in none of Nkomha Nkomha's six families did two brothers live
together. The 1962-64 Census of south-central Cameroon found even smaller
families among the Basa; the average number of persons in each lodging was
4.96. There were,however, an average of 1.27 households in each lodging,
and each household averaged 3.9 persons (Republique du Cameroun, 1964:120).
Information is scant about the amount of co-operation between the household
units, but there is no indication that it is high. The primary cash crop
raised by Basa farmers, oil palms, is a crop well adapted to both the forest
ecology and individualistic tendencies of the Basa. These palms are not
planted; rather oil palms growing wild in the forest are identified, are cared
for and the products then harvested and sold. The exploitation of these palms
is done on an individual level of adult males, who often prefer it to the cocoa
grown by their nieghbours. They get almost as much income with much less work
(Champaud, 1970) and retain more individual control over the sale of the
produce. Champaud (1970:309) writing on the Basa propensity to earn money from
oil palms again notes that although their social structure is fundamentally
similar to that of the neighbouring Bulu, the Basa are more in favour of personal
exploitation and individual success.

There have been some changes in social organization. There is slightly more nucleation of settlements than in traditional times. This is due both to the enforced movement of hamlets to nucleated settlements during a civil war in the late 1950's, and also to people's own decisions to live along the major roads to facilitate transport of their crops.

The average Manding household, in several different samples, was more than twice as large as the average Basa household. In my work on a sample of 60 families in two predominantly Malinke village groupings in the area of Kita, Mali, the average family size was 21.2 individuals.[8] in another survey of 88 Malinke villages, Hopkins (1971:102) found the average household size to be 18. In both these cases, the household unit so defined was also the primary economic unit: the group of persons that farms a subsistence and/or cash crop field in common, that eats from a common cooking pot, and recognizes a common head. The Malian census of 1960-61 (Republique du Mali, 1961:71) did find a smaller household size; in this census, Bambara (including both Malinke and Bambara, the major Manding groups in Mali) averaged 12.6 persons per compound. In turn, each compound averaged 2.2 households, and the average rural Bambara Household averaged 5.3 persons (Republique du Mali, 1961:89). However, for purposes of the census, a household was defined in terms of the nuclear family unit (Republique du Mali, 1961:85), not in terms of the actual functional economic unit, which comes closer to the census concept of compound. Compound size, in turn, is relatively large.

In spite of the concern over the breakdown of traditional family structure, evidence is that there is still a great amount of intra-family co-operation and reciprocity among the Manding. Preliminary evidence from the area of Kita suggests that larger extended families are those most likely to practise new modern agricultural techniques, and thus to reap the benefits of higher agricultural production, i.e., higher incomes. While those families that practised no new agricultural techniques had an average household size of 10.5, those who used the cheaper new techniques (fertilizer, selected seeds and/or seed treatments) averaged 14.9 members in their households. However, those that had the resources to obtain ploughs and draft animals averaged 40.3 individuals per household. The means by which and reasons why more successful households retain and/or gain old members, new members and clients remain unclear, but it is clear that there is some relationship between modern agricultural "success" and the maintenance of a

large extended co-operative family. It is clear that intra-familial
co-operation is maintained in these large households. Not only do all active
family members continue to work larger and larger communal fields, but the
use of agricultural equipment also depends on intra-familial co-operation.
It is usually only an older established household head who can afford to
purchase agricultural equipment, yet it is often a younger household member,
commonly literate, who actually knows how to use the equipment, and is
responsible for its being used properly. A large co-operatively structured
household is more indicative of a "modern" than a traditional farmer.

Again it should be noted that the major cash crop, peanuts, in the region
of Kita is one both adapted to the ecology and social organization of
agriculture in the region. The length of the growing season of the region's
peanut varieties is similar to but does not overlap the staple grain growing
season. Peanut planting follows grain planting and the harvest comes slightly
in advance; farmers first plant their staple grains and then turn to peanuts.
The two crops moreover use similar agricultural techniques and are planted in
a rotation which aids soil fertility. In practice the household often has two
major communal fields, one for peanuts and one for millet or sorghum and the
agriculturally active adults work in turn on these two large plots.

Family structure is related not only to agricultural production but also
has implications for the migration patterns found in these two societies. The
Manding are among those Sahelian groups particularly known for seasonal and
short term labour migration.[9] On the one hand, the large extended family with a
number of agriculturally active adults can more easily afford the loss of a
potential worker than can the smaller Basa family with only a few economically
active adults. Secondly, the savannah agricultural season lasts for five
well-defined months, and seasonal migration during the off season works well in
this environment as long as unskilled workers are needed in the dry season in othe
sectors of the economy. All groups benefit to some degree. The family has
fewer mouths to feed during the dry season and may get extra cash from
remittances by the migrant; the young male migrant can earn money to pay for
bridewealth or other cash expenses he may have; the employer who needs only
seasonal labour (especially for road work, and construction which are best
done in the dry season) does not need to pay his labourers all year. Although
the actual amount of (financial) reciprocity between migrant and home family

during the period of migration is unknown and may be small, the other
benefits are clear.[10] Once the period of migration is finished, the migrant
may return home and be re-integrated into the large farming family, which
reabsorbs his labour and perhaps sends out another son.

Among the Basa however, migration tends to be long term, and ties
between rural villages and the migrants are often minimal. Seasonal labour
migration is almost non-existant, in part because of ecological constraints.
In the equatorial forest, there are two rainy (and thus two growing) seasons
each year, the rains come regularly throughout most of the year, and there
is only a very short off season. Moreover the smaller economic unit can less
easily lose and re-absorb members than does the large extended savannah family,
although sometimes men will leave to work for years in the city, leaving
their wives and children behind on the farm.

A study of 35 female migrants on a Cameroonian rubber and oil palm
plantation shows the extremes of long term migration and the fragmentation of
families (Koenig, 1976).[11] These women averaged over ten years of work on
the plantation. Average household size was 2.7 with 10 of the 35 women living
alone. Most of the rest were women with husbands and their children, or women and
their children. Grandchildren or parents were sometimes included in the
household, but in only four of the 35 families did women share a household with
collateral relatives or care for persons other than their own children or
grandchildren. Reciprocity, especially monetary aid, between various sections
of the extended family was minimal; many migrants claimed that they simply had
no relatives left in the villages to give aid to or get aid from. In particular,
those who had adult children only rarely said that they were getting aid from
them, and several had completely lost track of children. Most children were
not living with their mothers on the plantation and only one adult male child
had returned to his village to farm. Rather adult children tended to be
unemployed or to be in semi-skilled jobs in urban areas. The only kind of
extended family reciprocity that was practised to any extent was fostering;
although plantation women rarely cared for the children of other kin, the
majority (13/19) of their own primary school age children were being raised by
relatives either in the home village or in urban areas. These women are
admittedly marginal, even among Basa migrants, but it is doubtful if this
situation could ever exist among the Manding with their strong traditional
and contemporary extended family structures.

Implications for Fertility

The implications of these different kinds of family structures for
contemporary fertility behaviour remains unclear. Yet there are clear
fertility differences. Manding women show higher fertility than do Basa
women. Birth rates in rural Mali were 61.3 per 1000 (Republique du Mali,
1961:106) while they were 41.7 among the Basa (Republique du Cameroun,
1964:70).[12] Individual fertility is also higher in rural Mali, where
women aged 30-34 showed a total fertility of 4.3 to Basa women's 3.29 at ages
30-34; at age 50 and older, rural Malian women showed a total fertility
of 5.38 to Basa women's 4.09 (Republique du Mali, 1961:111; Republique du
Cameroun, 1964:70). This may be due at least in part to higher sterility
rates among Basa women, for among rural Malian women aged 30-34, only
7.2% had never had a live birth, while among Basa women, this was 11%. At
age 45-49, 6.7% of Malian women never had a live birth, in contrast to 17%
of Basa women of this age (Republique du Mali, 1961:111; Republique du
Cameroun, 1964:77).

Yet the models of family structure presented above offer little clue to
why these fertility differences exist. In fact, some persuasive arguments could
be made for expecting similar fertility levels despite societal differences.
In neither society is land shortage a problem in the regions discussed;
children can always find land to farm should they wish to remain in the rural
area. In both areas, families do try to send their children to school, and so
children will cause at least some expense. In both cultures, a high premium
is put on being fertile and having descendants to carry on the family, so men
will want to have children. In both monogamous and polygamous families,
women will need to have children to maintain their identity as adult women;
in a monogamous family, a woman may want to have many children so her husband
will be less likely to take a second wife. In a patrilineal polygamous family,
each wife will try to improve her position over other wives, and one means to
do this is through having more children. The Manding family may be slightly
more likely to benefit from a large number of male children, some of whom
remain on the farm while others migrate, — both contribute to the upkeep of the
entire household. In the Basa family however, the son who migrates will
probably keep only minimal ties with his relatives in the village unless he is
highly successful. Some have assumed that extended families per se increase
fertility, but Burch and Gendell (1971:102) conclude, after looking at the

literature, that the extended family may depress as well as enhance
fertility.

The fertility differences may be linked to other than social structural
causes. Basa fertility may be lower since Basa country is close to the
central African sterility belt, although the Basa do show higher fertility
than many other Southern Cameroonian ethnic groups (Republique du Cameroun,
1964). But one cannot argue for better conditions of childbirth in either
society, since health care is not very good in either rural Mali or rural
Cameroon.

These are problems which could clearly benefit from further research
into the mechanisms by which different family structures may affect fertility
patterns. More detailed information on the knowledge, attitudes and practices
of adult men and women in regard to fertility would be a useful place to begin.
One could also usefully delve into the means by which women integrate
farming and child care responsibilities, and how these may differ in the two
societies. Finally a look at the roles of children in inter and intra-household
networks of co-operation and reciprocity would be most useful; in particular,
the roles of fostering and the provision of educational expenses may relate to
fertility differences among societies.

Conclusions

The aim of this paper has been to show some of the variety found among
traditional African family structures and to discuss some of the demographic
implications of this variety. In spite of similar values on the importance of
fertility, family co-operation, the family as a source of identification,
polygamy and seniority as a means of gaining power, there is a great variation
between the two societies discussed in the actual "on-the-ground" form and
extent of both intra and inter-familial co-operation and reciprocity.

The family found among today's contemporary rural Basa looks surprisingly
"Western", i.e., relatively small with a low degree of inter-familial reciprocity.
This is especially so in comparison with the strong extended families still
found among the rural Manding. Yet we have shown that this was a distinction
already there in traditional family structures. Neither type of familial
organization has changed radically; today, both structures seem closer to the

traditional structures within the society rather than to each other.

Why have these family structures remained so viable? Is this due simply
to the "strength of tradition" or is the strength of tradition, due, instead
to other factors? It seems that one factor contributing to the stability of
family structure is the stability of the ecological context which has
constrained family structure. Each society for example has adopted cash
crops which are adapted to both ecology and tradition social organization of
agricultural production. The Manding of Kita grow peanuts, which not only
grow well in the savannah growing season, but are also adapted to being
grown on large communal fields by extended family work groups. On the other
hand, the oil palms exploited by the Basa are so well adapted ecologically they gro
wild in the region; they are also successfully cared for by farmers working
alone. Thus traditional family organization fits well with agricultural success
in the contemporary situation. If however, a successful cash crop exploits
a new ecological niche, then family organization may be modified in response
to the new situation; this seems to have happened among some Manding groups
in the Gambia who have become heavily involved in rice cultivation (Weil, 1973).
However, among the two groups discussed here, cash crops exploit traditional
ecological niches and the family organization has remained viable. Given the
Basa preference for oil palm cultivation (which fits in well with traditional
social structure) as opposed to cocoa cultivation which can bring somewhat more
money, one can ask if people have a tendency to adopt those new agricultural
crops, or techniques which fit in well with traditional social organization,
when this is possible. Agricultural innovation which requires new radical
changes in social organization may require more rewards to encourage adoption.[13]

Due to its limited scope, this paper has not been able to delve deeply into
the implications of this persistence of very different familial attitudes and
values across different parts of Africa. Two lines of further research into these
implications suggest themselves immediately as important and potentially
fruitful: 1) how do the links maintained by successful (often educated) urban
migrants and their families remaining in rural villages differ between these
two ethnic groups, and again, how are the types of ties that exist conditioned
by either traditional or contemporary rural social structure? One might expect
to find more convergence of behaviour patterns among urban migrants, who have,
in both cases, left their traditional agricultural niches; 2) how do these
different familial values translate into different fertility patterns among

both urban and rural Malians and Cameroonians? The evidence shown above
suggests that very different fertility patterns do indeed exist, but the
mechanisms for micro-level differences in the effect of family structure
on fertility patterns remain to be elucidated further, if the findings in
this paper concerning family structure are to be of significant help to
planners.

REFERENCE NOTES

1. The primary Manding groups considered in this paper are the Bambara and
   Malinke of Mali. Usually considered two separate ethnic groups, the
   differences between them are primarily historical and cultural and the
   similarities in the family structure and general social structure are
   striking (Meillassoux, 1968:41-49). Furthermore, the Malian census of
   1960-61 treated them as one group which it referred to as Bambara
   (Republique du Mali, 1961:24,25).

2. The problem posed in this paper grew out of my own field experience with
   the two ethnic groups herein discussed. In spite of the fact that much
   of the literature stressed the similarities of family structure over all
   Africa, I was constantly struck by the differences in the family
   organization of the two groups, which led in turn to an interest in the
   systematic exploration of the differences among groups which are being
   influenced by the same rather large class of contemporary socio-economic
   changes. Neither raising the questions nor attempting answers would
   have been possible without my experience in the areas; therefore I
   would like to thank the organizations that made the fieldwork possible.
   I spent 16 months in 1974 and 1975-76 in Cameroon, supported by a
   National Science Foundation Doctoral Dissertation Research Grant, a
   National Defence Foreign Language Fellowship and a grant from the
   Program of African Studies of Northwestern University. I later spent
   6 months in 1977 in Mali, primarily in the Kita area, doing research on
   the socio-economics of millet-sorghum agriculture, supported by a US/AID
   contract given to Purdue University Department of Agricultural Economics.

3. General Basa social structure is not very different from that found
   among neighbouring acephalous groups, such as the Beti, Bulu, Bakoko or
   Mbam. Their family structure is however, the most fragmented of these
   groups. At times when data is unavailable on the Basa, comparable data
   will be provided from information on these other groups.

4. No comprehensive monograph exists on the social organization of Basa
   agriculture, in either traditional or contemporary circumstances. This
   does exist however for the Beti (Eton) who live in an area adjacent to
   the Basa and have a generally similar form of social organization. For
   an excellent discussion of Eton agriculture, see Guyer, 1977.

5. With the growing importance of cash crops and cash income in contemporary
   society, the internal household balance of power has shifted some, in
   favour of the household head who controls the biggest lump sum. For
   further information, see Guyer, 1977.

6. The distinction in social organization that I have presented here in the
   particularized way of Manding vs. Basa, may in fact relate to a more
   generalized distinction between forest and savannah societies. I myself
   do not have the data to discuss this, but the point has been convincingly
   argued by Meillassoux (1975). While I do not agree with all of the
   distinctions he makes, nor with all their implications, I do owe his
   model much for inspiring my own distinction between the Basa and Manding.

7. Although I shall present evidence that this is so, it must be noted
    that others would present evidence for the fragmentation of the
    extended family unit; see, e.g., Van der Belt, n.d.

8. Since the sample was chosen in a manner to include an equivalent number
    of peasants in various kinds of agricultural categories, the number
    of large families was slightly oversampled. Therefore, the average
    family size may in fact be slightly smaller, i.e. somewhere between 15 and
    20, but still much larger than among the Basa.

9. See Amin, 1974 and Berg, 1965 for economic interpretations of this
    phenomenon.

10. Meillassoux (1975) suggests also that the system allows the employer to
    pay lower wages, since the worker remains a member of his rural family.
    One might also suggest that the benefits to the employer are ultimately
    greater than those to either the worker or his rural family; for some
    estimates of the amounts and direction of cash flow between migrant
    workers and their families, see Amin. 1974.

11. Twenty-three (68%) of the women in this sample were Basa; the rest were
    all from other Southern Cameroon ethnic groups with similar social
    structure: Mbam, Ewondo/Eton and Bakoko.

12. The Malian census did not break down all figures by ethnic group, so in
    most cases we must make do with figures from rural Mali. Fortunately,
    Mali, as opposed to Cameroon, is quite ethnically homogeneous
    (Meillassoux, 1968), and where figures are given for the Bambara, they
    are quite similar to those given for rural Mali as a whole. For example, in
    rural Mali, women aged 50 and older showed a total fertility of 5.38
    while Bambara women aged 50 and older showed a total fertility of 5.50;
    in rural Mali 6.2% of women aged 50 and older had never had a live birth,
    while among Bambara women of this same age group, 6.1% never had one
    (Republique du Mali, 1961:111,113).

13. There may be a similar explanation for the different patterns of education
    and religion among the two societies. The Basa are overwhelmingly
    Christian while the Manding are primarily Moslem. The rate of school
    attendance among primary school age Basa children is very high, close to
    90%, while that among Manding children is much lower. Again, however,
    one may ask if the high degree of Christianity and education found among
    the Basa is something permitted by their traditional family and social
    organization rather than something that has changed their family structure.
    In other words, certain facets of traditional Basa family structure may
    have allowed the Basa to adopt certain more "Western" patterns of
    behaviour, but the adoption of these patterns does not necessarily mean
    that there is any greater split between traditional and modern values
    among the Basa than among Manding.

BIBLIOGRAPHY

Amin, S. 1974. _Modern Migrations in Western Africa_. London: Oxford University Press.

Berg, E.J. 1965. "The Economics of the Migrant Labor System". In _Urbanization and Migration in West Africa_. H. Kuper, (ed.) Berkeley and Los Angeles: University of California Press.

Burch, T.K. and M. Gendell 1971. "Extended Family Structure and Fertility: Some Conceptual and Methodological Issues". _In Culture and Population: A Collection of Current Studies_. S. Polgar (ed.), Cambridge, Massachusetts: Schenkman Publishing Co.

Caldwell, J.C. 1975. _The Sahelian Drought and Its Implications_. Paper No. 8. Washington, D.C.: Overseas Liaison Committee American Council on Education.

    1976 "Toward a Restatement of Demographic Transition Theory". _Population and Development Review_. 2:321-366

Champaud, J. 1970. "Mom (Cameroun) ou le Refus De l'Agriculture de Plantation". _Etudes Rurales_. 37-38-39:299-311

    1973 _Mom: Terroir Bassa_. Paris: Orstom.

Cisse, D. 1970. _Structures des Malinke de Kita_. Bamako: Editions Populaires.

Clignet, R. 1970. _Many Wives, Many Powers_. Evanston, Illinois: Northwestern University Press.

CRED (Center for Research on Economic Development)
    1976 _Le Secteur Agricole de la Republique du Mali_. Mimeo. Ann Arbor: The University of Michigan.

Franqueville, A. 1971. _Atlas Regional Sud-Ouest I_. Yaoundé: ORSTOM.

Goode, W.J. 1963. _World Revolution and Family Patterns_. Glencoe, Illinois: The Free Press.

Guyer, J. 1977. _The Woman's Farming System, The Lekie Southern Cameroon_. Mimeo. Yaounde: Ecole Nationale Superieure Agronomique.

Handwerker, W.P. 1977. "Family, Fertility and Economics". _Current Anthropology_. 18:259-287

Hopkins, N.S. 1971. "Mandinka Social Organization". In _Papers on the Manding_. C.T. Hodge, (ed.) Bloomington, Indiana: Indiana University.

Koenig, D. 1976. "Why Women Migrate: Agricultural Workers in Africa". Paper Presented at the 75th Annual Meetings of the American Anthropological Association, Washington, D.C.

Leibenstein, H. 1974. "An Interpretation of the Economic Theory of Fertility: Promising Path or Blind Alley?" _The Journal of Economic Literature_. 12:459-479

LeVine, R.A. 1966. Dreams and Deeds. Chicago: University of Chicago Press.

LeVine, V.A. 1964. The Cameroons from Mandate to Independence. Berkeley and Los Angeles: University of California Press.

Lewis, J. 1977. The Bambara family in the region of Segou. Personal Communication.

Mboui, J. 1971. "Essai sur la vie Domestique des Basa du Sud-Cameroun". These pour le Doctorat-es-lettres. Universite de Bordeaux: Faculte des Lettres et des Sciences Humaines.

Meillassoux, C. 1968. Urbanization of an African Community. Seattle: University of Washington Press.

   1975 Femmes, Greniers et Capitaux. Paris: Maspero.

Melone, S. 1972. La Parente et la Terre dans la Strategie due Developpement. Paris: Editions Klinksieck.

Nkomha Nkomha, M. 1974. "Rapport de Stage d'Observation et d'Analyse d'un Milieu Rural: Sonsimout". Mimeo. Yaoundé: Ecole Nationale Superieure Agronomique.

Page, H. 1975. "Fertility Levels: Patterns and Trends". In Population Growth and Socioeconomic Change in West Africa. J.C. Caldwell, (ed.) New York: Columbia University Press.

Paques, V. 1954. Les Bambara. Paris: Presses Universitaires de France.

Republique du Cameroun 1964. Enquete Demographique au Cameroun: Resultats Definitifs pour la Region Sud-Est, 1962-64. Paris: INSEE.

Republique du Mali 1961. Enquete Demographique au Mali, 1960-61. Paris: INSEE.

Van der Belt, H. n.d. "Agricultural Innovation and Village Structure: a Case Study among the Bambara of Koulikoro, Mali". Mimeo.

Ware, H. 1977. "Language Problems in Demographic Field Work in Africa: The Case of the Cameroon Fertility Survey". Scientific Reports, No. 2. London: World Fertility Survey.

Weil, P.M. 1973. "Wet Rice, Women and Adaptation in the Gambia". Rural Africana. 19:20-29

   1976 "The Staff of Life: Food and Female Fertility in a West African Society". Africa. 46:182-195

CHAPTER 6

PLURAL MARRIAGE,
FERTILITY AND THE PROBLEM
OF MULTIPLE CAUSATION

Oladele Arowolo

CHAPTER 6

PLURAL MARRIAGE, FERTILITY AND THE PROBLEM OF
MULTIPLE CAUSATION *

Oladele Arowolo

The relationship between plural marriage, or polygyny, and fertility has
been one area of conflicting propositions in the literature. Based on data of
varying degrees of acceptability and sometimes questionable estimates of
fertility, there are reports which indicate that the effect of polygyny on
fertility is positive, sometimes negative, or even neutral. On balance,
the relationship between polygyny and fertility is not clear, mystified by
the interplay of an array of socio-deomographic variables which are known to
be capable of either enhancing or depressing fertility.

It is the essence of this paper to:

(1) assess the state of knowledge on the issue of monogamy, polygyny
     and their relation to reproductive performance with a view to
     identifying problem areas especially with regards to limitations
     of reported data which confound the causal relationship and set
     a limit on comparability of findings;

(2) present fresh evidence from demographic survey data;   and

(3) employ a new methodology in the analyses of data which attempts to
     overcome the problem of multiple causation that seems to afflict
     almost all previous reports on this subject. This involves a
     multiple classification of factors and a step-by-step assessment
     of the effects of covariates in a regression model.

---

*   The research on which this report is based was funded by the University
     of Ibadan, Nigeria (Senate Research Grant, Paper 494). Facilities for
     data analysis were provided by the Population Studies Center,
     University of Pennsylvania.

1.   The Literature:

The findings reported in the literature on polygyny and fertility fall
into three broad groups. First, there are reports which indicate that women
in monogamous unions tend to show higher fertility than those polygynously
married.   Second, there are those reports claiming that polygyny enhances
fertility compared with monogamy. Third are those reports showing marginal,
if any differential in fertility between women in monogamous and women in
polygamous marriages.

The first category of reports includes those of Brebant (1954), Musham (1956)
and Page (1975).   In Brebant's report, based on the Belgian Congo, polygyny
is less prolific than monogamy. According to the report, "the effective
fertility rate", defined as the ratio of the live births registered during a
year to the number of married women of specified ages, probably 15-45 years,
"is lower in polygamous marriages than in monogamous marriages from 25-45
percent with an average of 31 percent".

In Musham's sample inquiry, in total fertility, (measured as number of
children aged 0 to 4 and 5 to 9 years per 1000 married women) monogamous
marriages show consistently higher ratios than polygynous unions. According
to the report, within polygynous marriages the first wives show lower fertility
ratios than second wives; and overall, the fertility of women in polygamous
marriages is said to be 32 percent lower than that of monogamous marriages.
Musham's study was conducted among the Beduin of the Negeb, a small Moslem
group in Southern Israel. Similar findings are reported for Central Niger
Delta, Upper Volta, Guinea and Zaire at various periods by Page. For each
of these countries, the ratio of polygynous to monogamous age specific
fertility rates are almost all below unity, and are said to decline fairly
steadily with age. There are scattered sources elsewhere (namely Brito,
1952; Ward, 1937, Beaujeu-Garnier 1966,pp.129-130), which give some kind of data
indicating the depressing influence of polygyny on fertility.

The problem with most of these reports and others reporting the opposite
or neutral positions is not the degree of differential between the fertility
of monogamous and polygynous unions but why the differential, if any? What
is it about polygyny that depresses reproductive performance of women in
such unions compared with those monogamously married?

114

Although not all the data presented for the various arguments are
entirely comparable, it is necessary to examine some of the factors
advanced in explaining observed differentials in the fertility of monogamous
and polygynous marriages. The need for wives to share a common husband
in a polygynous family involves, on the part of the man, a dissipation of
sexual energy and may set a limit on the probability of conception among
wives in such a family. This appears to be Musham's reasoning when he argued
that "Beduin women who share their husbands with one or more other women are
really less fertile than only wives of monogamous husbands". One of the
limitations of the sexuality argument in this regard is that it is biological,
and fertility analyses tend to treat biological condition as a random variable.
The curve relating coital frequency to conception probability is not
linear, but curvilinear because beyond an optimal point (defined as 5 per cycle)
increased coital frequency implies reduced sperm count and diminished
conception probability. Much depends on sperm count and virility, ovum
fertilizability, timing of ovulation, and the occurrence of cycles unfavourable
for coition to lead to conception. There is also a 'psychosomatic' factor
in conception probability which relates to psychological state of the couples,
anxiety to conceive or prevent conception which tends to operate in the
opposite direction.[1] Since demographers are not trained to measure these
biological/psychological factors, it is conventional to treat their variation
(and also variations in sexual frequency), whether or not they are
conditioned by polygyny, as random. In a situation where the man maintains
a monogamous family stance at home but has one or more female friends
outside as additional cohabiting partners[2], the claim of monogamy to
exclusive sexual practice is limited. For the society studied for this
report, this factor is of considerable relevance.

The higher fertility of monogamous marriages compared with polygynous
unions is also commonly attributed to higher incidence of sterility among
polygynous women. Page argues that subfecund women tend to be progressively
selected into polygynous unions as their husbands take additional wives in
order to satisfy their desire for progeny. She presents data from Zaire which
show a reduction in differential fertility when only women of proven
fertility are considered. In this paper attempt is made to control for this
factor by presenting data for women of proven fertility as well as for all
women to eliminate the relative infertility factor in the explanation of the
fertility of polygynous marriages.

In his review of the literature on fertility in Nigeria, Morgan notes that it appears that fertility may be somewhat higher in polygynous unions (p.204). Ohadike's study, based on Lagos women, shows a higher average number of children born to polygynists than to women in monogamous unions. According to him, the differential might be due to higher incidence of illiteracy among wives of polygynists, complemented by the lesser youthfulness of their age structure (pp.388-389). Age and education are measurable factors and it should be possible to control for their effects in an analysis of fertility differential among women in monogamous and polygynous unions.

Olusanya's report dismisses the observed 'minor' differences in fertility between polygynously and monogamously married women in Ife and Oyo(both Yoruba towns in Nigeria)(pp.165-78),as 'simply fortuitous'. He argues that even though wives in polygynous unions appear to be more fertile than wives in monogamous unions, the differential tends to disappear after controlling for differences in duration of marriage. No reference is made to the possible influence of education (or higher incidence of illiteracy among polygynists) which Ohadike's report emphasizes; and though Olusanya's data isolates women of proven fertility for analysis neither he nor Ohadike considered the possible effect of the rank order of wives in a polygynous family. While Page presents data on number of co-wives in relation to fertility of polygynous marriages, Musham considers the rank of a woman in a polygynous family as 1st, 2nd, etc. wife. In Page's report, the ratio of polygynous to monogamous age-specific fertility rates decline with increasing number of co-wives; and this result is not directly comparable to Musham's study in which second wives show a higher average number of children than first wives. One way of integrating the two efforts, which is attempted in this report, is to consider monogamists as a group and arrange polygynists in order of position among wives, ranging from the 1st, 2nd, --, to the nth wife as cohorts and compare their age specific fertility rates. In addition, this report attempts to analyse fertility of monogamists and polygynists by age of women and duration of marriage which Olusanya considered ideal but which regrettably he could not achieve in his analysis because of the nature of his data.

This report attempts to consider the factors that have been recognized as relevant to the polygyny/monogamy fertility argument but which no single report has combined together. These factors include age, education, duration of marriage, incidence of primary sterility, position of women among wives in a polygynous household, as well as other social and economic factors considered relevant to fertility analyses in general.

It may, indeed, be because these relevant dimensions have not been carefully considered that some researchers report absence of differential fertility between polygynists and monogamists. Busia (1954) gives the impression that in Ghana there is no significant difference in fertility between monogamously married women and those married to polygynists. And recently Podlewski (1975) has claimed that among the various ethnic groups of women in Cameroon, 'polygyny does not seem to influence fertility', but no further explanation is advanced. It is possible that there are no real differentials in the fertility of monogamous and polygynous unions as reported, but the evidence provided is not convincing. And for those reporting a higher fertility of monogamous marriages than polygynous unions, or vice versa, the polygyny effect has not been brought to bear on the evidence.

2.(a) Research Design:

This research was conducted between August and September, 1974 in Ibadan, Nigeria. At the time of survey the population of the city was estimated to be between 1.0 - 1.2 million, ranking it next to Lagos as the largest city in tropical Africa. The study was based on area probability sampling, with area units defined by grid squares superimposed upon a series of maps covering the entire city of Ibadan as defined by the 1963 census ward divisions. A total of 345 grid squares were listed and stratified into three zones corresponding to old, mixed, and new neighbourhoods into which the city is commonly divided in socio-demographic surveys of this nature. A 1 in 30 sampling fraction was adopted to identify the squares which constituted the primary selection units, resulting in selection of 12 grid squares. Although these grid squares were not known to contain equal number of elements, the pilot study indicated that each grid square contained, on the average, at least 100 eligible women. Eligible women were currently married Yoruba, aged 15-49 years, and resident in the city of Ibadan.

The pilot study listed 1,326 respondents, but due to refusals, invalid returns and respondents who could not be located, 957 eligible women were eventually interviewed. This report is based on these 957 women and it is expected that the social, economic and demographic categories deriving from this sample would provide a valid basis for some reference to overall marital fertility in Ibadan, and to a limited extent, to the population of urban married Yoruba women in Nigeria.

2 (b) The Survey Data:

The sample of currently married Yoruba women in the city of Ibadan incorporated a substantial proportion of women in polygynous unions to attest to the popularity of this custom among the Yoruba. About 35 percent of the married women interviewed were polygynous; and their distribution cuts across social and economic distinctions that are relevant to fertility analyses.

In order to control for possible influence of subfertility which as Page, Olusanya (op.cit.) hinted may be selective of type of marriage, we present fertility data on women of proven fertility as well as on all women. To be sure, the incidence of subfertility (or in this case primary sterility) is limited; 43 women in all reported zero live births, 34 of them are in monogamous unions and 9 are in polygymous unions.

TABLE 1: AVERAGE NUMBER OF CHILDREN EVER BORN ALIVE (CEB) BY AGE GROUP OF WOMAN, AND TYPE OF MARRIAGE (IBADAN, 1974)

Age Groups (in years)	Fertile Married Women				All Married Women				All Unions* Total	
	Monogamous		Polygynous		Monogamous		Polygynous			
	N	CEB	N	CEB	N	CEB	N	CEB	N	CEB
15-19	17	1.59	3	1.00	22	1.23	3	1.00	25	1.20
20-24	64	1.88	21	2.14	71	1.69	24	1.88	96	1.73
25-29	158	2.53	52	2.56	170	2.35	55	2.42	230	2.35
30-34	129	3.52	55	3.73	132	3.44	57	3.60	191	3.48
35-39	88	4.48	54	3.74	91	4.33	55	3.67	150	4.02
40-44	52	5.13	58	4.50	54	4.94	58	4.50	118	4.69
45-49	27	5.44	32	4.56	29	5.07	32	4.56	66	4.85

* Including women in ill defined/de facto unions.

Table 1 presents data on the average number of live births (CEB, for
short) reported by interviewed women classified by age, type of marriage and
fertility status. For both women of proven fertility and all married women
the ratios of polygynous to monogamous age-specific fertility rates are
consistently higher for the younger women and lower for the older women. In
other words, whether one considers fertile women only or all women in marital
unions, younger women (below 35 years) in polygynous unions are more fertile than
those monogamously married; but older polygynously married wives appear to
be less fertile than their counterparts in monogamous unions. The observed
pattern is best illustrated by the data on women of proven fertility, and is
comparable to Ohadike's report on Lagos women in which younger women in
polygynous unions exhibit higher average number of live births than their
counterparts in monogamous families.

In any discussion of fertility patterns in a rapidly modernizing society
the background characteristics of women residing in urban places should be
taken into consideration. Urban residents differ considerably in their family
formation attitudes depending on the extent to which they have acquired modern
values. Recent in-migrants into the city will ordinarily tend to be less
exposed to modern values than seasoned urban dwellers at the same level of
social and economic standing. Considering the fact that rural-to-urban
migration is a significant factor in the growth of cities in Nigeria, it is
necessary to control for differences in the background characteristics of these
women in order to understand the influence of plural marriage on the
fertility of women in the city of Ibadan.

Women are classified into Ibadan or outside origin depending on their
stated places of birth. Table II presents data on reported CEB, by age, place
of birth and type of marriage. Section (a) of the table refers to fertile
women only in order to control for varying incidence of subfertility among
polygynists and monogamists, while section (b) considers all married women in the
sample.

The first proposition here is this: given that in-migrants into the
city tend to be less 'modern' than life-time urban dwellers, regardless of
type of marriage, the age-specific CEBs of women born in Ibadan will ordinarily
be lower than the figures reported by those women born elsewhere. This

hypothesized pattern is evident from Table II; and the differential between
women born in Ibadan and those born elsewhere remains whether one considers
fertile women only or all women in the sample. Women in monogamous unions
present the largest differentials when the background factor is considered;
whereas polygynously married women are almost equally fertile in comparable
age groups whether born in Ibadan or elsewhere. Among women born in Ibadan
(whether all women in the sample or fertile women only) polygyny seems to
be related to higher fertility than monogamy. It is only among women of
'rural' or less urban origin that the ratios of polygynous to monogamous
age specific fertility rates do not vary systematically;   the ratios are
above unity at the younger ages but fall below unity after age 34 years.
It is also to be noted that monogamously married women born outside Ibadan
are distinctly more fertile than their counterparts of Ibadan origin, and
constitute over 70 percent of all women originating from outside the city of
Ibadan. Hence, when all monogamists are considered as a group, the impact
rural background becomes overwhelming and can outweigh the effect of
polygyny as such. By implication it is desirable to treat the women in
this sample as two groups in subsequent cross-classification by other social,
economic and demographic factors that are considered relevant to this
analysis. But by the time another dimension is introduced the number of
elements in each category becomes too small to be analyzable. So for the
present we proceed with a consideration of other factors in the explanation
of polygyny and fertility without the rural-urban dimension until later in the
analysis when we introduce the Multiple Classification/Regression Model
which will handle this problem more efficiently.

Perhaps of direct relevance to marriage itself as a factor in fertility
is the transition from monogamy to polygyny among women in polygynous
marriages. The first wife of a polygynous family can be considered monogamous,
at least until the second wife moves in. It is therefore hypothesized that
the effect of polygyny will tend to be delayed for the first wives of
polygynously married men and thus differential fertility between monogamists
and first wives of polygynists is likely to be more manifest at the older
than at the younger ages. If polygyny tends to enhance fertility, the
fertility of first wives in polygynous marriages will tend to be lower than the
overall average for all women in polygynous unions. Perhaps due to
differences in durations of marriage and the background factors the pattern

TABLE 1. AVERAGE NUMBER OF CHILDREN EVER BORN ALIVE (CEB) TO MARRIED
WOMEN BY AGE, PLACE OF BIRTH AND TYPE OF UNION

(a) Fertile Married Women Only

Age Group	Born in Ibadan				Born Elsewhere			
(in Years)	Monogamous		Polygynous		Monogamous		Polygynous	
	N	CEB	N	CEB	N	CEB	N	CEB
15-19	*	–	*	–	11	1.73	*	–
20-24	20	1.65	*	–	44	1.98	12	1.67
25-29	38	2.16	19	2.42	123	2.63	33	2.64
30-34	28	3.14	22	3.27	102	3.63	33	4.03
35-39	13	4.46	17	3.76	77	4.45	37	3.73
40-44	*	–	33	3.97	49	5.31	27	5.07
45-49	10	3.70	18	4.44	19	6.32	16	4.88

(b) All Married Women

Age Group	Monogamous		Polygynous		Monogamous		Polygynous	
15-19	10	0.80	*	–	12	1.58	*	–
20-24	22	1.50	11	2.27	49	1.78	13	1.54
25-29	43	1.91	20	2.30	130	2.49	35	2.49
30-34	30	2.93	24	3.00	103	3.59	33	4.04
35-39	15	3.87	18	3.56	78	4.40	38	3.63
40-44	*	–	34	3.85	51	5.10	27	5.07
45-49	11	3.36	18	4.44	20	6.00	16	4.88

is not clearly shown in Table III; it appears that the first hypothesis
is not confirmed but the lower age specific CEBs of first wives of polygynous
marriages than those reported by all polygynists are suggestive. The first
wives are not as polygynous as subsequent wives and it is possible that the
limited exposure to monogamous conditions is partly responsible for the
below average age-specific CEBs of first wives.

Of fundamental importance to marital fertility, regardless of type of
marriage, is the duration of marriage which is directly related to conception
probability and hence fertility. The age pattern of CEBs among marital
cohorts of women show an unexpected pattern: at almost each specified
duration of marriage and five-year age groupings, women exhibit higher
CEBs in monogamy than in polygyny. The pattern is the same whether one
considers all married women or only those of proven fertility (see Tables IV

TABLE 2. AVERAGE NUMBER OF CHILDREN EVER BORN ALIVE (CEB) TO MONOGAMOUS WOMEN, AND TO POLYGYNOUS WOMEN ACCORDING TO POSITION AMONG WIVES IN THE FAMILY

(a) All Women in Unions

Age Group	Monogamous Union	Position Among Wives in Polygynous Union		
		1st	2nd	All Women+
15-19	1.23	*	*	*
20-24	1.69	1.83	1.70	1.88
25-29	2.35	2.71	1.95	2.43
30-34	3.44	3.48	3.43	3.60
35-39	4.32	3.31	3.61	3.57
40-44	5.00	4.15	4.33	4.32
45-49	5.06	4.44	3.73	4.64

(b) Fertile Women in Unions

Age Group	Monogamous Union	Position Among Wives in Polygynous Union		
		1st	2nd	All Women+
15-19	1.59	*	*	*
20-24	1.88	2.20	*	2.14
25-29	2.52	2.81	2.06	2.57
30-34	3.52	3.61	3.59	3.73
35-39	4.46	3.44	3.82	3.71
40-44	5.18	4.28	4.33	4.40
45-49	5.40	4.44	3.73	4.64

+ Including 3rd, 4th etc. wives in the family.

* Number of cases less than 10, therefore CEBs not computed.

and V). Again it is possible that the background factors, over which no control is exercised are responsible for the enhanced fertility of monogamously married women. But it is clear that both the rural-urban background variable and duration of marriage are crucial to an understanding of marital fertility and the two factors as well as others will be jointly assessed in the Multiple Classification analysis that follows this section.

At this point, it is relevant to consider two factors that are known to be related to the decision from the point of view of a man to marry an additional wife, or from the woman's angle to live in a polygynous family.

These factors are education and religion.

As already cited, illiterate women and those with limited education tend to be drawn more into polygynous marriages than those with higher education. In this sample about 66 percent of women in polygynous unions are uneducated and barely 9.5 percent have more than nine years of formal education. On the other hand, 36 percent of those in monogamous unions can be considered illiterate and about the same proportion report higher than primary education. As shown in Table VI highly educated women are hardly found in polygynous families, only 6 percent of all women reporting 15-20 years of formal education are polygynously married.

If the relationship between education and fertility is negative, and knowing that polygyny is selective of the less educated, then an important factor in the fertility of polygynous marriages would be education. However, earlier reports have shown for this population that up to high school, education is positively associated with fertility and that higher education has a negative relationship with fertility. This is bound to complicate the problem of explanation further since polygynous women are largely illiterate and higher education appears to be the monopoly of women in monogamous marriages. The postulated relationship between education and fertility is revealed by data in Table VII, at least for monogamously married women; but it is difficult to guage the possible influence of education on the fertility of polygynously married women because of the lack of highly educated women in polygynous unions.

Religion is sometimes cited as a factor in the type of marriage contracted Moslems are said to have a religious basis for being polygynous as opposed to, say, the Christians. It is of interest to note here that the practice of polygyny cuts across religious groups. To be sure, about 52 percent of all Moslem married women in this sample are in polygynous unions but other Christian denominations show fairly substantial proportions in polygynous families; Aladura Christians 33%, Protestants 28%, and Catholics 20%. The relevance of a religious effect upon fertility here is questionable especially since polygynous families are ordinarily not expected to profess protestantism or catholicism. If Catholics are in polygynous unions they were not likely to have received church blessing, and in the absence of any

TABLE 4. AVERAGE NUMBER OF CHILDREN EVER BORN ALIVE (CEB) BY AGE GROUP OF WOMAN AND DURATION OF MARRIAGE

(a) Monogamous Unions

Length of Stay in Marital Union (in Years)

	0-4		5-9		10-14		15-19		20-24		All Women	
	N	CEB	N	CEB	N	CEB	N	CEB	N	CEB	N	CEB
15-19	19	1.11	*	-	-	-	-	-	-	-	22	1.23
20-24	43	1.09	27	2.63	*	-	-	-	-	-	71	1.69
25-29	66	1.53	86	2.58	14	3.64	*	-	*	-	170	2.35
30-34	*	-	52	2.94	55	4.04	14	3.93	14	5.86	132	3.44
35-39	*	-	14	2.86	32	4.09	27	4.85	20	5.70	91	4.33
40-44	*	-	*	-	*	-	17	5.06	11	5.36	54	4.94
45-49	*	-	*	-	-	-	*	-			29	5.07

(b) Polygynous Unions

	0-4		5-9		10-14		15-19		20-24		All Women	
	N	CEB	N	CEB	N	CEB	N	CEB	N	CEB	N	CEB
15-19	*	-	-	-	-	-	-	-	-	-	*	-
20-24	11	1.36	11	2.09	*	-	-	-	*	-	24	1.88
25-29	16	1.56	27	2.44	*	-	*	-	*	-	55	2.42
30-34	*	-	16	2.88	25	3.40	14	4.39	*	-	57	3.60
35-39	*	-	*	-	17	3.88	23	3.87	*	-	55	3.67
40-44	*	-	-	-	*	-	15	4.47	30	4.67	58	4.50
45-49	-		-		-	-	*	-	14	4.93	32	4.56

* Number of cases less than 10

TABLE 5.   AVERAGE NUMBER OF CHILDREN EVER BORN ALIVE BY AGE GROUP OF FERTILE WOMEN AND DURATION OF MARRIAGE

Duration of Stay in Union: Fertile Women Only

(a) Monogamous Unions

Length of Stay in Union (in Years)

Age Group (in Years)	0-4		5-9		10-14		15-19		20-24		All Women	
	N	CEB	N	CEB	N	CEB	N	CEB	N	CEB	N	CEB
15-19	14	1.50	*	–	–	–	–	–	–	–	17	1.59
20-24	36	1.31	27	2.63	*	–	–	–	–	–	64	1.88
25-29	57	1.77	84	2.64	13	3.92	*	–	*	–	158	2.53
30-34	*	–	51	3.00	55	4.04	12	4.58	*	–	129	3.52
35-29	*	–	13	3.33	32	4.09	27	4.85	14	5.86	88	4.48
40-44	*	–	–	–	*	–	17	5.06	20	5.70	52	5.13
45-49	*	–	*	–	–	–	*	–	10	5.90	27	5.44

(b) Polygynous Unions

Age Group (in Years)	0-4		5-9		10-14		15-19		20-24		All Women	
	N	CEB	N	CEB	N	CEB	N	CEB	N	CEB	N	CEB
15-19	*	–	–	–	–	–	–	–	–	–	*	–
20-24	10	1.50	*	–	*	–	–	–	–	–	21	2.14
25-29	15	1.67	25	2.64	*	–	–	–	*	–	52	2.56
30-34	*	–	15	3.07	24	3.54	14	4.93	*	–	55	3.73
35-39	*	–	*	–	17	3.88	23	3.87	*	–	54	3.74
40-44	*	–	–	–	*	–	15	4.47	30	4.67	58	4.50
45-49	–	–	–	–	–	–	*	–	14	4.93	32	4.56

* Number of cases less than 10

TABLE 6. DISTRIBUTION OF WIVES ACCORDING TO NUMBER OF
YEARS OF FORMAL EDUCATION AND TYPE OF UNION

	Years of Formal Education				
Type of Union	0-4	5-9	10-14	15-20	Total*
Monogamous	217(36.2)	166(37.7)	158(26.3)	59(9.8)	600(100.0)
	(50.3)	(67.2)	(85.4)	(93.6)	(64.8)
Polygynous	214(65.6)	81(24.8)	27(8.3)	4(1.2)	326(100.0)
	(49.7)	(32.8)	(14.6)	(6.4)	(35.2)
All Unions	431(46.5)	247(26.7)	185(20.0)	63(6.8)	926(100.0)
	(100.0)		(100.0)	(100.0)	(100.0)

* Excluding 31 women in poorly defined unions and/or
educational status

Figures in parentheses are percentages

TABLE 7. AVERAGE NUMBER OF CHILDREN EVER BORN ALIVE(CEB) TO MARRIED WOMEN
BY AGE, YEARS OF FORMAL EDUCATION AND TYPE OF UNION

(a) Fertile Married Women Only

Years of Formal Education

Age Group	0-4	5-9	10-14	15-20	0-4	5-9	10-14	15-20
15-19	*	*	-	-	*	*	-	-
20-24	2.00	2.00	1.57	*	*	1.70	*	-
25-29	2.93	2.48	2.42	1.93	2.67	2.55	2.36	-
30-34	3.32	3.71	3.66	3.41	3.44	4.11	*	*
35-39	4.52	3.57	4.76	3.92	3.49	4.29	*	*
40-44	4.73	*	5.75	*	4.29	5.22	*	-
45-49	4.67	*	6.20	-	4.38	5.75	-	-

(b) All Married Women

Age Group	0-4	5-9	10-14	15-20	0-4	5-9	10-14	15-20
15-19	1.18	1.27	-	-	*	*	-	-
20-24	1.92	1.66	1.47	*	*	1.42	*	-
25-29	2.55	2.38	2.27	1.71	2.43	2.43	2.36	-
30-34	3.11	3.71	3.66	3.41	3.21	4.11	*	*
35-39	4.31	3.13	4.76	3.92	3.30	4.29	*	*
40-44	4.33	*	5.75	*	4.20	5.22	*	-
45-49	4.12	*	6.20	-	4.38	5.75	*	-

* Number of cases less than 10

claim to Catholic religious support   there can hardly be anything
religious about the fertility of such 'catholics' or 'protestants'. In any
event, from our data on the age-specific CEBs of women by religion and type
of marriage it does not seem that there is any discernible pattern. Hence
the remainder of this analysis ignores the religious factor.

3.   Analysis:

This concluding section attempts to integrate all the factors
considered relevant to an understanding of the relationship between polygyny
and fertility. The model of Multiple Classification Analysis (MCA) is
employed. In this model factors considered relevant to the subject of
fertility and plural marriages are categorized into two groups; namely,
major factors, and covariates. The attempt is to be able to assess the
category effects on the age specific fertility (CEB) of currently married
women in monogamous and polygynous unions.

The independent variables in this analysis are age, type of marriage,
position among wives, place of birth and conjugal mobility (as major
nonmetric factors); and duration of marriage and years of formal education
(as metric covariates). In order to assess the effects of these factors on
the CEB of different age categories of women, the sample of women is divided
into two: young women aged 25-34 years, and older women, aged 40-49 years.
Based on the grand mean CEBs for each of the two age groups, deviation
values or category effects are computed for each nonmetric factor in
three forms:

(i)   unadjusted form, as gross deviations;

(ii) adjusted for variation accounted for by all other nonmetric factors
      in the design;   and

(iii) adjusted for variation accounted for by all nonmetric factors and
      metric covariates.

Ignoring all interaction terms, the covariates are processed after the main
effects and for each of the factors the category effects are shown as in (i),
(ii) and (iii) above. Tables 9 and 10 present the results.

TABLE 8. (a) AVERAGE NUMBER OF CHILDREN EVER BORN ALIVE (CEB) BY AGE GROUP OF WOMEN, TYPE OF MARRIAGE, AND RELIGION

Age Group (in Years)	Monogamous								Polygynous							
	Moslem		Catholic		Protestant		Aladura		Moslem		Catholic		Protestant		Aladura	
	N	CEB	N	CEB	N	CEB	N	CEB	N	CEB	N	CEB	N	CEB	N	CEB
15-19	*	-	*	-	*	-	*	-	*	-	*	-	11	1.27	-	-
20-24	15	1.60	16	1.94	36	1.61	*	-	11	2.45	*	-	21	2.43	*	-
25-29	34	2.38	17	2.88	92	2.29	29	2.14	19	2.00	*	-	20	3.85	*	-
30-34	30	3.00	19	3.58	69	3.68	11	3.00	20	2.90	*	-	16	4.06	12	4.42
35-39	16	3.75	14	4.21	45	4.29	15	5.13	25	2.88	*	-	30	4.90	10	4.70
40-44	*	-	13	5.46	30	5.40	*	-	25	3.92	*	-	12	4.92	*	-
45-49	*	-	*	-	17	5.76	*	-	13	4.69	*	-			-	-

(b) DISTRIBUTION OF INTERVIEWED MARRIED WOMEN BY RELIGION AND TYPE OF MARRIAGE

Type of Marriage	Religion				
	Moslem	Catholic	Protestant	Aladura	Others
Monogamous	128 (48.1)	88 (80.0)	310 (71.6)	72 (66.7)	6 (35.3)
Polygynous	138 (51.9)	22 (20.0)	122 (28.4)	36 (33.3)	11 (64.7)
All Unions	266 (100.0)	110 (100.0)	432 (100.0)	108 (100.0)	17 (100.0)

TABLE 9.   GROSS AND NET EFFECTS OF SELECTED DEMOGRAPHIC AND SOCIAL FACTORS
ON THE CEB OF CURRENTLY MARRIED WOMEN IN IBADAN, AGED 25-34 YEARS [*]

Independent Variable/ Categories:	Number of Women	Gross Deviation	Net Deviation D_1	D_2
1. Age:				
25-29 years	203	-0.58	-0.58	-0.22
30-34 years	183	0.65	0.64	0.25
2. Type of Marriage:				
Monogamous	278	-0.06	-0.10	-0.02
Polygynous	108	0.15	0.25	0.06
3. Position Among Wives:				
1st	333	-0.01	0.05	0.02
2nd	41	-0.12	-0.46	-0.28
3rd, etc.	12	-0.61	-1.21	-0.48
4. Place of Birth:				
Ibadan	114	-0.39	-0.40	-0.40
Elsewhere	272	0.16	0.17	0.17
5. Conjugal Mobility:				
Once	380	-0.01	-0.01	-0.01
Twice	6	0.63	0.51	0.44

---

[*]   Note:

Total Number of Women: 386
Grand CEB: 2.87

R^2, (adjusted for independents):   0.205

R^2, (adjusted for independents and covariables [+]):   0.380

D_1, Net deviation adjusted for independents

D_2, Net deviation adjusted for independents and covariates

[+]   The covariates are (1) Duration of Marriage and (2) Years of formal training in school

Covariate raw regression coefficient =
Duration of Marriage: 0.797
Years in School: 0.152

Fertile women only

TABLE 10. GROSS AND NET EFFECTS OF SELECTED DEMOGRAPHIC AND SOCIAL FACTORS ON THE CEB OF CURRENTLY MARRIED WOMEN IN IBADAN, AGED 40-49 YEARS[*]

Independent Variable/ Categories:	Number of Women	Gross Deviation	Net Deviation D_1	D_2
1. Age:				
25-29 years	110	0.29	0.17	0.39
30-34 years	58	-0.54	-0.33	-0.74
2. Type of Marriage:				
Monogamous	81	-0.18	-1.20	-1.18
Polygynous	87	0.17	1.12	1.10
3. Position Among Wives:				
1st	123	0.22	0.51	0.59
2nd	28	-1.26	-1.80	-2.00
3rd, etc.	17	0.13[a]	-1.70[a]	-0.82[a]
4. Place of Birth:				
Ibadan	58	-1.51	-1.85	-1.92
Elsewhere	110	0.79	0.98	1.01
5. Conjugal Mobility:				
Once	161	0.03	0.01	0.01
Twice	7	-0.65	-0.34	-0.32

---

* Note:

Total Number of Women: 168
Grand CEB: 5.37

R^2, (adjusted for independents): 0.039

R^2, (adjusted for independents and covariates[+]): 0.050

D_1, Net deviation adjusted for independents

D_2, Net deviation adjusted for independents and covariates

+, The covariates are (1) Duration of Marriage and (2) Years of formal training in school

a, refers to 10 women who are 3rd wives
Covariate raw regression coefficient =
Duration of Marriage: 0.800
Years in School: 0.099

Fertile women only

For the young women in the sample (aged 25-34 years) the average number
of children reported born live is 2.87, representing the grand CEB. Table 9
shows the effects of each category of factors. For example, monogamous
marriages show a -0.06 deviation from the grand CEB compared with a +0.15 for
women in polygynous marriages, implying of course that for the younger women
monogamy tends to be associated with below average fertility while polygyny
is associated with above average fertility. Among the older women (aged 40-49)
as shown in Table 10 the pattern is much the same, women in monogamous marriages
show an overall negative deviation of -0.18 and women in polygynous unions a
total positive deviation of 0.17 from the grand CEB of 5.37. It is also to be
noted that for both young and older women, being born in Ibadan is
associated with negative deviation from the group grand CEB and the category
effect is positive for women born outside Ibadan. The category effects of each
of the listed independent variables can easily be read from Tables 9 and 10.

Table 11, derived from Tables 9 and 10 shows a number of measures of
association. For example, the eta is the common correlation ratio which is
associated with the set of unadjusted category effects. This ratio is shown in
Table 11 for each independent variable or factor, and the square of eta indicates
the proportion of variance (in CEB) explained by a given nonmetric factor (i.e.
all categories of each variable combined). In this case type of marriage, which
gives eta values of 0.06 for young women and 0.02 for older ones, shows very
limited explained variance compared with, say, age among the younger women, or
place of birth in the young and older women.

Another measure computed from this analysis beta (shown as B^*, B^{**} in
Table 11). Beta is the partial correlation ratio which is associated with
the adjusted category effects for each factor, and can be viewed as
standardized partial regression coefficients in a very special sense. Multiple
R is the multiple correlation between the dependent variable (CEB) and all
factors (age, type of marriage, position among wives, place of birth and
conjugal mobility) and covariates (duration of marriage and years of formal
education) and factor-by-factor interaction terms.

In essence when all these factors are considered jointly (age, position
among wives, background residential status, conjugal mobility, relative
infertility, duration of marriage and years of formal schooling) it appears
that women in monogamous unions are slightly less fertile than women in

CHAPTER 7

EDUCATION AND FERTILITY
AMONG CAMEROONIAN
WORKING WOMEN

Dolores B. Koenig

TABLE 11.   COEFFICIENTS OF ETA, BETAS AND EXPLAINED VARIANCE (R)
IN CUMULATIVE FERTILITY OF MARRIED WOMEN

(a)   Aged 25-34 years

Independent Variables	eta	B^*	B^{**}
1. Age	0.40	0.39	0.15
2. Type of Marriage	0.06	0.10	0.02
3. Position Among Wives	0.12	0.14	0.11
4. Place of Birth	0.16	0.17	0.17
5. Conjugal Mobility	0.05	0.04	0.04
Multiple R		0.453	0.617

(b)   Aged 40-49 years

	eta	B^*	B^{**}
1. Age	0.05	0.03	0.07
2. Type of Marriage	0.02	0.15	0.15
3. Position Among Wives	0.08	0.12	0.14
4. Place of Birth	0.14	0.18	0.18
5. Conjugal Mobility	0.02	0.01	0.01
Multiple R		0.197	0.225

B^* beta, adjusted for independents

B^{**} beta, adjusted for independents and covariates

Covariates: Duration of marriage and years of education

Source: Based on Tables 9 and 10.

polygynous unions. The amount of variance associated with type of marriage
(that is, polygyny or monogamy) as a factor is very small: implying that even
though monogamy tends to depress fertility the pattern of variations in fertility
among Yoruba women in Ibadan has little to do with plural marriage.

REFERENCE NOTES

1. (a) V.Brebant, "Tendances de la fecundite au Congo Belge," Proceedings
    of the World Population Conference, 1954, (Rome, United Nations, E/CONF.
    13/413, 31 August-September,1954), pp.775-793;
    (b) H.V.Muhsam, "Fertility of Polygamous Marriages," Population Studies,
    vol.10, Part 1, July 1956, pp.3-16;
    (c) Hilary Page, "Fertility Levels, Patterns and Trends," in John C.
    Caldwell, et al. (eds.), Population Growth and Socioeconomic Change in
    West Africa, (New York, Columbia University Press, 1975), pp.29-57;
    see pp.50-51.

2. (a) E.Brito, "Poligamia e a natalidale entre os groupos Manjaco, Balanta
    e Brame," Bulletin Cultural de Guine Portuguesa, vol.III, No.25, 1952,
    pp.161-179;
    (b) Edward Ward, Marriage Among the Yoruba, (The Catholic University of
    America Anthropological Series, No.4, Washington,D.C.1937), see "Polygyny,"
    pp.24-40;
    (c) J.Beajeu-Garnier, Geography of Population, (translated by S.H.Beaver,
    Longmans, 1966), pp.129-130.

3. For discussion on coital frequency and probability of conception see
    (a) Peter A.Lachenbruch, "Frequency and Timing of Intercourse: Its
    Relation to the Probability of Conception," Population Studies, Part I,
    July 1967, pp.23-31;
    (b) Robert G.Potter,Jr., "Length of the Fertile Period," Milbank Memorial
    Fund Quarterly, vol.39, 1961, pp.132-162;
    (c) Colin Clark, Population Growth and Land Use (New York, Macmillan,
    St.Martin's Press, 1967).

4. See Morgan, reference to Lagos, Nigeria: Robert W.Morgan, "Fertility
    Levels and Fertility Change" in John C.Caldwell et al.(eds.), op.cit.,
    see pp.204-205.

5. R.W.Morgan, ibid.,p.204.

6. P.O.Ohadike, "A Demographic Note on Marriage, Family and Family Growth
    in Lagos, Nigeria" in John C.Caldwell and C.Okonjo, (eds.) The Population
    of Tropical Africa, (London: Longmans, Green and Co., and New York:
    Columbia University Press, 1968), pp.379-392, see pp.388-389.

7. P.O.Olusanya, "The Problem of Multiple Causation in Population Analysis,
    with particular reference to the Polygyny-Fertility Hypothesis," The
    Sociological Review, 19,2,May 1971, pp.165-178.

BIBLIOGRAPHY

Beaujeu-Garnier, J., Geography of Population, (translated by S.H.Beaver, Longmans, 1966).

Brebant, V., "Tendances de la fecundite au Congo Belge", Proceedings of the World Population Conference, 1954, Rome, United Nations, E/CONF. 13/413, 31 August-September, 1954. pp.775-793.

Brito, E., "Poligamia e a natalidale entre os groupos Manjaco, Balanta e Brame", Bulletin Cultural de Guine Portuguesa, Vol.III, No.25, 1952, pp.161-179.

Busia, K.A., "Some aspects of the relation of social conditions to human fertility in the Gold Coast", in Frank Lorimer (ed.), Culture and Human Fertility, UNESCO, Paris, 1954, pp.341-350.

Clark, Colin, Population Growth and Land Use, New York, Macmillan, St.Martin's Press, 1967.

Lachenbruch, Peter A., "Frequency and Timing of Intercourse: Its Relation to the Probability of Conception", Population Studies, Part I, July 1967, pp.23-31.

Morgan, Robert W., "Fertility Levels and Fertility Change" in John C.Caldwell, et al.,(eds.), Population Growth and Socioeconomic Change in West Africa, New York, Columbia University Press, 1975.

Muhsam, H.V., "Fertility of Polygamous Marriages", Population Studies, Vol.10, Part 1, July 1956, pp.3-16.

Ohadike, P.O., "A Demographic Note on Marriage, Family and Family Growth in Lagos, Nigeria", in John C.Caldwell and C.Okonjo, (eds.), The Population of Tropical Africa, (London: Longmans, Green and Co., and New York: Columbia University Press, 1968), pp.379-392.

Olusanya, P.O., "The Problem of Multiple Causation in Population Analysis, with Particular Reference to the Polygny-Fertility Hypothesis", The Sociological Review, 19, 2, May 1971, pp.165-78.

Page, H., "Fertility Levels, Patterns and Trends", in John C.Caldwell, et al., (eds.), op.cit., pp.29-57.

Podlewski, A., "Cameroon", in John C.Caldwell, et al.,(eds.), op.cit., pp.543-564.

Potter, Robert G., Jr., "Length of the Fertile Period", Milbank Memorial Fund Quarterly, Vol.39, 1961, pp.132-162.

Ward, Edward, Marriage Among the Yoruba,(The Catholic University of America Anthropological Series, No.4, Washington, D.C. 1937), 24-40.

CHAPTER 7

EDUCATION AND FERTILITY AMONG CAMEROONIAN WORKING WOMEN[1]

Dolores B. Koenig

Writers on fertility have stressed the association between higher levels
of education and the desire of families to have fewer children. Empirical
studies in turn have documented an inverse relationship between fertility and
education in many areas throughout the world, including West Africa. Yet the
data which is presented here on working women in Cameroon show precisely the
opposite relationship. Women with higher levels of education have on the
average more living children than those with no education. It is suggested
that the situation in Cameroon is not simply an aberrant case. Rather a
consideration of the causes of this pattern will lead to a specific discussion
of the means by which education influences fertility, thus aiding an
understanding both of those situations where education is associated with
lower fertility and those cases where it is associated with higher fertility.

The Literature: Education and Fertility

In a review of the literature concerning the influence of work on
fertility, Birdsall (1976) says that the major arguments are of two basic
types: economic and psycho-social. The same two divisions are equally important
in discussions of the impact of education on fertility.

Economic Arguments

The economic arguments for lower fertility have been developed most
completely by the Chicago School of the "New Home Economics". In general
they start from the assumption that children bring both costs and benefits.
A family will have fewer children when the costs of children (i.e.,
childrearing, housing and education) exceed the benefits (i.e., the joys
of children in general, input of labour to the family and old age security).
In rural areas the costs of children are assumed to be relatively low and the
benefits high. However in urban areas, the situation is reversed and the
costs of children become high (especially if they are given extensive, high
quality education) and the benefits low, since children in school cannot

contribute much to the family income (Birdsall, 1976:704). Children may present not only direct costs, but may also lose income for the mother who gives up work to care for children (Leibenstein, 1974). The more education a woman has, the greater the income she may expect to forfeit by not working, and the greater the opportunity cost of children.

The major direct cost of children is assumed to be education yet some critics have questioned this cost in countries with free educational systems (Leibenstein, 1974:467). If education is free, the direct costs of education may be low for the whole population. However, this is not relevant for most of Africa, where secondary education incurs relatively high costs for parents, even for children in government schools. Secondly, even if schooling is free, the parents must contribute longer to the child's maintenance and forgo his or her earning power for the longer period of time that the child is in school.

There is a second part of the economic argument, which concerns aspects other than the costs of children themselves. In the words of these theorists, higher income parents will tend to substitute the purchase of other goods for the purchase of children. On the one hand they will emphasize quality rather than quantity in child rearing and will purchase for their children high quality education, health and other services (Leibenstein, 1974:462). On the other hand, they may also decide to purchase other consumption items such as travel and better housing in place of additional children. This presupposes that the population favours highly educated children, prefers conspicuous consumption to large families. Although the latter may be true in some cultures, it may not be true everywhere. The importance of cultural values in childbearing decisions will be discussed further below.

The particular form of economic constraints will likely vary with the cultural context. In Africa, for example, the extended family may strongly influence the distribution of economic costs. For example, Handwerker (1977:263) notes that as women become more dependent on their husbands' wages in urban areas, they may want smaller families, for, with a large family, a man will have difficulty in maintaining assistance to his kin and also properly caring for his own wife and children. This becomes particularly important when the wife has no income of her own.

Psycho-Social Arguments

Economics does not function in a vacuum and the economic costs and benefits of children will be assessed within a context of a particular frame of values. In particular, insofar as a woman's social status depends on the number of children she bears, she will continue to bear children even though costs may appear to be high and the economic benefits relatively few. Only when women have means other than childbearing through which they can achieve status and prestige will they use these means and thus lower the number of children they bear (Germain, 1975:192). One means to alternative status achievement is to educate women and to give them the possibility of entering the labour force to gain prestige and social recognition through their careers. Presumably the higher the level of education, the higher the status of the occupations a woman may enter, and the less need she has for children. Women will presumably continue to bear children but at a lower rate and for different reasons than when they could only gain social status through childbearing.

This argument assumes that educated women will be able to enter the work force. However, education may still have an influence in and of itself. Even when women do not begin working in large numbers, it is still found that the wives with influence inside the home are those who had either a high level of education or high status employment.(Birdsall, 1976:702,710). This is important in terms of the economic argument posted above. If educated women do perceive economic constraints against large families, then they are more likely to be able to translate their feelings into action and convince their husbands to accept their views.

Finally it should be noted that prolonged education may have a purely mechanical effect on fertility. Insofar as women continue to go to school for a longer period of time, their age at the initiation of childbearing should be raised. Thus their actual reproductive period will be likely to be shorter and they will probably bear fewer children (Okediji, 1973:252).

It is likely that as individuals become more educated, they also have greater access to higher incomes, and are more likely to live in urban areas. In this situation their aspirations for their children will become higher, and thus the costs of producing children of the type that they want will

increase. At the same time the benefits of children will decrease. Children
will no longer contribute to the family economy in the positive way that they
did on the family farm. Furthermore, educated women are likely to have less
need of many children to validate their social position as adults, as the
more educated they are, the more alternative pathways to social reward and
recognition they should have. These theories lead us to expect that with
increasing education and the greater income and social status that usually
accompany it, fertility levels should decline.

The Empirical Evidence

In the great majority of cases, the evidence shows that education is
indeed inversely correlated with fertility. Increasing income, higher levels
of education, urbanization and the change from an agricultural to an industrial
economy all correlate in general with lower fertility. Although fertility may at
times increase with husband's level of income, it almost always decreases with the
wife's (Birdsall 1976:705). In many parts of Africa where fertility studies have
been completed, these trends were also observed. In particular, a number of
studies in Ghana have shown a negative correlation between education and
fertility: fertility is also in general lower in urban areas (Page, 1975:54).
Caldwell (1968:605) found that the ideal family size in rural Ghana was 7.5,
while that of urban elite men was between 4.5 and 6.1, and that of urban elite
women was between 4.3 and 5.5. Furthermore, the better educated Ghanaian wives
were also more interested in family planning. Only 32% of illiterates expressed
interest, as compared with 53% of those with primary schooling, 65% of those
with secondary schooling and 100% of those with a post-secondary education.
Similar trends were also discovered in Nigeria (Caldwell, 1968: 613,615).

In most of West Africa, there appears to be an inverse correlation between
education and fertility at some levels and some life cycle stages, but there
has more recently been some question as to just how general this is. For
example, Clignet and Sween (1974:236) found an inverse correlation between women's
level of education and fertility in Cameroon. However, there was a slight
increase in the average number of children born to the wives of more educated
men. Handwerker (1977) argues from his Liberian data that in the capital
there is a curvilinear relationship with those with a moderate level of
education having the highest fertility. Furthermore, the negative correlation

between urbanization and lower fertility is not universal. Although urban
fertility is lower than rural fertility in the Ivory Coast, Upper Volta,
Niger, Chad, Benin and Sierra Leone, it is higher in Zaire, Gabon and perhaps
Nigeria (Caldwell, 1975:9). This suggests that although the main lines of
the theory proposed above may be correct, the situation may be more
complicated than first suggested.

The Data from Cameroon

The above theories of education and fertility will be discussed in light
of some data collected among working women in Cameroon in 1975-1976. As the
study was primarily designed to collect information on women's educational
and occupational patterns, no direct information was collected on fertility,
i.e. number of pregnancies or number of live births. However, data were
systematically collected on the number of living children, and the researcher
often discussed with informants their attitudes toward children and family.
Thus the data presented - on numbers of living children - are not directly
comparable to data in fertility surveys which usually deal with live births.[2]
Furthermore, the samples are small and the data not easily generalizable.
However, they can provide useful indicators of directions to pursue in more
rigorous fertility studies.

Three groups of working women were interviewed. These groups were
stratified by occupational categories which in turn were defined by reference
to their average educational level. As representatives of the group of
uneducated working women, a group of wage labourers on a large French-owned
rubber and oil palm plantation were interviewed. Representing a group of
workers with middling level of education were bank workers in the two major
cities of Yaounde and Douala. Representing women with a high level of
education were a number of elite women who were in a variety of fields;
however, all except one were in administrative positions of one kind or
another. The one who was not an administrator exercised an independent
liberal profession. Plantation workers averaged .46 years of education while
bank workers averaged 11.1 years and elites averaged 16.7 years. There was
some overlap between bank workers who were themselves in administrative
positions and the elites in terms of the level of education. However, the
average level of education of the bank workers was clearly lower than that
of the elites.

This sample cannot be used to examine the impact of work on women's fertility, since all women in the sample were not only working, but were salaried permanent workers.[3] It can, however, be used to look at the impact of education within the population of working women. For example, one can hypothesize that the occupations of the more educated women will offer them more prestige than those of the plantation workers and thus we might expect that they would have less need to have large families than the plantation workers, who although they work, do not occupy positions that give them any significant social recognition. Since the uneducated women lived in a rural area most fed themselves to some degree from their own farms; one might also hypothesize that the cost of children would be less among the plantation workers than amongst the bank and elite women, who lived in major cities. In light of both these arguments, one might expect to find a higher average number of children among the plantation workers than among bank workers and elites.

However, the data show just the opposite (Table 1). The average number of living children per woman increases directly with occupational category. While plantation workers averaged 2.03 living children per woman, bank workers averaged 2.15 and elites 2.91. However, if only women who had any living children are counted, bank workers show the highest number of living children, 3.73 compared with 3.35 among the elites and 2.37 among the plantation labourers. This reverse in the trend occurs because of the high number of childless bank workers, 43%, as opposed to 13% and 14% among the elites and plantation workers respectively. It is likely that the childlessness of bank workers is due in large part to their young age; 8 of 11 of the childless women are under age 30. There are a certain number of women in each sample who can have no children, but except for the bank workers where data are questionable, the women show lower sterility rates than the population as a whole, where 30% of women in urban centres and 26% of Basa women (the ethnic group most highly represented on the plantation) had had no live births (Republique du Cameroun, 1964:77).

Because of the small size of the samples (35,26 and 22),no controls were placed for age. Thus the figures are not strictly comparable since women are at different points in their childbearing lives. Among both plantation workers and elites, most women have completed their childbearing years or are near to it.

TABLE 1

MEAN NUMBER OF LIVING CHILDREN

	Plantation	Bank	Elite
All Women	2.03 (N=35)	2.15 (N=26)	2.91 (N=23)
Women with Children Only	2.37 (N=30)	3.73 (N=15)	3.35 (N=20)
Proportion With Children	86%	57%	87%

Plantation workers averaged 43.5 years of age, while elites averaged 37.5.
Among bank workers on the other hand, the average age was 28.9; most were
relatively young and many were in the midst of their reproductive lives.
Final figures for bank workers at the end of reproductive lives would probably
show an increase, perhaps to a relative fertility equal to or even greater
than that found among the elites. This would lead to a pattern similar to
that found by Handwerker (1977) in Liberia where lower level white collar
workers had more children than either elites or working class.[4]

There are also differences in marital status distributions which may
affect childbearing. Elites show the most "normal" distribution, 17 out of
23 being married. Only 8 plantation workers out of 35 were married as were
12 out of 26 bank workers. While most bank workers were single (11 out of
26), most plantation workers were widowed (17 out of 35). Different marital
statuses have different implications for each group, and these will be
discussed below. A rigorous fertility study would also control for this
variable.

Although one cannot rigorously compare these figures either between occupational groups (due to lack of age or marital status controls) or with other surveys (because of the live births/living children distinction), they are nonetheless interesting. This is particularly true in light of the fact that this is a pattern confined to not only one generation, but which appears across generations. In general plantation workers came from full sibling groups (same mother, same father) that were smaller than those of the other two groups. Plantation workers averaged 1.4 full siblings, while bank workers averaged 4.4 and elites 4.5. Again the gap may be somewhat exaggerated since this refers to full siblings living at the time of the interview. Because of their relatively older age, plantation workers were more likely to have lost siblings who had nevertheless survived childhood. The differences are nonetheless striking.

A Model for the Effects of Education on Fertility

Previous theories have suggested that various economic and value changes have led to a decrease in the desire for a large number of children. Although this may be the indirect result of increased education (as posited in the above theories), greater levels of education have other more direct consequences. In particular increased education leads to (1) increased information about modern birth control techniques or at least a knowledge of where to get that information; and (2) higher education offers immediate access to well paid jobs, and thus lead to increased financial resources. These resources can be used for many things, but in terms of fertility consequences, one highly significant use is to assure better medical care. In Cameroon, one of the perquisites of increased wealth is indeed in better medical care.

While increased education leads directly to an increased ability to control births, it need not also lead directly to a change in the values about the ideal number of children to bear.

The Control of Births in Central Africa

Is there evidence that the more education women have, the more they are able to control the number of children they bear? As noted above, since we lack direct evidence on either the number of children desired or the number of live births per woman, the arguments in this section will be based on the number of children alive at the time of interview and the spacing between these children.

Indirect evidence suggests that the small number of children born to the uneducated is due to their inability to control their fertility in a positive direction rather than to any desire for small families. Most women would like to have had larger families, but either experienced periods of sterility or were unable to afford good medical care for children who were born. Their children were thus less likely to survive childhood. Furthermore the women in this sample were from a region of the country affected by a civil war in the late 1950's and early 1960's in which a large number of men were killed and a large number of women were widowed. Although few widows gave up sexual contacts completely, their migration from the village to work on the plantation made their sexual contacts more irregular and probably also exposed them to a greater possibility of venereal disease. Thus uncontrolled fertility in this group does not imply large families of eight or nine children but rather smaller families, where few children were born and where fewer survived. Thus almost half of this sample have either no children (5) or 1 child (12). Among those with more children, some do show the regular spacing of children (every 2 to 3 years) that would be expected of relatively traditional women with uncontrolled fertility. In particular, among the families with five or more children, the spacing between children is fairly regular (Table 2). For the one woman with four children where the ages of the children are known, however, there is 6 years between the first and second, and 4 years between the second and third. Among those with three children, more have regular spacing than do not. But among those six with 2 children only, where the age of the children is known, five have 4 years difference or more between the two children. The evidence is that women either have irregular fertility or that a percentage of their children do not survive.[5]

Furthermore, the number of living children of plantation workers is below the average number of live births recorded for women of their age and ethnic group in traditional villages. Most of the plantation workers are Basa women and their average age is 43.5. Among Basa women aged 40-44, the average number of live births was 3.55 in 1962-64 (Republique du Cameroun, 1964).

TABLE 2

SPACING OF CHILDREN

(For Children with Known Ages Only)

Number of Children	Ages of Children in Each Sibling Group		
	Plantation	Bank	Elites
7	19,17,15,13,13, 4,3	17,15,13,12,11, 6,2, 16,11,9,7,5,3, 1 16,14,12,10,8 6,4	17,14,13,11,9, 7,3
6			22,20,18,16,14,13
5	24,23,21,18,16	15,13,11,9,7 8,7,6,4.1 16,15,11,6,3 12,10,7,5,1	18,18,15,13,8 11,9,7,5,3
4	13,7,3,1	19,17,15,12	23,21,19,17 10,8,6,3 ·12,9,5,4 8,5,4,4
3	23,21,14 19,17,14 18,15,13 18,15,13		7,5,4 13,12,10 17,15,4 19,16,14
2	11,6 22,6 10,6 14,8 15,9 21,19	8,7 4,2 11,1 2, 3 months	16,10 8,8 7,4 11,10

Note: Two siblings of same age denote twins.

Uneducated women who migrate to do plantation labour tend to be extremely marginal people, pushed into wage labour by a combination of circumstances which force them to rely primarily on their own resources and cut them off from substantial kin support.[6] That they show such a low number of living children is, to a great degree, just one more reflection of that marginality. Among these women, uncontrolled fertility does not lead to large families but rather to very small ones.

What happens, then, among more educated women who work? Given their greater financial resources, it would be expected that they would be able to get better medical care and thus have larger families. However, this tendency may also be counteracted if women deliberately limit the size of their families.

In general the bank workers seem to be highly fertile. Those who have children usually began childbearing at an early age; 18 was the average of these women at the birth of their first child. The oldest age at which a bank worker who had living children bore her first child that survived was 22. Furthermore, women continue to bear children at fairly regular intervals once they have begun (Table 2).

There is little evidence that these women wish to limit the number of children they bear, although a number of the younger, single, more highly educated bank workers may postpone having children until they marry. More commonly, they have a child or two and then wait. Almost half (5 of 11) of the single women have had children, but most of them seem to have controlled childbearing after their first pregnancy or two. Many of these were schoolgirl pregnancies and/or the girls thought they would marry the child's father. For various reasons, these marriages did not occur. Most seem to have learned to control fertility after this experience and are now waiting until marriage to have more children. Not being married in this culture does not exclude childbearing, but it does limit it. A number of the single women with no children (perhaps 4) remained single because of an inability to bear a living child.

The women did have some knowledge of modern birth control techniques; one woman recounted how her last child was the result of a mistake she had with her pills; another single woman with no children told me how she had advised her sister to use the pill. Other young women simply made general comments on how they do not plan to have children (or any more children) until they marry. However, their childbearing patterns show little evidence of much use of contraception to limit sizes of families once they marry. Of the women who had two children only, three out of four had a youngest child who was less than two years old at the time of the interview.[7] Of the three women with seven children, all had youngest children who were age four or younger. As noted above, the bank workers may in fact show the highest cumulative fertility of the women in this study if all women could be compared at the end of their childbearing years. This is perhaps surprising in light of the fact that these women, especially those in lower level clerical jobs are perhaps those most subject to the economic constraints discussed in the first section of the paper. While they have many of the aspiration of the elite, their incomes are significantly lower. However, they may be the group most conscious of the traditional positive values of large families, as suggested by Handwerker (1977), and as described by Harrell-Bond (1975).[8] Although they have knowledge of modern birth control, they still find the value of children higher than the economic constraints of the urban setting.

The elites are the women in the country who have both the greatest knowledge and also the greatest economic resources. They are continuing to have relatively large families although perhaps ultimately not quite as large as those of bank workers. They show the same relatively regular spacing between children. However, they also seem to control their fertility at some point. Not one of the women interviewed had a child younger than two years and eight out of the twenty with children had not had a child for more than five years (as opposed to only three bank workers).[9] They also seemed to postpone childbearing, presumably because of extended schooling. In contrast to the bank workers who bore their first child at the average age of 18, elite women had their first child at the average age of 24. They also showed the most concern to bear children only within the context of marriage. Although a few did bear children before marrying, no widows or divorcees had children after the termination of the marriage, an occurence found in both other groups.

Although they talked less about use of birth control than did bank workers, 11 of 23 were trained in medical fields (nurses, doctors,

pharmacists) and were knowledgeable about modern techniques of birth
control. Several women were involved in population, maternal and child
health programmes and clinics.

Although they control family size, elite women still prefer relatively
large families. The women who had really small families tended to be those
who were not living with their husbands. Of the ten women who had two
or fewer children, six were single, divorced, separated or widowed. Of the
four remaining, one claimed that she intended to have more children at
some time. The only woman who admitted to deliberately having a small
family (one child) said she did this because her husband had to support
15 children of his three unmarried sisters, and she considered this enough
children for the family to support.

In general, in the central African situation where traditional
fertility has been relatively low rather than high (as in western Africa)
a likely initial effect of education and the increased income that goes
with it is to increase fertility. Very poor people have neither the
knowledge nor resources to improve low fertility, and thus have few living
children, due to a combination of sterility and infant and child mortality.
They would like to have more, but this is often not possible. Not
surprisingly then, one of the priorities of individuals when they do get
incomes is good health care. Thus among the more educated, fertility has
risen. Although they may know how to control fertility, the middle classes
may often choose not to. The reasons for this will be discussed below.
Finally, very highly educated women are also able to ensure their fertility
to a high degree, but there is some evidence that they also control their
fertility, in order not to have families that they would consider too large.
However, the families that they do have continue to be large by Western
standards, and elite women tend to have families larger than those of the
other two samples. The ability to control fertility does not necessarily
mean that values will immediately change so that people will want small
families.

A Question of Values

What then are the values that lead Cameroonian women to prefer large
families? At one level, there is undeniably the "traditional" importance

of a large family in African society. Harrell-Bond (1975) describes these
values among the professionals of Sierra Leone, the reasons for them, and
their implications. Handwerker (1977) discusses similar values among
educated city dwellers in Liberia and suggests that tradition may retain
importance longer among the white collar and skilled blue collar "sub-elite".
The data comparing bank workers and elite women suggest that this might
also be true for Cameroon. However, both groups continue to have relatively
large families, and one important factor for both groups of women is the
continued positive value of children.

One of the mechanisms by which education is assumed to limit fertility
is through the opportunity cost of the woman's time when she feels she must
leave her employment to care for her children. This argument assumes either
that child care is expensive or unavailable or that there is a cultural value
that it is better for a mother to care for her own children. It is impossible
to discuss the working time lost to the women in this sample through child
raising since they have continued in paid employment through their numerous
pregnancies. Cameroonian law supports women's rights to have children as
well as employment through the provision of generous maternity leave.[10]
Furthermore, for both bank workers and elite women, child care is relatively
inexpensive. Income distribution is such that the cost of a full time
housemaid who may also cook and clean as well as care for the children makes
a small dent in the wife's income.[11] The salary of a maid averages about 8-10,000
francs CFA/month full time, while the bank worker's average salary is 46,000
francs. No exact salary data were available for the elite women, but it is
likely that salaries were at least 100,000 francs CFA/month. Moreover, there
is no cultural value that says that a mother should be home all day to care
for her children. Although women do admit that they have more chores if
they work, they usually feel that the benefits of the work far outweigh the
disadvantages.

A second reason proposed for the inverse correlation of education with
fertility is that the costs of childraising, particularly education, rise
with a parent's education, as he/she wants better quality education for
his/her children. Although this may be true in general in Cameroon, it is
less so at some levels than others. At the primary school level, elites'
educational costs were likely to be higher, as they were more likely to send

their children to prestigious private schools. However, at the secondary
level, this was no longer true since the children of elite women were more
likely to get into government schools where there were no fees, while the
children of the lower and middle classes were more likely to pay high tuition
at private schools. Also as more educated parents were more likely to live
in the city, these children were more likely to live in their own homes and
thus less likely to have boarding fees.[12]

Finally in Africa, one reason suggested for the gradual reduction of
family size is the difficulty of supporting both one's children and one's
greater kin network in the style to which they have become accustomed. Although
this may be a problem for both elite women and bank employees, it becomes
less of one in families where both husband and wife work, and where there
are two incomes. Both husband and wife can more easily aid kin without
serious damage to nuclear family necessities.

In light of these arguments, one might expect that the economic
constraints toward smaller family size would appear first among the middle
classes rather than among elites, since a greater proportion of their
salaries is spent on child care and they are slightly less likely to be able
to send their children to the free government secondary schools. In fact,
the data suggest that precisely the opposite is happening. The traditional
values supporting high fertility may still be more important than economic
constraints in determining fertility at this point in time. While many
middle level city dwellers pay lip service to the necessity of some
family limitation, evidence is slight that they are implementing this.

Government policy may also be an important factor. The Cameroon
government is in favour of the use of family planning for child spacing
to conserve the health of the individual mother, but has a strongly pro-
natalist population policy. Women are urged to have as many children as
they can while remaining healthy. Six is the ideal (Lantum, 1973), as the
government would like to increase its present population of approximately
6 million to 15 million before it even begins to consider limiting it
(Gwatkin, 1975:173). Although pockets of the country are very densely
populated (e.g., over 100 per square kilometer in parts of North and West),
the population density in the country as a whole is a relatively low 13 per
square kilometer and in much of the south ranges between 2 and 10 per square

149

kilometer. In general this population policy is accepted by the people,
including educated women. Given the general lack of population pressure
in their country, they make decisions about family size for essentially
individual and familial reasons.

On the one hand, a number of considerations related to both
traditional values and to government policy, lead women to want to have
large families. On the other, the economic constraints on educated women
are simply not strong enough to encourage them to radically limit the size
of their families. Thus educated women continue to have families that are
large by Western standards and are also larger than those of their
uneducated counterparts.

Conclusions

In general, data from all over the world have shown a trend toward
lower fertility with higher education. One case suggesting the opposite does
not contradict the general tendency. However, it does point up some of
the general assumptions behind the theories proposed to explain this trend.
While these assumptions are often true, they are not universally so, and
in a situation where a number of the assumptions do not hold concurrently,
one will find contradictions to the general trend.

The Cameroonian data highlight, in particular, three assumptions.
Firstly, there is a baseline assumption of high birth rates in a situation
where fertility is uncontrolled. Although infant and child mortality may
account for most of the low growth rate under traditional conditions, there
are situations where women also show low fertility. This is particularly
true in parts of central Africa where there is apparent sterility among
significant sections of the population. One cannot always argue from a
baseline of high fertility.

Secondly, among proponents of the influence of education and economic
constraints on fertility, there is an unfounded assumption of homogeneity
in two different areas. The first is in the value placed on children, or
in the words of the theorists in tastes in children. As Leibenstein
(1974:468) says, the theorists assume that people of all socio-economic
statuses will have the same tastes for children, but this may not be a

reasonable assumption. If this is not a reasonable assumption across classes in one culture, it is even less reasonable to expect similar tastes in children across cultures. Rational decisions are made about how many children to have, but within the context of the values of a particular culture, which may place a positive value on large families for a variety of reasons. As Leibenstein (1974:460) proposes, it may be more realistic to develop a general model for comparisons of costs and benefits in regard to decisions about a marginal child (i.e., a fifth rather than a fourth) rather than for

Secondly, the theories assume homogeneity in terms of which situations constitute economic constraints. As this paper emphasizes, women who do remain in the labour force do not have lost income for an extra child as an important constraint. Furthermore, in a situation where finding child care is relatively easy, either through extended family or because it is cheap, this also need not be an economic constraint. Finally, in the African situation where both spouses are expected to contribute to natal families, this might form an important economic constraint on the size of their own nuclear family but is eased to some degree when both spouses work and there are two salaries. The particular situations which constitute economic constraints upon large families vary from culture to culture.

This paper has not presented any rigorously tested new findings. However, by discussing the assumptions behind current theories on the relationship between fertility and education, it has pointed out some new directions of inquiry that will hopefully be followed up by more systematic research.

REFERENCE NOTES

1. I would like to thank the National Science Foundation, National Defence Foreign Language Fellowships and the Program of African Studies at Northwestern University who financed the fieldwork upon which this study is based.

2. In Africa, the number of live births will be significantly higher than the number of living children. A high estimate (probably too high, say the authors) is that 83% of Cameroonian children born are still living at age 5 (Republique du Cameroun, 1964:86). The comparisons to other surveys presented here should be evaluated with this in mind.

3. The data on this are themselves ambiguous. When figures on urban working women are compared to fertility figures for urban centres in the Center-South (from Republique du Cameroun, 1964:70), evidence suggests that working women may have lower fertility. Women aged 25-29 averaged 2.37 live births to 2.15 living children for bank workers in my sample (average age 28.9). Women aged 35-39 averaged 3.63 live births to 2.91 living children for elites in my sample (average age 37.5). However, data from Clignet and Sween's (1974) analysis of the censuses of Yaoundé and Douala (with no control for age) show just the opposite; as opposed to an average 2.51 living children among all urban women in my sample (i.e., bank employees and elites), they found an average 2.40 births for all monogamously married women and 1.87 for those women who had completed primary school. However, educated women are certainly considerably younger than the illiterate. Almost all women in my samples are monogamously married, when married.

4. There is some internal evidence suggesting that the final fertility of bank employees will be higher. This sample of 26 interviewed in 1975/76 was selected from a larger sample first interviewed in 1974. At the time of the original interviews, these same women averaged 1.8 living children, and only 13 out of 26 had children. Only a year and a half later, 15 women had children (one woman had two in the interval) and the mean increased to 2.15.

5. I have no knowledge of the use of traditional abortificants or contraceptives.

6. For a more complete discussion of the characteristics of female plantation workers and their marginality, see Koenig (1976).

7. One of these three was known to be pregnant at a time after this survey was done.

8. Harrell-Bond discusses elite attitudes in Freetown; however, these attitudes are quite similar to those expressed by mid level bank workers.

9. In part this is simply an artifact of the older age of the elite. A larger sample which would allow for age controls could test this proposition more rigorously.

10.   Some women may cease work once children are born, but more commonly
      women who begin childbearing quite young may wait until children
      are older to begin working, as was the case with some bank workers.

11.   Neither fostering nor use of relatives to provide in-home child care
      were very common among either bank workers or elites. A few single
      women had mothers or other relatives care for their children;
      otherwise a servant was usually hired.

12.   Francophone Africa never had the great emphasis on boarding schools
      that was found in Anglophone Africa.

BIBLIOGRAPHY

Birdsall, N. 1976. "Women and Population Studies". Signs. 1:699:712

Caldwell, J.C. 1968. "The Control of Family Size in Tropical Africa".
Demography. 5:598-619
1975. "Introduction". In Population Growth and Socioeconomic
Change in West Africa. J.C. Caldwell,(ed.) New York: Columbia
University Press

Clignet, R and J. Sween 1974. "Urbanization, Plural Marriage and
Family Size in Two African Cities". American Ethnologist.
1:221-242

Germain, A. 1975. "Status and Role of Women as Factors in Fertility
Behaviour: A Policy Analysis". Studies in Family Planning.
6:192-200

Gwatkin, D.R. 1975 "Governmental Population Policies". In Population
Growth and Socioeconomic Change in West Africa. J.C. Caldwell,
(ed.) New York: Columbia University Press

Handwerker, W.P. 1977. "Family, Fertility and Economics". Current
Anthropology. 18:259-287

Harrell-Bond, B. 1975. Modern Marriage in Sierra Leone. The Hague:
Mouton

Koenig, D. 1976. "Women and Migration: Plantation Workers in
Cameroon". Paper presented at the 75th Annual Meeting of the
American Anthropological Association, Washington, D.C.

Lantum, D. 1973. "A KAP Survey on Cameroon Women in 1973". Mimeo

Leibenstein, H. 1974. "An Interpretation of the Economic Theory of
Fertility: Promising Path or Blind Alley?". The Journal of
Economic Literature. 12:459-79

Okediji, F.O. 1973. "Social Cultural and Economic Determinants of
Fertility in Africa". Pan-African Journal. 6:252-262

Page, H. 1975. "Fertility Levels Patterns and Trends". In Population
Growth and Socioeconomic Change in West Africa. J.C. Caldwell,
(ed.) New York: Columbia University Press

Republique du Cameroun, 1964. Enquete Demographique au Cameroun:
Resultates Definitifs pour la Region Sud-Est 1962-64. Paris: INSEE

CHAPTER 8

THE RELATIONSHIP BETWEEN
EDUCATION AND FERTILITY

Susan H. Cochrane

CHAPTER 8

THE RELATIONSHIP BETWEEN EDUCATION AND FERTILITY

Susan H. Cochrane*

A number of recent reviews on the determinants of fertility have come out with statements that the inverse relationship between education and fertility is one of the most consistent and best documented in the literature.[1] Such statements tempt policy makers to consider using educational policies to contribute to fertility reduction. However, an extensive review of the evidence shows that the relationship between education and fertility is not always inverse. The earlier generalizations about such a relationship probably resulted from a scarcity of data in the poorest, least literate societies and in rural areas. It is in such areas that inverse relationships are less likely to be observed. While further studies may show that the results to date for such areas are invalid, there is theoretical and empirical evidence which indicates that education in the poorest regions may be associated with an increase in biological supply of children (and births). In the short run this increase would tend to increase actual fertility. In the long run adjustments to new circumstances might be expected to bring about a reduction in fertility. The length of time needed for this adjustment to occur under various circumstances is yet to be determined. This paper summarises the empirical evidence, presents a theoretical model supporting the hypothesis of a lagged adjustment and discusses the policy and research implications of the results.

Findings

Population policy is directed at the rate of population growth and thus at aggregate levels of fertility as measured by crude birth rates.

---

*   This paper summarizes the results of a monograph entitled Fertility and Education: What do we Really Know? World Bank Staff Occasional Paper No.26, 1979. The Paper does not necessarily represent the views of the World Bank.

From a policy perspective the relationship of greatest interest is that
between the aggregate level of education in a country and the crude birth
rate. Such relationships are almost invariably inverse when one compares
countries with different levels of education. The causal significance of
such relationships is, however, highly uncertain, given the many other
factors which tend to be associated with various levels of development.
If one controls for the age structure of the population and the level of
income or development then statistically significant inverse relationships
are only observed in 70 percent of the cases. (See Table 1). Rather than
using the nation as the unit of aggregation one can use subnational
geographical areas. Using such cross regional data from within developing
countries and controlling for the age structure and extent of urbanization
one observes statistically significant inverse relationships in only
60 percent of the cases in which significance was reported. (See Table 2).

This aggregate data, both cross-national and cross-regional, tends to
indicate that inverse relationships are less likely to be observed in the
least developed countries. Unfortunately given the lack of well developed
national statistical systems in the poorest countries, it is impossible to
find a sufficient number of aggregate studies relating education and
fertility in these countries. Therefore, to further explore that
relationship one must rely on studies relating individuals' education and
fertility. Such studies can be based on sample surveys which are too
small or too localized to provide cross regional comparisons.

The cross-individual studies of the relationship in developing
countries are of two kinds (1) those simply comparing the fertility
(adjusted for age) of those at different levels of education and (2)
multiple regression studies in which fertility is the dependent variable,
education and income are two of the independent variables and a control
is introduced for age. The first kind of study shows inverse relationships
(not necessarily significant) in 49 percent of the cases. (See Table 3).
The second type of study shows inverse relationship in about 58 percent
of the cases. (See Table 4). These aggregate percentages are somewhat
irrelevant however, because of great differences revealed in both kinds
of studies in the relationship in different subgroups. Both kinds of
studies show that: (1) Female education is more likely to be inversely

TABLE 1. CROSS-NATIONAL STUDIES, ARRANGED BY METHODOLOGY USED

Study (date published)	Sample	Age control	Income Control	Direction of relation
Simple correlation				
Bogue (1969	80 DC and MD			inverse
Heer (1966)	41 DC and MD			inverse
Ekamen (1974)	32 DC			inverse[c]
Kirk (1971)	25 Latin American			inverse[c]
	17 Asian			inverse[c]
	15 Islamic			inverse[c]
Kasarda (1971)	42 DC and MD (1950-59)			inverse[c]
	60 DC and MD (1960-69)			inverse[c]
	42 DC and MD	X		inverse[c]
	60 DC and MD	X		inverse[c]
Repetto (1974)	64 DC and MD	X		inverse
Multiple regression				
Anker (1975)	69 developing	X		inverse[a]
	29 African	X		inverse[a]
	19 Asian	X		inverse[a]
	21 American	X		inverse[a]
Janowitz (1976)	30 DC	X		inverse[a]
Russet (1964)	38 DC and MD		X	inverse[a]
Ekamen (1974)	32 DC		X	inverse[a]
Gregory (1973)	25 MD		X	inverse[c]
	15 DC		X	inverse[a]
McCabe and Rosenzweig (1976)	48 DC		X	inverse[a]
Freedman and Berelson (1977)	46 DC		X	inverse
Friedlander and Silver (1967)	all countries		X	inverse[c]
	most developed		X	direct[a]
	middle level		X	inverse[c]
	least developed		X	mixed[a]
	allcountries	X	X	inverse[a]
	most developed	X	X	direct[b]
	middle level	X	X	inverse[b]
	least developed	X	X	mixed[a]
McCabe and Rosenzweig (1976)	38 urban DC	X	X	inverse[c]
Janowitz (1976)	54 DC and MD	X	X	inverse[c]
Repetto (1974)	64 DC and MD	X	X	inverse[c]
Heer (1966)	41 DC and MD	X	X	inverse[a]
Adelman (1963)	37 DC	X	X	inverse[c]
	developed	X	X	inverse[b]

NOTE: DC = developing country; MD = more developed country

a. Not significant

b. Significant in less than 50 percent of the cases

c. Significant or significant in 50 percent or more of the cases

Source: Cochrane, Susan H. Fertility and Education: What Do We Really Know? World Bank Staff Occasional Papers No. 26, 1979.

TABLE 2. CROSS-REGIONAL STUDIES, ARRANGED BY METHODOLOGY USED

Study (date published)	Location	Age control	Control for degree of urbanization	Direction of relation
Simple correlation				
Merrick (1974)	Brazil	X	none	inverse[c]
Stycos (1968)	Argentina	X	urban	inverse
		X	rural	inverse[b]
	Bolivia	X	urban	direct[b]
		X	rural	direct
	Chile	X	urban	inverse
		X	rural	inverse
	Colombia	X	X	inverse
	Costa Rica	X	urban	inverse
		X	rural	inverse
	Guatemala	X	urban	inverse
		X	rural	direct
	Honduras	X	urban	direct
		X	rural	inverse
	Mexico	X	urban	inverse
		X	rural	direct
	Nicaragua	X	urban	inverse
		X	rural	direct
	Panama	X	urban	direct
		X	rural	inverse
	Venezuela	X	urban	inverse
		X	rural	direct
Zarate (1977)	Mexico	X	urban	inverse[a]
Caldwell (1968)	Ghana	X	urban	inverse[c]
Multiple regression				
World Bank (1974)	India		X	inverse[c]
Schultz (1969)	Peurto Rico		X	inverse[c]
Drakatos (1969)	Greece	X	X	inverse[a]
Li (1970)	Taiwan	X	cities	inverse[c]
		X	urban towns	inverse[c]
		X	rural towns	inverse[b]
Hicks (1974)	Mexico (states FFR)	X	X	direct[c]
	children ever born (rural)	X	rural	direct[a]
	children ever born (states)	X	X	direct[a]
Schultz (1972)	Taiwan	X	X(M)	inverse[a]
			X(F)	direct[c]
	(adjusted for multi-collinearity)	X	X(M)	inverse[c]
			X(F)	inverse[c]
Ben-Porath (1973)	Israel	X	(Jewish towns)	
			(M)	direct[a]
			(F)	inverse[c]
		X	(Jewish rural)	
			(M)	inverse[c]
			(F)	inverse[c]
		X	(kibbutzim)	
			(M)	direct[a]
			(F)	direct[a]
		X	(non-Jewish, urban)	
			(M)	direct[c]
			(F)	inverse[c]
Traina and Bontrager (1977)	Costa Rica	X	X	inverse[c]
Siever (1976)	Mexico	X	X	inverse[c]
Schultz (1972)	Egypt - intermediate school			
	children under 5	X	X	inverse[b]
	children 5 to 9	X	X	inverse[b]
	-literacy			
	children under 5	X	X	direct[c]
	children 5 to 9	X	X	direct[a]
Cochrane (1978)	Thailand (1960)	X	X	direct[c]
	(1970)	X	X	direct[c]
	change between 1960 and 1970	X	X	inverse[b]

NOTE: (M) = education of men; (F) = education of women
a. Not significant
b. Significant in less than 50 percent of the cases
c. Significant or significant in more than 50 percent of the cases

Source: Cochrane, Susan H. Fertility and Education: What Do We Really Know? World Bank Staff Occasional Papers No. 26, 1979.

TABLE 3. CROSS-TABULAR STUDIES ON THE RELATION BETWEEN AGE-ADJUSTED FERTILITY AND EDUCATIONAL LEVEL, BY ILLITERACY RATE

Study (date published)	Location	Illiteracy rate (percent)	Data source (sample size)	Characteristics	Direction of relation	Number of reversals in relation [a]	Percent difference in fertility between educated and not educated
CELADE[b] (1972)	Buenos Aires	(A) 10	1964 survey (2,136)	(F)	irregular	3	ND
				(M)	irregular	3	ND
CELADE (1972)	San Jose	(A) 14	1964 survey (2,132)	(F)	curvilinear	4 + years	+1
				(M)	inverse	0	ND
Chung (1972)	Korea	(F) 19	1971 (1,883)	(F)	inverse	0	-20 to -17
Carelton (1965)	Puerto Rico	(F) 22	1960 cnesus	(F)	inverse	0	-15
CELADE (1972)	Panama City	(F) 25	1964 survey (2,222)	(F)	inverse	1	ND
				(M)	inverse	0	ND
CELADE (1972)	Caracas	(A) 27	1964 survey (2,087)	(F)	inverse	1	-22.9
				(M)	inverse	2	-16.6
Knodel and Prachuabmoh (1973	Thailand	(F) 29 (urban-18; rural-31.7)	1969 survey (1,064F; 675M)	(F) urban	curvilinear	1-3 years	+29
				(F) rural	curvilinear	1-3 years	+29
				(M) urban	irregular	3	+10
				(M) rural	curvilinear	4-6 years	+4
CELADE (1972)	Bogota	(A) 30.5	1964 survey (2,259)	(F)	inverse	1	-13
				(M)	inverse	2	-35
CELADE (1972)	Quito	(A) 34.6	1964 survey (1,082)	(F)	inverse	2	ND
				(M)	inverse	0	ND
CELADE (1972)	Guayaquil	(A) 34.6	1964 survey (1,243)	(F)	inverse	0	ND
				(M)	inverse	0	ND
CELADE (1972)	Mexico City	(F) 35	1964 survey (2,353)	(F)	inverse	0	-12.5
				(M)	inverse	2	-33
Stycos (1968)	Peru	(A) 39	1960/61 survey (1,078)	(F) Lima	inverse	0	-7
				(F) Chimbote	curvilinear	1-2 years	+22
				(F) Viru-Huaxlay	inverse	0	-16
Goldstein (1972)	Thailand	(F) 44	1960 census	(F) Bangkok	inverse	1	-8
				(F) other urban	inverse	0	-11
				(F) urban agric.	inverse	0	-3
				(F) rural non-agric.	curvilinear	1-2 years	+0.1
				(F) rural agric.	inverse	0	-8
CELADE (1972)	Rio de Janeiro	(F) 40.6	1964 survey (2,512)	(F)	inverse	1	-22.3
				(M)	inverse	3	-26.6
Gendell and others (1970)	Guatemala	(A) 45.3	1964 census (urban)	(F) domestics	curvilinear		+14
				(F) other active	inverse	0	-55
				(F) inactive	inverse	0	-8
Palmore (1969)	West Malaysia	(F) 50.4 (urban-42.1; rural-54)	1966-67 (5,467)	(F) metropolitan	inverse	0	-11
				(F) nonmetropolitan urban	curvilinear	1-5 years	+7
				(F) rural	curvilinear	1-5 years	+12
Hull and Hull (1977	Indonesia	(F) 51 (urban-30.2) rural-55.5)	1971 census	(F) urban	curvilinear	(complete)	+15
				(F) rural	curvilinear	(primary)	+21
Ewbank (1977)	Tanzania	(F) 85	1967 census	(F)	curvilinear	1-4 years	+12
Srinivasan (1967)	India	(F) 87		(M) rural	curvilinear	6-8 years	+1
Ohadike (1969)	Lagos, Nigeria	(A) 89	1964 Lagos survey (596)	(F) urban	inverse	0	-3
				(M) urban	curvilinear	primary	+8
El Badry and Rizk (1967)	Cairo, Egypt	(F) 91 (A) 80	1960	(F) upper Egypt	curvilinear	literate	+12
				(F) lower Egypt nonurban	curvilinear	literate	+13
				(F) lower Egypt urban	inverse	0	-14

NOTE: (F) = education of women; (M) = education of men; (A) = education of adults; ND = no data.
a. Number of reversals in general inverse relations; if the relation is nonlinear, this column reports on the level of education with highest fertility.
b. United Nations Regional Center for Demographic Training and Research in Latin America.

Source: Cochrane, Susan H, Fertility and Education: What Do We Really Know? World Bank Staff Occasional Papers No.26, 1979.

TABLE 4. MULTIPLE REGRESSION STUDIES OF AGE-ADJUSTED FERTILITY AND EDUCATIONAL LEVEL, CONTROLLING FOR RESIDENCE AND INCOME

Study (date published)	Location	Illiteracy rate (percent)	Data source (sample size)	Equation	Education Sign	Education Measurement	Income Sign	Income Measurement	Other significant variables
McCabe and Rosenzweig (1976)	Puerto Rico	(F) 13.4	1970 census	35-44 working women	(F)	− years completed	+	male wage	predicted wage of males and females
Davidson (1973)	Caracas	(G) 27	1963-64,CELADE (2,087)	20-24 25-29 30-34 35-39	(F) (F) (F) (F)	− − −ᵃ years completed −	− −ᵃ − −	husband's income	age of marriage age of marriage; desired family size
Encarnación (1974)	Philippines	(G) 28	1968 National Fertility Survey (used 3,629 single family households)	total urban rural lower income upper income	(F) (F) (F) (F) (F)	+ −ᵃ +ᵃ years completed +ᵃ −ᵃ	− − +ᵃ +ᵃ −	family income	age of and duration of marriage
Rosenzweig (1976)	Philippines	(G) 28	1968 National Fertility Survey (1,830)	35-39	(F) (M)	−ᵃ years of + schooling		predicted income of husband	age of marriage infant mortality wage of children
Kogut (1974)	Brazil	(G) 29	1960 census	northeast south east	(F) (M) (F) (M) (F) (M)	−ᵃ −ᵃ −ᵃ years of −ᵃ schooling −ᵃ +ᵃ	− − −ᵃ −ᵃ −ᵃ	household income	locale; age; duration of marriage locale; age; duration of marriage; religion
Iutaka (1971)	Brazil	−	1959-60 urban survey (1,280	total urban natives urban migrants	(M) (M)	+ᵃ + years −	−ᵃ +ᵃ	social status	age; age at marriage; city; size; color
Chernichovsky (1976)	Brazil	−	rural (170)	mortality control no mortality control	(F) (M) (F) (M)	− years −ᵃ literacy − years − literacy	+ᵃ +ᵃ	land owned or cultivated	age; age at marriage extended family
Davidson (1973)	Mexico City	(F) 35	1963-64 CELADE (2,353)	20-24 25-29 30-34 35-39	(F) (F) (F) (F)	− − years completed −ᵃ	− − − 0	husband's occupation	age at marriage age and work status age at marriage age at marriage
Khan and Sirageldin (1975)	Pakistan	(G) 61	1968-69 survey 35-49 want no more (2,910)	total urban rural	(F) (M) (F) (M) (F) (M)	−ᵃ literacy + years −ᵃ literacy + years − literacy + years	− − + +	family income	education desired for child; child deaths; family planning
Knowles and Anker (1975)	Kenya	(G) 70	1974 survey (1,074)	all women	(F)	+ years	+	household income	land owned; urban residence; years married
Kelley (1976)	Kenya	−	401 urban nuclear households	all women	(F) (M) (F) (M)	+ primary + primary −ᵃ secondary + secondary	+ᵃ	earned household income	age of wife
Chernichovsky (1976)	India	(G) 71	rural survey (212)	all women	(F) (M)	+ literacy + years	+ᵃ	income from agriculture and other occupation	mother's age; age at marriage; number of child deaths
Kocher (1977)	Tanzania	(G) 85	1973 survey northeastern region (800)	20-29 30-39	(F) (M)	−ᵃ −	− +	household crop production	building quality index; no variable significant in demand; equation; all significant in supply
Cochrane and others (1977)	Nepal	(F) 97.4	1976 rural (122)	all women	(M) (M) (M) (M) (M) (M)	+ years +ᵃ literacy +ᵃ literacy score +ᵃ numeracy + picture vocabulary + induction of classes	− − − − − −	imputed farm income plus other income per household member; land area worked per capita has positive coefficient	duration of marriage

NOTE: (F) = education of women; (M) = education of men
a. Statistically significant

Source: Cochrane, Susan H. Fertility and Education: What Do We Really Know? World Bank Staff Occasional Papers No.26, 1979

related to fertility than male education. In the first kind of study in 56% of the cases female education was inversely related to fertility while this was true in only 31% of the cases for males. In our multiple regression studies the percentages inversed were 79 and 32 respectively for females and males. (2) Education in urban areas is more likely to be inversely related than in rural areas. In the first kind of study 57% of the studies of urban regions showed inverse relationships while only 20% of the rural studies did. In the multiple regression studies the percentages were 67% and 41% respectively. (3) Education in countries with literacy rates above 40% are more likely to be inversely related than in less literate countries. In the first kind of study when illiteracy was under 40, 52% of the cases were inverse while only 29% were if illiteracy exceeded 60%. In the multiple regression studies the percentages were 79 and 25 respectively. Thus the percentage of inverse relationship observed overall depends very much on the distribution of studies in various categories.

In general there are far fewer studies of rural than urban areas, of males than of females and in less literate as opposed to more literate societies. In addition the studies in the least literate societies are more likely to be based on very small sample sizes. It is expected that the World Fertility Survey will correct this imbalance and provide a much firmer empirical base for generalizations about fertility at various levels of development. Unfortunately most of the WFS surveys are restricted to ever married women and thus would tend to understate the total effect of education and fertility if education significantly increases the proportion of women who never marry.

The simple replication of studies relating education and fertility in a wider variety of countries with fairly uniform data will help clarify the situations in which education is inversely related to fertility. Such studies however will not clarify the issues of the casual relationship between the variables. A model is needed of how education affects fertility. Such a model is needed to establish if the observed association between the variables is in fact causal. In addition such a model needs to be able to explain why education has different impacts on fertility in different situations. The model of fertility determination presented here is based

TABLE 5. EVIDENCE ON THE EFFECT OF INTERVENING VARIABLES
ON COMPLETED FERTILITY

Intervening variable	Direction of relation	Empirical support
Supply factors		
Probability of marriage	+	Schultz (1972), Mazur (1973) Maurer (1973)
Wife's age at marriage	−	McGreevey-Birdsall, Encarnación (1968), Kim and others (1974), Davidson (1973), Yaukey (1972), Palmore and Ariffin (1969)
Health	+	Butz (1976), Baird (1965)
Separate location of spouse	−	Williams (1976)
Joint family living	?(−)	United Nations (1973), Williams (1976)
Legal, monogamous marriage	?(+)	Mason and others (1971)(+), Nerlove and Schultz (1969)(+), Miro and Mertens (1968) (mixed), United Nations (1973) (mixed)
Taboos on sexual activity	−	United Nations (1973) (several studies cited)
Infant and child mortality	+	McGreevey-Birdsall (1974), Snyder (1974), Williams (1976)
Demand factors		
Preferences for children	?(+)	
Husband's wage	?	Simon (1974), Williams (1976)
Money cost of children	−	Mueller (1972), Bulatao (1975), Arnold and others (1975)
Wife's wage	−	Mason and others (1971), DaVanzo (1972), Snyder (1974), Rosenzweig and Evenson (forthcoming)
Incompatibility of wife's work	−	Goldstein (1972), United Nations (1973), Bindary and others (1973), Williams (1976)
Cost of child care substitutes	−	Cain and Weinenger (1973), McCabe and Rosenzweig (1976)
Economic benefits of children	+	Mueller (1972), Harmon (1970), McGreevey-Birdsall (1974)
Fertility regulation		
Husband's marital power	?(+)	Weller (1968) (+), Mitchell (1972) (+)
Husband-wife communication	−	Mitchell (1972), Michel (1967), Hill and others (1959) Ramakumar and Gopal (1972)
Knowledge of birth control	−	
Attitude toward birth control	−	
Access to birth control	−	Mason and others (1971), Schultz (1972)

Source: Cochrane, Susan H. Fertility and Education: What Do We Really Know? World Bank Staff Occasional Papers No.26, 1979.

TABLE 6.   EFFECT OF EDUCATION ON FERTILITY THROUGH INTERVENING VARIABLES

Intervening variable	Effect of education on the intervening variables		Effect of intervening variables on fertility	Effect of education on fertility through intervening variables	
	Male	Female		Male	Female
Supply factors					
Probability of being married	+	−	+	+	−
Wife's age at marriage	?	+	−	?	−
Health	+	+	+	+	+
Separate location of spouse	−	?	−	+	?
Joint family living	−	−	?(−)	? (+)	?
Legal, monogamous marriage	?	+	?(+)	?	? (+)
Taboos on sexual activity	−	−	−	+	+
Infant and child mortality	−	−	+	−	−
Demand factors					
Preferences for children[a]	−	−	?(+)	−	−
Husband's wage	+	0	?	?	0
Money cost of children	+	+	−	−	−
Wife's wage	0	+	−	0	−
Incompatibility of wife's work	0	+	−	0	−
Cost of child care substitutes[b]	0	+	−	0	−
Economic benefits of children	−	−	+	−	−
Fertility regulations					
Husband's marital power	+	−	?(+)	?	?
Husband-wife communication	+	+	−	−	−
Knowledge of birth control	+	+	−	−	−
Attitude toward birth control[a]	+	+	−	−	−
Access to birth control	+	+	−	−	−

a.   Depends in part on whether the education is religious or secular.

b.   Depends on community level of female education.

Source: Cochrane, Susan H. Fertility and Education: What Do We Really Know? World Bank Staff Occasional Papers No.26, 1979.

on the premise that education does not directly affect fertility but acts
through a large number of variables which in turn determine fertility.

Fertility is determined by three primary factors: the biological supply
of children, the demand for children, and the regulation of fertility. Each
of these factors are in turn influenced by a large number of variables.
Figure 1 presents a simplified version of such a model. The model represents
a situation in which the current number of living children is compared with
demand for children. If that number equals or exceeds demand, then there is
a possibility that fertility regulation will be used to limit further
fertility. Whether regulation is in fact used, however, also depends on
attitudes towards, knowledge of and access to fertility regulation. In
addition effective use also depends on husband-wife communication. The
effect of education on fertility depends on how education affects the demand
for children, the supply of children and the use of fertility regulation if
another child is not desired and in turn how these variables affect fertility.
Table 5 shows the hypothesized effect of the intervening variables on
fertility and lists studies which give evidence on these relationships.
Table 6 shows the hypothesis set forth on the relationship between education
and these intervening variables (columns 1 and 2) and through these intervening
variables, its relationship to fertility (columns 4 and 5).

Not all the variables in Tables 5 and 6 have been well studied in
their relationship to education. Table 7 summarizes the results of numerous
studies for those variables which have been studied in relation to education.
Education acts through the demand for children, child mortality, the
biological supply of children and fertility regulation. Table 7 shows that
education tends to reduce the demand for children as measured by desired
family size by reducing preferences for children, and perceived benefits
of children. However, education also tends to increase the perceived ability
to afford children which counters these negative effects to some extent but
does not outweigh them.[2] The relationship between education and perceived
or actual costs of children is poorly documented but existing evidence
supports the hypothesis set forth above. Education also reduces the number
of births needed to achieve a particular desired family size by lowering
infant and child mortality. The evidence is also very strong that education
increases contraceptive use by improving attitudes towards and knowledge of
contraception. The greatest uncertainty in terms of education's effect on

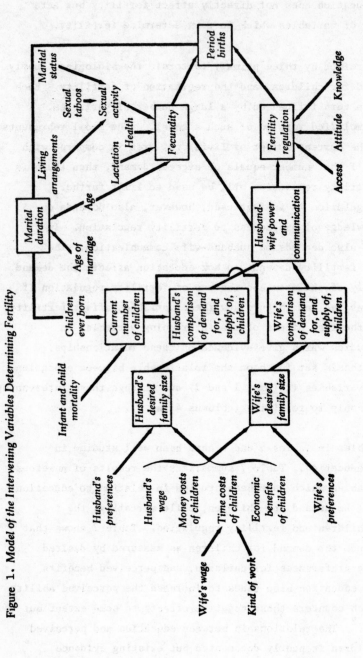

Figure 1. Model of the Intervening Variables Determining Fertility

Source: Cochrane, Susan H. Fertility and Education: What Do We Really Know? World Bank Staff Occasional Papers No.26, 1979.

TABLE 7   EVIDENCE SUPPORTING THE RELATION BETWEEN EDUCATION AND FERTILITY THROUGH THE INTERVENING VARIABLES

Variable	Relation of education and variable	Probable relation of education through the variable	Results Supporting (number of cases)	Not Supporting (number of cases)
Potential supply of births	?	?	-	-
Probability of marrying	inverse	-	6	5[a]
Age of marriage	direct	-	59	12[a]
Health	direct	+	2	0
Lactation	inverse	+	6	0
Postpartum abstinence	inverse	+	2	0
Infant or child mortality	inverse	-	16	7
Demand for children (desired family size)	inverse	-	17	8[a]
Preference for children	inverse			
Ideal family size		-	20	7[a]
Desired number of sons		-	8	1
Perceived benefits of children	inverse	-	17	2
Perceived costs of children	direct	-	2	0
Perceived ability to afford children	direct	+	9	3
Fertility regulation (contraceptive use)	direct	-	26	11
Attitudes toward birth control	direct	-	28	4
Knowledge of birth control	direct	-	28	1
Husband-wife communication	direct	-	9	0

a. Relation of male education to the variable is much weaker than that of female education.

Source: Cochrane, Susan H. Fertility and Education: What Do We Really Know? World Bank Staff Occasional Papers No.26, 1979.

fertility is related to the effect of education on the potential biological supply of births or fecundity. While female education seems to reduce the years married by raising the age of marriage and at least in some countries reducing the probability of marriage, education's effect on the fecundity of married women appears to operate in a different direction. It appears that education improves the health of women sufficiently to improve either their chances of conceiving or their ability to carry births to term. In addition more educated women tend to give up traditional behaviour such as prolonged lactation and post-partum abstinence which tend to suppress fertility.

Therefore education's effect on fertility through the intervening variables tends to be negative except for possible effects through natural fertility (through biological and behavioural factors) and the ability to afford children. Therefore education should increase fertility only in those environments where these factors are quite important in determining fertility. Those countries with the poorest health and nutrition combined with traditional reliance on antinatal practices such as lactation and post partum abstinence would be most likely to experience strong positive effects of education on fecundity. The most immediate factor countering this increase in fecundity is probably education's effect on the age of marriage. However, if the age of marriage is very young, raising that age by a year or so may have little effect on fertility because few very young women give birth due to the high incidence of adolescent sterility. Also marriages involving young girls often involve an interval of some years between the marriage ceremony and the consumation of the marriage. Only once the age of marriage is in the late teens can one expect further increases in the age of marriage to reduce fertility.

Increased fecundity can of course be offset by increased contraceptive use, but there are very good reasons for expecting this effect to be lagged. First the supply of births and the survival of children must increase more than any possible increase in demand occasioned by a greater ability to afford children. Once such changes have occurred, time will be needed for individuals to adapt to new conditions or even in some cases to perceive the demographic changes necessitating behavioural changes.

Research Implications

The above review suggests that several kinds of research are needed to clarify these issues. First, more studies need to be done relating education and age adjusted fertility in certain under-researched areas. Second, the effect of education on several variables which are important in determining fertility have not been studied sufficiently.[3] Third, work needs to be done to test the model presented above in its entirety to determine the relative importance of the many channels through which education affects fertility. Fourth, little or no work has been done to determine which of the various results of education are most important in reducing fertility. Each of these research needs are discussed briefly in the following paragraphs.

As mentioned above there is a scarcity of research relating to the age adjusted fertility and the education of individuals in the poorest countries and in rural areas within most countries. In addition, an insufficient amount of work has been done exploring the relationship of education and fertility for males. The World Fertility Survey should provide the data needed for such studies in the poorest countries and in rural areas. In addition it will provide data on the husband's level of education. Such studies will help establish whether the patterns observed in the relationship between education and fertility at the individual level are in fact correct. To understand why these different patterns are observed several other kinds of research are needed.

The simplest kind of work that needs to be done is work which examines education's effect on intervening variables separately for men and women in urban and rural areas. Age of marriage, ideal and desired family size and contraceptive knowledge and attitude are perhaps the most important variables that need to be examined in this detail. If a large part of the effect of female education on age of marriage results from the opening up of attractive, good-paying jobs which are not compatible with marriage, then it should be expected that female education will probably have little effect on age of marriage of those who remain in the rural sector where such jobs do not exist. Education, however, may even in the rural sector, raise the overall age of marriage of the country by encouraging migration of educated women to the urban sector where such jobs are available. Thus, it would not be sufficient to examine only education and current residence in various relationships, but also previous residence.

Education may have differential impacts on ideal and desired family size in urban and rural areas because the costs and benefits of children may well differ in these circumstances. There appears to be little evidence on this, although data on desired family size in rural areas of West Malaysia and Iran show that education does not have the expected effect.

The fertility regulation variables showed very consistent relationships with education, but these data were generally not broken down by urban-rural residence. There was some indication that education differentials in contraceptive usage tended to be larger for cities than for whole countries, but this is highly tentative.

In addition to fairly simple comparisons of the links of education to intervening variables such as sex and residence, more complex forms of research need to be conducted. The effect of education on the biological supply of children is very little understood. More research needs to be done on finding measures of fecundity and relating these to education. Education of males and females may have differential effects on health and thus the potential supply of births and children. Education may improve health through the access that higher income gives   medical care and better nutrition. If this is the case, male education may have strong effects on the supply of children. Alternatively, education may affect health by giving individuals better knowledge of good health and nutrition practices. Here female education may be most important. If a strong link is established between education, health and fecundity, this might provide an explanation of the lack of a negative (and occasionally a positive) relationship between education and fertility at low levels of development or income (possibly also low levels of literacy). This is a hypothesis advanced by Encarnacion in his study of the Philippines.

A set of relationships need to be further explored which have considerable intuitive appeal and theoretical support. These are the relationships between female education, market opportunities, women's wages and fertility and age of marriage. Although much work has been done on female labour participation and fertility, this work has shown both positive and negative relationships (See Shields, 1977). In addition, Dixon has shown that while female

labour force participation has a positive effect on age of marriage and
proportion of women never married in Eastern Europe, the Middle East and
Asia, it has no such effect in Western Europe and English overseas areas.[4]
Both of these factors suggest that one must not simply look at labour
participation, but at the compatibility of work with marriage and
childbearing and the wages in that work. Compatibility of work and marriage
and/or childbearing depends on a multiplicity of factors, social definitions
of appropriate roles, location of work, rigidity of hours, costs of child
care, availability of contraceptives, etc. Wages in work are important
because economic models suggest that fertility, marriage and labour supply
are jointly determined by the wife's market wage. Thus there is the possibility
that labour force participation and fertility are not causally related but
dependent on other factors. Both the effect of education on wages and on
the compatibility of work and family roles and the effect of these variables
on fertility need to be more fully explored. One possible explanation of
the inter-action between the individual's level of education and the aggregate
level of literacy and fertility is that as long as overall female literacy or
education is low, substitutes for the mother's time are cheaply available
so that more educated women can enjoy the benefits of more education (market
work or other alternative activities) without reducing fertility.

The strong relationship between education and fertility regulation also
needs to be more fully explored if meaningful policies are going to be
developed with respect to education. Among the major questions to be
answered are the extent to which mass-media campaigns and free family planning
services can substitute for education in increasing contraceptive knowledge
and use. These issues are fairly complex. Macro relationships between
education, fertility regulation and contraceptive availability and mass media
content need to be established as well as micro relationships which include
data on community level family planning variables.

For the fertility-education relationship to generate policy implications,
it is necessary to know not only the extent to which other factors can
substitute for education's effect, but also to know what characteristics of
education result in the inverse association with fertility. It may be that
education per se has no effect, but that it is the selectivity of the educational
system which results in individuals with certain background characteristics,
e.g. intelligence, ambition, high socio-economic status, etc. going further

in school and these characteristics may lead to lower fertility even if higher education were not obtained. Alternatively, education may provide explicit skills, such as literacy and numeracy, which result in lower fertility either through better job opportunities or improved abilities to acquire new information and implement complicated technologies. Education may provide primarily changes in attitudes, resulting in more modern attitudes towards the control of one's life, the possibilities of social mobility, or the proper roles of men and women. Education may provide explicit knowledge that will result in lower fertility. Finally, education (particularly secondary education) may serve as a simple alternative to early marriage in societies where there are very few alternatives.

All of the above factors are probably operative to some extent. If education is to be considered as a policy instrument for reducing fertility, one needs to know the relative importance of the various aspects of education. In addition, since the various characteristics of education probably operate differentially on the various intervening variables, it is necessary not only to know these differential impacts,but also to know the relative impact of the intervening variables on completed fertility. A path analysis of the system presented in Figure 1 with the various dimensions of education appropriately added would provide such information. The data requirements of such a model are, however, enormous. Not only would background information on the family, literacy, numeracy, modernization and knowledge have to be collected as well as the intervening variables, but the sample sizes required would be quite large. However, if an education module could be added to surveys similar to the World Fertility Survey, the data requirements could be approximated.

Implications for Policy

The research needed to further explore the relationship between education and fertility is quite substantial. Therefore the policy conclusions that can be drawn from the existing work must be fairly tentative. First, we cannot expect education to lead to an automatic reduction in fertility in all circumstances. Second, we should expect that increases in female education will be more likely to reduce fertility than increases in male education. Third, education in urban areas is also more likely to reduce fertility than in rural areas. Fourth, education in the more literate countries is more likely to reduce fertility than in the least literate, at least in the short run.

The major policy dilemma posed by the evidence presented here is what policy should be pursued in those areas where education is unlikely to be associated with an immediate reduction in fertility and may in fact be associated with an increase in fertility in the short run. If as hypothesized here increases in education increase fertility by improving the health of women, increasing the perceived ability to afford children and reducing adherence to traditional antinatal practices such as prolonged lactation and post-partum abstinence, then it would seem that even if education is not increased, fertility will rise from these factors as a result of any programme to improve the well-being (health and income) of individuals and by the very process of modernization which leads to the abandonment of traditional behaviour. Since the tendency for fertility to increase from these causes seems to be the inevitable product of development, the appropriate policy should probably be to minimize the time lag between these factors increasing fertility and countervailing forces which tend to reduce it. Education would seem to be one factor which might have strong effects in minimizing such a lag. Once people's desired family size falls it is quite evident from the literature that education enables people to better achieve these smaller sizes.

172

REFERENCE NOTES

1. See Simon (1974), McGreevey and Birdsall (1974) and Mason et al (1971).

2. Since desired family size represents the resolution of costs, benefits
    and the ability to afford children, the fact that such desires are
    inversely related to fertility establishes this point.

3. This is shown by the scarcity of a number of kinds of studies
    summarized in Table 7. In addition some variables considered to be
    important in the general model and included in Table 6 are so little
    studied in relationship to education that they were not included in
    Table 7.

4. The small effect that exists is negative in the West.

BIBLIOGRAPHY

Adelman, Irma. 1963. "An Econometric Analysis of Population Growth". American Economic Review. 53:314-339.

Anker, Richard. 1975. "An Analysis of Fertility Differentials in Developing Countries". International Labor Review. (ILO) Population and Employment Working Paper, No. 16.

Arnold, Fred. and others. 1975. The Value of Children: A Cross-National Survey. Vol. 1. Introduction and Comparative Analysis. Honolulu: The East-West Center.

Baird, Dugald. 1965. "Variation in Fertility Associated with Changes in Health Status". Public Health and Population Change. Pittsburgh: University of Pittsburgh Press.

Ben-Porath, Voram. 1973. "Economic Analysis for Fertility in Israel: Point and Counterpoint". Journal of Political Economy 81 (supplement 2): S202-233.

Bindary, A. and others. 1973. "Urban-Rural Differences in the Relationship between Women's Employment and Fertility". Journal of Biosocial Science. 5:159-167.

Bogue, Donald. 1969. Principles and Demography. New York: Wiley

Bulatao, Rodolfo. 1975. The Value of Children: A Cross-National Survey. Vol. 2. The Philippines. Honolulu: The East-West Center.

Butz, William P. and Jean-Pierre Habicht. 1976. "The Effects of Nutrition and Health on Fertility: Hypotheses, Evidence and Intervention". In Ronald Ridker (ed.). Population and Development: The Search for Selective Interventions. Baltimore: Johns Hopkins University Press.

Cain, Glen and Adriana Weinenger. 1973. "Economic Determinants of Fertility: Results from Cross-Sectional Aggregate Data". Demography. 10:205-221.

Caldwell, John C. 1968. Population Growth and Family Change in Africa: The New Urban Elite in Ghana. New York: Humanities Press.

Carelton, Robert O. 1965. "Labor Force Participation: A Stimulus to Fertility in Puerto Rico". Demography 2:233-239

Celade (United Nations Regional Center for Demographic Training and Research in Latin America) and CFSC (Community and Family Study Center). 1972. Fertility and Family Planning in Metropolitan Latin America. Chicago: University of Chicago.

Chernichovsky, D. 1976a. "Some Socio-Economic Aspects of Fertility Behavior in Northeast Brazil: A Note". World Bank Mimeo. ND. 1976b. "Fertility Behaviour in Developing Economies: An Investment Approach". Paper presented at IUSSP Seminar on Household Models of Economic-Demographic Decision-Making. Mexico City, November 4-6.

Chung, Bom Mo, and others. 1972. Psychological Perspective: Family Planning in Korea. Seoul: Hollym Corporation.

Cochrane, Susan, Bal Gopal Baidya, and Jennie Hay. 1977. "Memo on Fertility in the Parsa Pretest in Rural Nepal". World Bank Division of Population and Human Resources.

Cochrane, Susan. 1979. The Population of Thailand: Its Growth and Welfare. World Bank Staff Working Paper, No. 337.

DaVanzo, Julie. 1972. The Determinants of Family Formation in Chile, 1960: An Econometric Study of Female Labor Force Participation, Marriage, and Fertility Decisions. No. R830-AID. Santa Monica, California: Rand Corporation.

Davidson, Maria. 1973. "A Comparative Study of Fertility in Mexico City and Caracas". Social Biology. 20:460-496.

Drakatos, Constantine. 1969. "The Determinants of Birth Rate in Developing Countries: An Econometric Study of Greece". Economic Development and Cultural Change. 17:596:603

El-Badry, M.A. and Hanna Rizk. 1967. "Regional Fertility Differences among Socio-Economic Groups in the United Arab Republic". World Population Conference, 1965. Vol IV. New York: United Nations.

Ekanem, Ita. 1974. "Correlates of Fertility in Eastern Nigeria". Nigerian Journal of Economic and Social Studies. 16:115-127.

Encarnación, Jose, Jr. 1974. "Fertility and Labor Force Participation: Philippines 1968". The Philippine Review of Business and Economics. Vol. 11.

Ewbank, Douglas. 1977. "Indicators of Fertility Levels in Tanzania: Differentials and Trends in Reported Poverty and Childlessness". Paper presented at the Annual Meeting of the Population Association of America, April 21-23, St. Louis, Missouri.

Freedman, Ronald and Bernard Berelson. 1977. "The Record of Family Planning Programs". Studies in Family Planning. 7:1-40

Friedlander, Stanley and Morris Silver. 1967. "A Quantitative Study of the Determinants of Fertility Behaviour". Demography. 4(1): 30-70.

Grendell, Murray, and others. 1970. "Fertility and Economic Activity of Women in Guatemala City 1964". Demography. 7:273-286

Goldstein, Sidney. 1972. "The Influence of Labor Force Participation and Education on Fertility in Thailand". Population Studies. 26:419-436.

Gregory, Paul; John Campbell, and Benjamin Cheng. 1973. "Differences in Fertility Determinants: Developed and Developing Countries". Journal of Development Studies. 9:233-241.

Harmon, Alvin. 1970. Fertility and Economic Behavior of Families in the Philippines. Santa Monica, California: Rand Corporation.

Heer, David. 1966. "Economic Development and Fertility". Demography. 3 (2):423-444.

Hicks, W. Whitney. 1974. "Economic Development and Fertility Change in Mexico, 1950-1970". Demography. 11:407-422

Hill, Rueben and others. 1959. The Family and Population Control. Chapel Hill: University of North Carolina Press.

Hull, Terence and Valerie Hull. 1977. "The Relation of Economic Class and Fertility: An Analysis of Some Indonesian Data". Population Studies. 31:73-87.

Iutaka, S., E.W. Bock, and W.G. Varnes. 1971. "Factors Affecting Fertility of Natives and Migrants in Urban Brazil", Population Studies. 25:55-62.

Janowitz, Barbara. 1976. "An Analysis of the Impact of Education on Family Size". Demography. 13:189-198.

Kasarda, John D. 1971. "Economic Structure and Fertility: A Comparative Analysis". Demography. 8:307-318.

Kelley, Allen. 1976. "Interaction with Economic and Demographic Household Behavior". Paper presented at the National Bureau of Economic Research Conference on Population and Economic Change in Less Developed Countries, Philadelphia, Pennsylvania.

Khan, M. Ali and Ismail Sirageldin. 1975. "Education, Income and Fertility in Pakistan". Paper presented at the Applied Research Institute, University of Karachi and Research Department of United Bank, Ltd., September 30.

Kim, Mo-Im. 1977. "Age at Marriage, Family Planning Practices and Other Variables as Correlates of Fertility in Korea". Demography 1:413-498.

Kirk, Dudley. 1971.   "New Demographic Transition?", in Rapid Population Growth, National Academy of Sciences. Baltimore: Johns Hopkins Press.

Knodel, John and Visid Prachuabmoh. 1973. The Fertility of Thai Women. Bangkok; Institute of Population Studies, Chulalongkorn University.

Knowles, James C. and Richard Anker. 1975.   "Economic Determinants of Demographic Behavior in Kenya". International Labor Review (ILO) Population and Employment Working Paper No. 28.

Kocher, James E. 1977.   "Rural Development and Fertility Change in Northeast Tanzania". Paper presented at the Annual Meeting of the Population Association of America, April 21-23, St. Louis, Missouri.

Kogut, Edy Luiz. 1974.   "The Economic Analysis of Fertility: A Study of Brazil". International Labor Organization (ILO), Population and Employment Working Paper, No. 7.

Li, W.L. 1970.   "Temporal and Spatial Analysis of Fertility Decline in Taiwan". Population Studies 27:97-104.

Mason, Karen and others. 1971.   Social and Economic Correlates of Family Fertility: A Survey of the Evidence, Research Triangle Park, N.C.: Research Triangle Institute.

Maurer, K. and others. 1973.   Marriage, Fertility and Labor Force Participation of Thai Women: An Econometric Study. No. R829-AID/RF. Santa Monica, California: Rand Corporation.

Mazun, D.P. 1973. "Relation of Marriage and Education to Fertility in the U.S.S.R." Population Studies. 27(1): 105-115.

McCabe, James L. and Mark R. Rosenzweig. 1976.   "Female Employment Creation and Family Size", in Ronald Ridher (ed.) Population and Development, Baltimore: Johns Hopkins University Press.

McGreevey, W.P. and Nancy Birdsall. 1974. The Policy Relevance of Recent Social Research on Fertility, Washington, D.C.: Interdisciplinary Communications Program, Smithsonian Institute.

Merrick, Thomas. 1974.   "Interregional Differences in Fertility in Brazil, 1950-1970", Demography 2:423-440.

Michel, A. 1967.   "Interaction and Family Planning in the French Urban Family". Demography 4(2): 615-625.

Miro, Carmen and Walter Mertens. 1968.   "Influences Affecting Fertility in Urban and Rural Latin America". Milbank Memorial Fund Quarterly. 46(3)2: 89-120.

Mitchell, Robert E. 1972.   "Husband-Wife Relations and Family Planning Practice in Urban Hong-Kong". Journal of Marriage and Family. 34:139-146.

Mueller, Eva. 1972.   "Economic Motivations for Family Limitation", Demography. 26(3): 383-403

Nerlove, Marc and Paul T. Schultz. 1970. "Love and Life between the Censuses: Model of Family Decision-Making in Puerto Rico, 1950-1960". No. RM-6322-AID., Santa Monica, California: Rand Corporation.

Ohadike, Patrick. 1969. "The Possibility of Fertility Change in Modern Africa: A West African Case". African Social Research. 8:602-614

Palmore, James A. and M. Ariffin. 1969. "Marriage Patterns and Cumulative Fertility in West Malaysia: 1966-1967". Demography. 6:383-401

Palmore, James A., Jr. 1969. "The West Malaysian Family Survey, 1966-1967". Studies in Family Planning. 40:11-20

Ramakumar, S.R. and S.V.S. Gopal. 1972. "Husband-Wife Communications and Fertility in a Suburban Community Exposed to Family Planning". Journal of Family Welfare. 18:30-36.

Repetto, Robert. 1974. "The Relationships of the Size Distribution of Income to Fertility and the Implications for Development Policy", in Timothy King (ed.), Population Policies and Economic Development. World Bank Staff Report. Johns Hopkins University Press.

Rosenzweig, Mark R. 1976. "Rural Wages, Labor Supply and Land Reform: A Theoretical and Empirical Analysis". Discussion Paper No. 20. Princeton: Research Program in Development Studies, Princeton University.

Rosenzweig, Mark R. and Robert Evenson. 1977. "Fertility, Schooling and the Economic Contribution of Children in Rural India: An Econometric Analysis". Econometrica, 45:1065-1079.

Russett, B.M. and others. 1964. World Handbook of Social and Political Indicators. New Haven: Yale University Press.

Schultz, T. Paul. 1969. "An Economic Model of Family Planning and Fertility". Journal of Political Economy. 77:153-180.
1972a. Disequilibrium and Variation in Birth Rates over Space and Time: A Study of Taiwan. Santa Monica: Rand Corporation.
1972b. "Fertility Patterns and Their Determinants in the Arab Middle East". In Charles A. Cooper and Sidney Alexander (eds.) Economic Development and Population Growth in the Middle East, New York: Elsevier.

Shields, N., 1977. "Female Labor-Force Participation and Fertility: Review of Emperical Evidence". Population and Human Resources Division of World Bank.

Siever, Daniel. 1976. "Comment on W. Whitney Hicks. Economic
    Development and Fertility Change in Mexico, 1950-1970".
    Demography 13:149-152.

Simon, Julian L. 1974. The Effects of Income on Fertility,
    Chapel Hill: North Carolina Population Center.

Snyder, Donald W. 1974. "The Economic Determinants of Family
    Size in West Africa". Demography 11:613-628

Srinivasan, K. 1967. A Prospective Study of the Fertility Behavior
    of a Group of Married Women in Rural India - Design and Findings
    of the First Round of Enquiry". Population Review. 11:46-60.

Stycos, J. Mayone 1968. Human Fertility in Latin America. Ithaca:
    Connell University Press.

Traina, Frank J. and Herman D. Bontrager. 1977. "Statistical
    Determinants of Fertility Decline in Costa Rica". Paper
    presented at the Annual Meeting of the Population Association
    of America, April 21-23. St. Louis Missouri.

United Nations. 1973. The Determinant and Consequences of
    Population Trends. New York: United Nations.

Weller, Robert. 1968. "The Employment of Wives, Role Incompatibility
    and Fertility: A Study among the Lower and Middle Class Residents
    of San Juan, Puerto Rico". Millbank Memorial Fund Quarterly.
    46:507-526.

Williams, Anne D. 1976. "Review and Evaluation of the Literature"
    in Michael C. Keeby (ed.). Population, Public Policy and
    Economic Development. New York: Praeger.

World Bank. 1974. "Population Policies and Economic Development",
    World Bank Staff Report. Baltimore: Johns Hopkins University
    Press.

Yaukey, David and Timm Thorsen. 1972. "Differential Female Age
    at First Marriage in Six Latin American Cities". Journal of
    Marriage and Family, 35:375-379.

Zarate, Celvan. 1977. "Fertility in Urban Areas of Mexico.
    Implications for the Theory of Demographic Transition".
    Demography. 4(1):363-373.